More praise for

GET YOUR OWN DAMN BEER, I'M WATCHING THE GAME!

"Girls, this is a must-read! Score some major points with your guy
when it comes to his second love—football!"

—VIVICA A. FOX, actress

"This book reflects the same depth of understanding and expertise that Holly
displays as an actor. She explains the nuances of the game in a manner that all
can comprehend. Much like the mantra we have at *FOX NFL Sunday*,
Holly sugarcoats the education pill."

—JAMES BROWN, *FOX NFL Sunday*

"Only Holly Robinson Peete combines the terminology, strategy, and history of the
game with her pinpoint portrayal of life in the NFL, on and off the field.
You can't help but understand and love pro football once you read this book."

—ANDREA KREMER, ESPN national correspondent

GET YOUR OWN DAMN BEER, I'M WATCHING THE GAME!

A Woman's Guide to Loving Pro Football

HOLLY ROBINSON PEETE

with DANIEL PAISNER

Foreword by NFL Hall of Famer Ronnie Lott

RODALE

Illustrations by Kelly Hume/Deborah Wolf Associates
Play diagrams on pages 93, 94, 96, 97, 98, 99, and 103 by Rodney Peete

Book design by Christopher Rhoads

Library of Congress Cataloging-in-Publication Data

Peete, Holly Robinson.
    Get your own damn beer, I'm watching the game! : a woman's guide to loving pro football / Holly
Robinson Peete with Daniel Paisner ; foreword by Ronnie Lott.
       p.   cm.
    Includes index.
    ISBN-13 978–1–59486–163–5 paperback
    ISBN-10 1–59486–163–3 paperback
    1. National Football League.   2. Football—United States—Terminology.   3. Football—Social
aspects—United States.   4. Peete, Holly Robinson.   I. Paisner, Daniel.   II. Title.
GV955.5.N35P44 2005
796.332'64'0973—dc22
                                               2005013614

Distributed to the trade by Holtzbrinck Publishers

8   10   9   7   paperback

We inspire and enable people to improve their lives and the world around them
For more of our products visit **rodalestore.com** or call 800-848-4735

This book is dedicated to my daddy.

Thanks for teaching me to love the game.

How I miss Sundays with you . . .

Contents

Why Are We Here?

CHEAT SHEET: 10 All-Time Annoying Things We Should Never Say to Our Men during the Game

1

Where It All Began (for Me)

CHEAT SHEET: 10 All-Time Greats of the Game (pre-1970)

2

Kickoff

CHEAT SHEET: 10 All-Time Greats of the Game (post-1970)

3

Assume the Position

CHEAT SHEET: 10 All-Time Great Football Names

4

Three Teams in One

CHEAT SHEET: 10 All-Time Great Coaches of the Game

Foreword

Back when I played football in college and the NFL, and I was trying to knock someone out on the field, I knew it was an awesome hit when the crowd went, *Wo-o-o-o!* I say that now myself when I spot something that's the real deal, like a great movie or a sweet set of wheels. After reading Holly's book, I knew it was a *Wo-o-o-o!* book.

I've been in this game since I was 10 years old, and I've seen all kinds of football books. But I've never seen one that made me say *Wo-o-o-o!* Well, this book is about a lot of *Wo-o-o-o!* In this one volume is everything you need to know about the game of football, its history, the players, the coaches, the fans, and more.

I guess that doesn't mean much coming from a guy who grew up playing football and already knows everything about the game. After all, this is a book for women, not pro football players. So I asked the women in my life what they thought, and they all agreed with me. "This is a '*Wo-o-o-o!*' book," they said. "It's the real deal."

My mom has watched me play since I started playing football, and she learned a lot over those 15 years. In the beginning she used to say to me, "Now don't you get hurt, son." (We all know I never did listen to my mom.) But by the end of my career mom was saying things like, "Why didn't you blitz on that play? You should have been reading the guard's hand! You could tell he was leaning backwards and that he was going to pass block." Then she would add, "Why did you let Eric Dickerson run over you?"

My wife, Karen, also learned about football the hard way—play by play, year by year. And she says that if she'd had this book back when we first got together, she might have been able to understand more clearly what I was doing on the field. When I told her about my day at the "office," she might have had a better idea what I was talking about!

In this book, Holly gives you the gift of what she knows from living the

NFL life. This kind of savvy takes years to learn—just ask my mom and my wife—but Holly makes it easy to understand. Everything from great Super Bowl moments, to the language of the game, to "football butts" worth watching (which I have to remind my wife to STOP watching!).

Who better than Holly to give you this gift? She really knows what goes on behind the scenes. She's been there—literally—in the locker room after Rodney busted his knee in 1995, and when he won a championship game in 2003. She knows the high points of the football life, and the low points. She knows what it feels like to win a big game and what it feels like to rush to the hospital after a season-ending injury.

Most of all, Holly genuinely loves football. And you will, too. I guarantee, this book will make you say, *Wo-o-o-o!*

—Ronnie Lott
   NFL Hall of Fame Safety

Acknowledgments

To my little linemen: Rodney, Robinson, and Roman. Mommy wrote a book about football—isn't that cool?! To my gridiron princess: Ryan Elizabeth, as passionate a football fan as there ever was. To my QB: Rodney. Honey, the integrity, poise, and passion you have consistently displayed on and off the field have mesmerized me. Thanks for letting me ask all the dumb questions. Edna and Willie Peete, Rebeca and Skip Peete, thanks for the love. Matt Robinson, number one NFL bro-in-law. Holla' Swaad! Dolores Robinson: Mommy, you have become a truly great football fan and a wonderful NFL mother-in-law. You make me proud! Robinson/Peete crew: I love you all ferociously!

Dan Paisner, thank you for your talent, compassion, and friendship. Mel Berger, thank you for helping me to finally realize this project. Thank you Patti Webster and everyone at W&W Public Relations. Big shout-out to Leah Flickinger and everyone at Rodale—your belief and guidance have made this rookie process so pleasant. Thank you for the opportunity.

Much love to the following fabulous NFL couples for their support: Karen and Ronnie Lott, Deanna and Brett Favre, Brenda and Kurt Warner, Sherice and Tim Brown, Tina and Sean Jones, Cindy and Jon Gruden, Pat and Emmitt Smith, Linda and John Lynch. Shout-out to Kim Porcher, for being my first NFL-wife friend.

Derrick Heggans, Jim Steeg, Tom Murphy, Mark Richardson, Tracy Pearlman, Andrea Kremer, Marcus Allen, James Brown, Vivica A. Fox, Dan Fogleman, Yvette Bowser, Chris Voelker, Valerie Harrell, Adam Christopher—thanks for your consistent gracious support. Star Jones Reynolds—the best girlfriend to watch a game with! And Lianne Cashin, thanks for always being there.

Finally, to all the women who love football, want to love football, or just want to fake it better in an effort to find some harmony and bonding time with your man on the weekend . . . I wrote this with you on the brain. I hope you like it!

Why Are We Here?

An Introduction

Green Left Close, F Right, Pass 14 Solid, Z-Slam Drag on Two!
Far West Right Slot, A Right, 322 Scat, Y Stick Lion!
Cowboy Right, Flip 50 Gap, X Slant Dallas!

Chances are, you took one look at these opening lines and thought you grabbed a book of trigonometry proofs instead of a book on football. I set the damn lines to paper myself, and even I thought I was working on the wrong book project. But make no mistake: These are lines I pulled from some of my husband Rodney's playbooks going back a couple seasons, lines he could bark out in the huddle to 10 of his teammates and expect them to understand. And it wasn't just these few lines; it was a couple thousand of them, spread over a couple dozen seasons, reaching all the way back to high school and college. Back when Rodney played for the Oakland Raiders, there was a sequence of offensive plays in the team's playbook called *Spider 2 Banana 2 Over*. Every time I heard him studying his plays, I used to think he was ordering some new Ben & Jerry's ice cream flavor.

So, what's the deal with this bizarre, secret language? What do these cryptic codes have to do with our ability to understand and appreciate the game of football? Is it possible to consider ourselves diehard fans if we don't have the first idea what these guys are talking about down there on the field? And more to the point, where's the Ben & Jerry's ice cream, and can we get it with extra sprinkles?

Well, I'll answer my own questions one at a time. First off, nobody *really* knows what the deal is with this bizarre, secret language—not even the coaches who come up with this stuff. Best I can figure, it's just like hand signals in baseball, or a set of counterintelligence codes, or any other secret signs you don't want your opponent to decipher. The words themselves don't serve any real purpose but to trigger a series of set plays and alignments your teammates have committed to reflex memory, so that every man on the field knows what's expected of him at any given time. "The play is the thing." That's a line from Shakespeare, which is about what you can expect from an actress-turned-football-expert, but it gets straight to the point: It's not what you call it so much as it is the play itself. You have to realize, a team's plays won't change that much from one week to the next, and its tactics and strategies will also be pretty much the same; but the *names* of those plays and tactics and strategies will frequently undergo a complete overhaul if coaches believe the other team has figured them out. Football is war, ladies, and it simply won't do to have the enemy listening in on your plan of attack.

Next, we fans don't need to understand the play-calling preferences of our favorite team to fully understand or appreciate the game. Save that for the experts—and for the players. We can know a team's strengths and weaknesses, and we can know a team's tendencies, and the names of each play can still be all kinds of Greek to us. Our ability to cheer our lungs out shouldn't be affected either way, and we should still be able to spot a lapse on defense or an outstanding cut-back on a busted running play.

Also, there's no reason to expect that we could have the first idea what these guys are talking about in the huddle, or on the sidelines. That's the whole point behind these ridiculous calls and signals. We're not *supposed* to figure it out. After all, if it were so easy for mere fans to pick up on the plays, then defensive coordinators would know what the other team was up to every time the ball was put in play—and if that were the case, there wouldn't be much point to playing the whole game, now would there?

And finally, regarding the ice cream, *Spider 2 Banana 2 Over* was not, in fact, a Ben & Jerry's flavor. Neither was *Spider 2 "Z" Banana "X" Over,* or *Spider 2-3 "Y" Banana "U" Basic,* or any other variation on the theme. There is, however, always ice cream—and yes, I'll take mine with sprinkles, please. (Can you tell I was pregnant while writing this?) The snacks are one of the best parts of the game for us fans. They're part of the fun. Ice cream is always key, along with the chips and dip, and sandwiches, and beer. As a matter of fact, there's room for every basic food group at a true fan's training table, and room for something to wash it all down with as well.

Football is, at bottom, a game. It's supposed to be fun and challenging, strategic and exciting. As it's played on the professional level, it can be fairly complicated, and there's usually a whole helluva lot at stake; but as fans we'll do well to let someone else worry about that. Our job, really, is to root, root, root for our favorite team and to have a good old time doing it.

I believe it's about time we shatter the old myth that tells us women don't really understand football, or that we *can't* really understand it. And while we're at it, there's another myth that suggests we don't really care to understand it—so we might as well shatter that one, too. Did you know that more than 50 million American women watch the Super Bowl each year, and that more than 45 million of us tune in to at least a part of an NFL game each weekend during the regular season? Or that football ranks as the favorite sport among U.S. women—ahead of baseball, basketball, NASCAR, and even figure skating? That's a whole lot of myth-shattering right there.

Sure, it's true enough that for countless women across the country, football season looms on the calendar as one of the most dreaded times of the year. For them (for *you,* perhaps), fall weekends are given over to long stretches in front of the television set, waiting for some guy to set down the remote, get up off his butt, and start paying some attention to the kids, or to the yard, or to little old *us.* But there's a silent army of women out there who want to learn about the game—to *really* learn about the game, to where the Xs and Os on a coach's chalkboard mean something other than kisses and hugs.

Have you ever heard the expression, *If you can't beat 'em, join 'em*? Well, if you've been dreading football season, this book will turn your weekends around. And, if you've been learning the game in bits and pieces and are becoming more of a fan each time you check out a game or open the sports pages in your daily newspaper, this book will help you along the way. I'm convinced that if women understood the game of football—if they were hard-wired to it like most men—they'd come to enjoy it as much as any guy. They could even become hooked! I know I am. Truth is, I'm probably more in my element talking football with the guys on my television crew at work than I am gossiping with my girlfriends about the new shoes they just bought—even if they happened to buy them on sale! Once you're bitten by the game, you might find that you're the same way. Just imagine, actually looking forward to a long Sunday afternoon, snuggling in front of the television set with your man, watching the games, and connecting as equals instead of being relegated to chips-and-beer detail. Imagine, too, a day when your husband or boyfriend no longer calls all his guy friends over to watch the game on his big screen television, because there's no one he'd rather watch it with than you. Hey, it could happen—and I'm betting that it will. In any case, it'll be worth the effort.

Professional football can be exhilarating, fun, intricate, and edge-of-your-seat suspenseful—not just for men, but for women as well. I've heard some of my girlfriends describe the game as "barbaric." Others have suggested that it's nothing more than "a bunch of guys running around and patting each other on the butt." (As if there's anything wrong with *that!*) But it's not like that at all. Football is a great, thinking-man's game—or, I should say, a thinking *person's* game. It's like an intricate match of full-contact chess. Everything is planned and plotted and thought through to the nth-degree—and after that, there's still a whole lot of room for improvisation and seat-of-the-pants desperation moves. Athleticism and grace and brute strength are all-important, but so, too, are memory and method and timing. There is precious little room for error. Games can be won or lost on a missed signal.

Over the years, I've developed an enormous respect for what it takes to develop and implement a game plan each week, and for the supreme effort that goes into conditioning. At the same time, I've never lost the excitement I felt as a little girl rooting for my Philadelphia Eagles, knowing that if the team played well, I could probably score a toasted almond ice cream bar from the Good Humor truck after the game. (See, I told you there was always ice cream!) That's the beauty of a game like football. You can know the basics and still find something to cheer about, or you can know a whole lot more and keep finding new aspects of the game to appreciate. You get out of it what you put into it—and let me tell you, I've put a lot into it. I learned the game at my father's knee, cheering on our team; but it took years to understand it in such a way that I could share it with others. And after that it took a whole damn career, learning the game all over again as the wife of a now-retired NFL quarterback, to feel confident enough about what I was seeing on the field to want to share it with others through a book such as this one.

I've also developed a real appreciation for the history of the sport, and I believe a good working knowledge of football's origins, its pioneers, and its most influential moments can add immeasurably to our enjoyment of the game. (Not to mention the fact that it impresses the pants off our know-it-all men.) Context is everything, and it helps to know the difference between the Steel Curtain and the Purple People Eaters, just as it helps to be able to distinguish Peyton Manning from his brother Eli—and to tell the two of them from their father, Archie. I hope to leave behind enough bread crumbs to give even the most casual fan a bare-bones, need-to-know short-course on all things football—sort of an "Everything You Always Wanted to Know about the NFL, but Were Afraid to Ask Your Condescending Man."

Remember those teachers back in grade school who used to tell you there were no such things as stupid questions? Well, try telling that to some of the guys out there who get all bent and bothered every time we ask them something about the game they think we should know. I sometimes think they don't know the answers themselves, and they don't like the thought of being found out— which could be why they give us such a hard time. But the great thing about a book like this is that I've asked all the stupid questions, so you don't have to. I've tried to anticipate your questions on each aspect of the game and present the answers in a clear, straightforward way that leaves nothing to chance or guesswork. And if you still feel the need to ask a follow-up question or two, you'll at least have a pretty good working knowledge of the subject at hand, so no put-out or put-upon guy can make you feel inadequate for pumping him for information.

This book is for women who are new to the game, and for those who grew up on it, as I did. It's our own personal handbook, a place we can turn to for answers to questions that seem to annoy the heck out of our men, especially when we ask them during the game. And, at the other end, we'll come away as fans, sophisticated enough to describe to our men how their favorite wide receiver cut his route short on a timing pattern, causing the QB to throw a pick to the DB, who returned it for six. Then we'll send them to the fridge to grab *us* a beer!

10

ALL-TIME ANNOYING THINGS WE SHOULD NEVER SAY TO OUR MEN DURING THE GAME

1. "O-o-oh, those shoulder pads are so eighties!"

2. "Remember when your butt used to look like that?"

3. "Honey, I just peed on the stick, and I'm glad you're sitting down."

4. "Good news! My folks are on the way over and they've got their vacation videos!"

5. "I still look good enough to wear one of those cheerleader outfits, don't I?"

6. "So does this mean the trash is going to take itself out?"

7. "I'm sorry, but this was the only time the decorator could come. And besides, it's only a few dozen swatches."

8. "You've already watched three quarters. Why can't we spend the last one talking about us?"

9. "Hey, I used to date that wide receiver. And they're right, he does have good hands."

10. "You never told me Billy Dee Williams used to play for the Bears."

1

Where It All Began
(for Me)

Bleeding Eagles Green

I suppose a bit of a personal introduction is in order before we get too deep into this thing. After all, it doesn't just happen that a little girl grows up in Philadelphia rooting for the Eagles, only to wind up marrying an Eagles quarterback. But that's the short version of how it happened for me.

Here's the (somewhat) longer version. My dad was a big-time football fan. It was his thing. It wasn't his only thing, mind you, but it was a big deal. Man, he loved his Eagles, and I grew to love them right alongside him. Again, it wasn't the only thing we shared, but it was something special.

My father's name was Matt Robinson, and he was an incredible writer. He wrote and produced a bunch of local television shows in

Philadelphia, but he also commuted to New York for a lot of the time I was growing up. He wrote scripts for *Sanford and Son,* and *The Waltons,* and *Eight Is Enough,* and he wrote several children's books, plays, and screenplays. Later on, he was a writer and producer on *The Cosby Show.* But he was probably best known for creating the role of Gordon, which he played from 1969 to 1972 on the original *Sesame Street.* He still turns up from time to time in the repeat segments they sometimes air, with his big pork chop sideburns and bushy moustache. Could a 4-year-old have asked her daddy to have a cooler gig?

He's gone now, my dad, after a long, difficult bout with Parkinson's disease, but football is at the heart of my memories of him. It was our common ground. I watch his old *Sesame Street* tapes with my children and think about how it was when I was their age, when my dad first started hanging out with Oscar, Big Bird, and the rest of the gang—and when I first discovered Harold Carmichael and Norm Snead, who were two of the more popular Philadelphia Eagles players throughout my growing up. My dad had a pretty busy taping schedule up in New York as I recall, but he was around on weekends and we made the most of our time together. Sundays were our special time during football season. My brother and I would sit at his knee, watching the game on television. Plus, we loved to watch him roll over in laughter each draft day as he scouted the proceedings—not for the best players, mind you, but for the hippest, most unusual names of the latest crop of college stars. Remember William "The Refrigerator" Perry? Well, we knew all about him in our household even before he burst onto the NFL scene, thanks to my dad's love for crazy-cool football names. That was always one of his favorite things, to collect the wildest and most unique football names that crossed his radar. And as a special tribute, I'll present a list of some of his all-time favorites (plus a few new ones he would have loved) a bit later on in these pages.

My earliest football memory (to which I alluded earlier) is from when I was 5 or 6 years old and more interested in spending time with my father than in the game he was watching or the players on the field. The game itself was probably nothing more than background noise to me when I was that little. If you'd have asked me, I'd have told you Jim Ringo was a Beatle before I pegged him for an Eagle.

Anyway, one late fall afternoon, I heard the jangle of the Good Humor ice cream truck coming up the block in my Mount Airy neighborhood, and I started tugging on my father's shirt to get his attention at some crucial point in the game. All I cared about was a strawberry shortcake ice cream bar. All he cared about was a field goal the Eagles were attempting, to take the lead as time ran out on the clock. In an effort to hush me up for another beat or two, he turned to me and said, "Honey, if that kicker makes this field goal, you can get your strawberry shortcake."

I started cheering for Dad's Eagles right then and there, and from that moment on, I think I associated everything I ever wanted in life with an Eagles' victory. (I guess that explains a lot.) In any case, there was usually a strawberry shortcake ice cream bar to help us celebrate at the end of each win. We started watching games together every week during the season; and in the beginning, it really did have more to do with my love of ice cream than my love of football. Soon after that, it was more about hanging with my father than anything else; but after a while, the lines got blurred and I was hooked on the game. I loved the adrenaline rush of excitement that seemed to flow from that field, the artistry of the wide receivers, and the crunch of brute strength at the line. I loved the sheer thrill of an open field run. I wasn't the most sophisticated fan in the world right out of the gate, but my father was a patient teacher and I paid close attention. In time, I learned the basic rules, and eventually I was able to pick up a little strategy and subtlety. When I moved from Philly to L.A. at the age of 9, and years later when I left the house after high school, I still managed to follow the Eagles. They were my team by that point, and it didn't matter if I was away at school or studying for a year in Paris—whenever the Eagles were playing, I was doing my best to catch the game and cheer them on.

And then life just kinda happened. I caught my first big break in 1986 on a television show called *21 Jump Street* for the upstart Fox Network, opposite a then-unknown Johnny Depp, and from there I managed to keep finding steady work. My mom, Dolores Robinson, already a prominent talent manager started managing my career—and she kept me busy and out there and happening. And all along, I kept my eye on my Eagles. My dad was a true die-hard fan, who counted it a real frustration whenever his team came up short. But I was turning out to be more of a die-easy fan (not quite sure if that's the opposite of die-hard, but you get the idea). If the Eagles managed to win a couple of games, that was just fine with me. If they managed to string together a successful season, even better. And if they lost a heartbreaker, I still treated myself to a strawberry shortcake ice cream bar at the other end. Why not? Life went on, pretty much as it would have if they had won the heartbreaker. Truth is, it wasn't always so easy to root for the Eagles; and if you ask any of today's fans, it hasn't gotten any easier—no matter how well they're playing. Anyway, I kept at it. I never lost faith. I figured if the Philadelphia Eagles could go to the trouble of suiting up and giving it their all each week, the least I could do was pull for them from my couch in L.A. or wherever I happened to be at the time.

In 1993, while I was shooting a sitcom called *Hangin' with Mr. Cooper,* I was introduced to a quarterback. His name was Rodney Peete, and he was something—good-looking, God-fearing, and more charming than any man had a right to be. Plus, he had a golden arm and a killer smile—in all, a totally winning package. He won me over in about the time it took to run a 2-minute offense. (Well, okay, maybe not that quick. There was a female friend—or 10!—I had to send into exile first, but that's for another book. . . .)

Rodney had been drafted by the Detroit Lions out of USC and had started on a promising career before the Lions cut him loose. He eventually wound up in Philadelphia, calling the plays for my beloved Eagles. I thought, "How cool is that?" Just think, to root for your hometown team as a star-struck little kid and to somehow wind up with the quarterback on your arm. Let me tell you, it was a fairy-tale wrapped inside a storybook wrapped inside a dream. I couldn't wait to introduce Rodney to my father—not least because he'd given me a lot of crap about the guys I'd been dating, and because short of Dr. J (Julius Erving, the Philly basketball legend who was a bit too old and a bit too married for me), I couldn't have brought home a more perfect guy than the new

Eagles quarterback.

We got married in 1995, but I'll save the details of our courtship for our grandchildren and keep the focus on the football aspects of our time together. You see, for the longest while I'd thought of myself as a football fan; but now that I had met Rodney and listened in on his conversations with his friends and his teammates, I came to realize that I didn't know all that much about the game. Sure, I could recite the rules, identify most of the Eagles starting roster, and run about three or four deep into the rosters of our opponents, but that was about it. I didn't know from play-calling, or defensive schemes and formations, or West Coast offenses. And keeping up with Rodney was one thing; I also had to contend with his entire family. There was my father-in-law, Willie Peete, an assistant coach in the NFL from 1983 to 1999 for the Chiefs, Packers, Bucs,

HISTORY OF THE GAME

IT'S GREEK TO ME

Most of the die-hard football fans in my acquaintance don't know the first thing about the game's origins. After all, in our lifetimes, there has always been football in one form or another. I grew up with the game in something very much like its present form. It was a part of our family scenery. Clearly, though, the game didn't drop fully realized into our laps. Like other sports, it evolved over a period of time, and a lot of folks suggest it grew from a game the Ancient Greeks used to play. The game was called *harpaston,* and—best anyone can tell—the object was to kick, throw, or run a ball across a goal line. Crossing that goal line was key despite the game's other objectives such as to lash, maim, or otherwise injure your opponent and to stand tall and proud in the face of such brutality.

This primitive version wasn't quite football as we know it—more like a distant cousin, once removed. There was no limit to the number of players allowed on each side, and there were no real rules to govern acceptable styles of play. It was a down-and-dirty, no-holds-barred, anything-goes contest, and there was more than a little bloodshed on those fields before the outcome of each game was decided.

and Bears; my brother-in-law, Skip, currently the running-backs coach for the Oakland Raiders; and my mother-in-law, Edna, the coach's wife, the coach's mother, and the quarterback's mom! (Let me tell you, Edna has had to endure countless Peete vs. Peete matchups, and watching those games with her could be nerve-wracking, to say the very least.) I scrambled to keep up. At first, I was out of my element; but eventually I picked up a thing or two, and with that extra effort I was able to send Rodney the all-important message that what he was doing was all-important to me as well.

And now, jumping ahead to my best football memory: 1995, wildcard play-off game, Eagles vs. Lions. Rodney's new team up against the team that let him go. My father couldn't have written a better script to set up this showdown. The Lions had just gone on an incredible late season run to win a play-off spot, and they came into the game as the heavy favorites, with all kinds of momentum. The talk in the press and all over Detroit was that the Lions were going to really take it to Rodney and the Eagles. But Rodney and the Eagles weren't having any of it. They came out like they were on a mission.

As it happened, Rodney's personal mission happened to coincide neatly with the team's objective: To win—big. You have to realize that whenever a player is cut or traded by a team, he really wants to stick it to them, to get his former employers to think they made a terrible mistake. And here Rodney felt he had something to prove. All week long leading up to the game, he kept hearing, "Oh, Rodney Peete can't do this," or "Rodney Peete can't do that," and it lit him up inside. So he came out and did this-and-that-and-then-some to those Lions. By the end of the first half, the Eagles were leading with a delicious score of 38–7, the icing on the cake coming from Rodney's "Hail Mary" pass that somehow wound up in the hands of one of his receivers in the end zone as time ran out. He ended up throwing for three touchdowns and over 300 yards, that's how fired up he was about this game.

Next day, I scoured the Internet for everything I could find in the Detroit papers about the game and about Rodney. I entered every Lions chat room I could find online and basked in everyone's misery. Evil as it makes me sound, I just loved it. Posts like "How could we let Peete destroy us?" absolutely made my day. Rodney had a play-off game with Dallas to worry about, but I reveled in that win over the Lions for the longest time, because those Detroit fans were so hurt by the loss. They were devastated, but it wasn't just the loss that got them going: It was the fact that they had been run ragged by a guy they had written off and sent packing. That was the strawberry shortcake ice cream bar for me.

My worst football memory also involves Rodney in an Eagles uniform, and it reinforces how fickle we fans can sometimes be—especially in a hard-nosed city like Philadelphia. It was a Monday Night Football game the following season, and the Eagles had gotten off to a flying start. Rodney was playing with a big new contract, which I'm sure had a lot to do with that kick-butt performance against his old team in the 1995 play-offs. There were great expectations all around. And then, all of a sudden, Rodney dropped back to pass and somehow got his cleat caught in that godawful AstroTurf they used to have at Veterans Stadium. (I used to call it "loopy green cement.") He twisted his knee in all kinds of weird ways. I couldn't see what happened from where I was in the stands; but later on, when I caught a replay on television, I had to look away—that's how painful it was just to watch. That night at the stadium, all I could see was this big huddle around Rodney, and the trainer calling for a stretcher, and Rodney laying on the field in obvious agony. I knew it wasn't good. The real tell, though, was when I got waved down from the stands to join Rodney in the locker room. Even a newlywed football wife knows that's not a good sign—they don't wave you down from the stands to the locker room unless it's serious. Right there, I knew Rodney's season was over. I just prayed his career wasn't through as well.

By the time I got down to the locker room, the team had already made plans to rush Rodney to the hospital. I sat next to him while trainers and coaches and players swarmed around him on the table. My poor honey's kneecap was up in his thigh. As a rookie wife, I was panicking, and I struggled to say and do all the right things. To make matters worse, I remembered I was in the locker room—that forbidden vat of testosterone into which no woman (with the exception of a few brave female sportswriters) was allowed. There I was, the *only* woman among some 40 (mostly) naked men, all of them more concerned with their QB than where my eyes might uncontrollably shift. Whew, it was some litmus test for me that night.

Rodney needed surgery straightaway, and I jumped in the ambulance right along with him. What else was I gonna do? We had no kids at that point, so I was very much standing by my man—which of course I still do to this day, only it was a lot easier back then without four kids to worry about as well. My focus was completely on Rodney. I was frantic with worry. Plus, I hadn't thought to grab a comb or brush, or any lipstick or makeup, and the only reason I mention my appearance at all is because 3 or 4 days into Rodney's unexpected hospital stay, I looked a mess. I hadn't left Rodney's side, and at one point I walked into one of the waiting room areas and noticed a television tuned to an episode of *Hangin' with Mr. Cooper*. The nurse on duty took one look at me, and then she looked up at the screen, and then back at me. Then she crinkled up her face as if to say, "That can't be you." Really, I looked more like a homeless woman than a sitcom star, and it must have made an incongruous picture—but there it was.

Turned out Rodney had torn his patellar tendon, and we were in that hospital for 5 days while he recovered from surgery, and at the end of those 5 days, I looked even more of a mess. It was such a terrible time, and adding to the anguish of those long days in the hospital was the way the talk-radio guys kept hammering Rodney like his career was over. No question, his season was over, but he still had a ton of football left in him (8 more seasons, to be exact). He'd just come off a terrific season. His doctors didn't see any reason why Rodney couldn't be back at full strength by training camp, and I didn't see any reason why all these sportswriter-types couldn't just leave him alone until then. No one deserves that kind of negative energy, but I guess that's part of the deal when you sign on to play in an over-the-top, sports-mad city like Philadelphia.

Eagles fans can be the best fans on the planet when things are going well, but they'll turn on you in a flash when things go sour. Men, women, children . . . across the board. They're tough, and this knee injury was a prime example. One night, we were watching the local news in Rodney's hospital room when the sports anchor went to a man-on-the-street piece on the Eagles' uncertain quarterback situation in the wake of Rodney's injury. Some folks ex-

HISTORY OF THE GAME

THE MODERN CONNECTION

According to most football historians, the early Greek form of football found its way to England in the 19th century, where it branched off in two distinct directions. One branch developed into the sport we now know as rugby, in which players advanced the ball by running with it or kicking it, and defenders stopped their opponents' forward progress by running with them and kicking them to the ground. There were also full-body tackles and thinly disguised blows to the head—and both sides took turns generally beating the tar out of each other in the name of sport.

The other branch developed into what we Americans call soccer and the rest of the world calls football, in which players also advanced the ball by kicking it but were forbidden to use their hands. Eventually, they were banned from kicking each other. Both games became wildly popular throughout Europe.

All of which takes us to the late 1800s, when versions of these two time-honored schoolboy games began to be played on American college campuses. In Princeton's version, players used their fists to ward off tacklers. At Harvard, the game—typically played between freshmen and sophomores on the first Monday of the school year—was called "Bloody Monday" for the way its players looked when they left the field at its conclusion. Accounts of those early games read more like slugfests than anything else, and I don't know that I'd have had the patience or the stomach to marry the guy on the target end of most of those blows. And yet over time there emerged a series of rules and innovations that helped to standardize play from one region to the next, to level the playing field, and to protect the players.

pressed concern that the backup quarterback was unproven. Others hoped Rodney might be back in time for the play-offs. And then they cut to a woman in a shoe store who said, "Kneecap or no kneecap, he shouldn't have dropped the ball."

Now, Rodney happened to fumble the football when he went down on that Astroturf, and the loss of possession turned out to be key; but I stared at that television and thought, "Man, what a rough place to play!" That was harsh. The guy's kneecap all but popped off his knee, he winced in pain and grabbed at it, and this woman in a shoe store was on him about dropping the ball. I'd like to see how she'd react if someone took a tire iron to her knee in that shoe store to see if she would've dropped those shoes in her hand!

The truth is, when it comes to defending my man, my knowledge of the game has served me better than any weapon I could ever imagine. Here's an example. In 2002, Rodney was several weeks into a resurgence-type season with the Panthers, after most everyone in football had written him off. I was watching *Fox NFL Sunday* during a game in which Rodney had struggled a bit in the first half, along with the rest of his Carolina teammates. At halftime the show's hosts—Howie Long, Terry Bradshaw, Jimmy Johnson, and my buddy "J.B." (James Brown)—were talking up a storm about the game. At one point, Coach Johnson started running his mouth about "that rag-armed Rodney Peete," suggesting Rodney might want to forget about Gatorade and start drinking Geritol, and I grew livid. I know these guys joke around all the time and that the players are fair game, but Rodney had been on such a tremendous roll. He'd led the team to a 3–0 start and helped turn things around for the Panthers after an abysmal 1–15 season the year before, and the talk struck me as mean and personal and below the belt. Right or wrong, it got my back up.

So what did I do? I put a call in to J.B., assuming that he was doing his thing on live television and wouldn't get my message until later that evening. Still, I needed to vent, so I left a message. "J.B.," I said, "you tell Coach Johnson to stop picking on Rodney. This is the first bad half he's had this season."

About an hour later, after the Panthers had lost and the late afternoon games had begun, my phone rang. Sure enough, it was J.B. on the line.

He was still in the studio, still taking in all the live feeds from the games around the league, still preparing his updates and recaps.

"I've got some guys here who want to talk to you," J.B. said, clearly bemused.

Then Terry Bradshaw got on the line. "Coach Johnson wants to talk to you," he said in that infectious drawl of his. "Give 'em hell, Holly!"

Then Howie Long got on the line and told me not to go easy on Coach.

Then it was Coach's turn. "Now, Mrs. Peete," he said, like he had it rehearsed, "comes a time in every player's career when he can't perform the way he used to . . ."

I cut him off. "Come on, Coach," I shot back. "With all due respect, did you see how porous that offensive line was? He was getting killed back there."

Coach Johnson hadn't expected me to challenge him on his opinion. After all, he was one of the best coaches to ever roam a sideline, and I was just a lowly wife. What did I know? But I kept at it. I told Coach that Rodney had been hitting his receivers square between the numbers, and they were dropping balls left and right. I told him a mess of other things, too, and when I was finally done, he made a sheepish reply.

"I have to admit, you do know your stuff, Mrs. Peete," he said, and in the background I could hear the other guys laughing at the way they'd hung Coach out to dry. They'd fed him to the lioness wife and let me tear him to pieces.

The next week, J.B. invited me to the Fox studios in Los Angeles, so I drove over to meet him. I took a seat off-set and started watching all the games that were playing on the many monitors. The Panthers were playing well, and Rodney was having a nice game.

At one point, during the on-air halftime show, the *Fox NFL Sunday* guys started baiting Coach all over again, asking him how he thought Rodney Peete was doing. Of course, Coach knew full well that I was in the studio that day and ready to pounce on him if he sold my man short a second time, but he also knew that Rodney was kicking butt on the field. And so he said, "Fellas, Rodney Peete keeps playing like this and he's going to the Pro Bowl."

Next thing I knew they cut away to an off-set shot of this sweet-suffering wife to let the audience at home in on their little inside joke. Thank God I looked halfway presentable, and I was able to laugh the whole thing off as they explained to the viewers what was going on, counting myself lucky that I could stand up for Rodney in such a cool (and informed!) way.

The point here is that a woman can be just as hard-core and hard-hearted and hardheaded as any man when it comes to football. This can be a good thing and a not-so-good thing, depending on your perspective; but for the purposes of this book and these opening remarks, let's just accept it on its face. We're

Courtesy of Anita Bartlett / Fox Sports

Here I am at the studio with (*from left*) James Brown, Terry Bradshaw, Jimmy Johnson, and Howie Long.

fans, no different than any guy—except we usually smell better. We may have learned the game at our daddy's knee, and in some cases we might have awakened to the harsh realities of the game in a Philadelphia hospital—but a lot of us have come to the game in our own way, on our own terms.

And my terms are these: Play hard and play fair, and ease up on the quarterback if he can't hang onto the ball in the midst of a season-ending injury. Oh, and while you're at it, pass the ice cream.

CHEAT SHEET

10

ALL-TIME GREATS OF THE GAME (PRE-1970)

A true football fan can spot a legend a mile away, at least by reputation, and you'll do well to have a passing knowledge of at least this handful of gridiron greats. Of course, for every All-Pro I've included here, there are dozens I've had to leave out . . . but we sideline analysts have to draw the line somewhere.

As you'll see when you read on in this book, so much has changed about the game in the modern era, so I've decided to break these all-time greats into two groups—those who roamed the field prior to the AFL-NFL merger in 1970 and those who came after. It's virtually impossible to compare an impact player from today's game to a star of yesteryear, so why bother? (Some players, like Chicago Bears teammates Dick Butkus and Gale Sayers, straddle both eras but wind up here because they made their lasting impacts in the 1960s.) Today's athletes are bigger, stronger, faster, quicker, and far better conditioned; coaches and strategies are more sophisticated, more intricate, and more nuanced than ever before; and fans have come to expect the high-energy thrills and excitement that these better athletes and more tactically demanding coaches now provide.

Also, in assessing the impact of legendary players since 1970, I've limited the discussion to players who have retired from the game. This is primarily because I don't want to put myself or Rodney in any kind of awkward position if we run into any current teammate or opponent who wonders why he wasn't included (or any wife who wonders the same on her husband's behalf), but also because it's impossible to judge the historical impact of a player's career until it has concluded. No question, guys like Jerry Rice, Brett Favre, and Peyton Manning will one day round out these lists, but for now they'll just have to keep up the good work and wait their turn.

Here are 10 need-to-know Hall of Famers from football's early days, up to and including my early childhood, presented in no particular order but the one in which they occurred to me.

RED GRANGE (1925-1935): One of the best-known players of the game's early days, halfback Red Grange is widely credited with helping to put the NFL on the map . . . dubbed "the Galloping Ghost" by sportswriters during his All-American collegiate career at the University of Illinois for his breakaway speed and elusive open-field moves . . . for a time, Grange was one of the most popular athletes in the country, in any sport . . . played primarily for the Chicago Bears in an abbreviated professional career that never matched his success at the college level, but his name and reputation live on as one of the first icons of the game . . .

DON HUTSON (1935-1945):

Football's first great wide receiver, known for his leaping ability, his big, soft hands, and his monumentally long reach . . . the centerpiece of Green Bay's innovative "quick strike" offense of the 1930s and '40s . . . recorded the NFL's first 1,000-yard season (actually 1,211) in a 1942 campaign that saw 17 of his then-record 74 catches go for touchdowns . . . retired with 488 career catches, dwarfing the next-highest total (298) and establishing a benchmark that would last for generations . . . Hutson was virtually impossible to defend, leading opposing coaches to double- and triple-team him on pass patterns, an unusual strategy at the time. . . .

GINO MARCHETTI (1952-1966):

The prototypical defensive end of the 1950s, Marchetti manned the line for the Baltimore Colts with tremendous speed and upper-body strength, and a wild ferocity that left opponents dizzy . . . it was Marchetti who pioneered the practice of pressuring the quarterback from the defensive end position, and nobody did it any better . . . led the Colts to two NFL championships, on his way to 10 Pro Bowl appearances and a reputation that grew with each menacing tackle and explosive charge . . . this guy was so good that opposing coaches sometimes avoided his side of the field completely on the game-changing theory that, if you can't beat 'em, you can at least avoid 'em . . .

SAMMY BAUGH (1937-1952):

"Slingin' Sammy" is probably best known for the way he almost single-handedly reinvented the passing game . . . in an era dominated by quarterbacks who looked to pass only sparingly and running attacks that operated as the default means of advancing the ball, Baugh introduced a ball-control passing game that caught opponents by all kinds of surprise . . . in his rookie season, led the Washington Red-skins to their first-ever league championship . . . Baugh pulled double-duty in his first seven seasons as an outstanding defensive back who, in one game, grabbed a then-record four interceptions . . . he was also one of the game's best punters . . . retired with a record 187 touchdown passes and an incredible 21,886 passing yards, along with a 56.5 pass completion percentage that eclipsed his closest rivals by double-digits . . .

JOHNNY UNITAS (1956-1973): Another Baltimore legend and an icon to generations of die-hard Colts fans . . . a composed and imposing presence on his side of the line, with an uncanny ability to read opposing defenses and isolate weak spots . . . he was also famous for his willingness to hang back in the pocket until the last possible moment, daring pass rushers and linebackers to leave their marks and delivering letter-perfect passes the moment they did . . . retired with more meaningful career records than any other quarterback in NFL history, including 2,830 completions, 40,239 yards, and 290 touchdowns . . . his most impressive stat is probably the 47 consecutive games in which he threw at least one touchdown pass, an indication of his great consistency and his competitive toughness over the long haul . . . on a personal note, Rodney took an award named for him for best college QB in 1988 . . .

JIM BROWN (1957-1965): Cleveland Browns running back widely considered the greatest fullback to play the game, and arguably the greatest athlete . . . (he was also a standout basketball and lacrosse player) . . . won the league rushing title a record eight times . . . named the NFL's Most Valuable Player in 1957, 1958, 1963, and 1965 . . . retired at the top of his game in 1965, after only nine seasons, establishing a career rushing record of 12,312 yards that stood for nearly 20 years . . . known in retirement for a series of Hollywood action films, and for occasionally boasting (into his fifties, no less) that he could still compete on the professional level, a claim no one who had seen him play cared to dispute . . .

GALE SAYERS (1965-1971): Running back Sayers charged into the NFL in 1965 with one of the greatest rookie seasons in any team sport, tallying an incredible 22 touchdowns and becoming an immediate and lifelong darling of Chicago Bears fans . . . most incredible of all was his versatility: 14 of his 22 rookie scores were rushing touchdowns, six were touchdown receptions, one was a kickoff return, and one came on a punt return . . . the man seemed to run at full-tilt, all-out, all the time, and yet he could switch gears and side-step defenders and glide artfully across the field in such a way that you never quite knew where his powerful legs would take him next. . . . those who played with him called him the greatest athlete they'd ever seen . . . those who played against him wished they hadn't . . . his career was cut painfully short by a series of knee injuries at the age of 28 and his legacy dimmed by the fact that his Bears never reached the post-season on his magical watch, but there was no dimming the sparkle he brought to the game . . . still, his career totals stand among the all-time best: 5.0 yards per carry, 11.7 yards per catch, 30.6 yards per kickoff return, and 14.5 yards per punt return . . .

OTTO GRAHAM (1946-1955):
The consummate quarterback of his generation, Graham led the Cleveland Browns to a dominant 47-4-3 record and four consecutive league championships from 1946-49 in the upstart All-America Football Conference . . . Graham and the Browns jumped to the more competitive NFL in 1950, but kept on winning, reaching the NFL championship game for another six years in a row and collecting three titles . . . in all, Graham's 10 straight league championship appearances and 105-17-4 record over that span are unmatched for a quarterback at the professional level . . . forget unmatched, it's downright unheard of . . .

DICK BUTKUS (1965-1973):
Ranks among the greatest linebackers in the history of the game and one of the preeminent stars of the NFL in the late 1960s . . . played his entire career for the Chicago Bears . . . like his great teammate, Gale Sayers, he never played for a winner but dominated the middle of the field on his way to eight Pro Bowl appearances . . . according to many football historians, helped to reinvent the position with his hard-hitting style of play and overall athleticism . . . also known as one of the best ball-stripping tacklers of his generation, with a stunning 27 opponent fumble recoveries and 22 interceptions in just 119 professional games . . . became famous to a new generation of fans in retirement with appearances in a wildly popular series of beer commercials for Miller Lite . . .

DICK "NIGHT TRAIN" LANE (1952-1965):
The "godfather of cornerbacks," according to fellow defensive back Lem Barney, Lane was a force in the secondary for the Los Angeles Rams, the Chicago Cardinals, and the Detroit Lions in a 14-year career that began in 1952 . . . a walk-on who had never played above the junior college level, he wowed the Rams coaching staff and became a fixture in the defensive backfield, posting a record-shattering 14 interceptions in his rookie season, running two of them back for touchdowns . . . Lane, who took his headline-friendly nickname from a popular song, became known around the league for his tenacious hits . . . his trademark clothesline and facemask tackles forced NFL rule makers to ban such moves, but Lane adapted to every rules change and remained a hard-edged, hard-charging, hard-hitting force throughout his career . . .

2

Kickoff

Terms of Engagement

When it comes down to it, the object of the game of football is not to beat your opponents senseless, or to take out the other guy's legs, or to dodge and stiff-arm past would-be defenders until you've run out of field. These, girlfriends, are merely the happy accidents of the game, but not the object of the game itself.

Simply put, the object of the game is to score more points than the other guys. Of course, the same is true in baseball, basketball, soccer, volleyball, and pretty much every sport I can think of except golf, where the lowest score prevails—so I suppose that last line isn't all that helpful.

Let me try again. The object of the game is to advance the ball the length of the field, toward a goal line defended by your opponents, and to prevent your opponents from doing the same. Naturally, your opponents' objective runs entirely counter to yours—they're out to prevent you from advancing the ball or to run circles around your defense, take your pick. It's a classic stalemate: The team in possession of the ball can attempt to run with it, or pass it to avoid or outmaneuver the defenders, while the defending team must be able to "read" or anticipate its opponents' plays in order to deny them forward progress. Theoretically, if each side runs its game plan to perfection, nobody will accomplish anything.

Ah, but therein lies the beautiful truth of the game. There is no such thing as theoretically. No team ever executes its game plan to perfection. It's never happened and it never will. Sure, from time to time, a team might run a perfect play, or slot in the perfect defensive scheme for a given situation, but over the course of an entire game someone on one side of the ball or the other is bound to miscalculate, misread, or misstep. It's these mistakes that can cause a quarterback to make an unscripted yet brilliant play or a cornerback to make an interception and run it back for a touchdown. Mistakes can change the whole complexion of the game. They're exciting, and they keep fans coming back for more. That's football, baby. Mistakes happen. And they can happen anywhere on the field, at any time.

What is scripted, however, are the rules and regulations, the terms of engagement, if you will. This chapter covers the basics—the field, the ball, the clock, the scoreboard, the teams and officials, and the rules—leaving room for an open-ended discussion of the game's merits a bit later on in the book.

The Field

Let's address this anywhere-on-the-field business straight out of the gate, because we need to get the lay of the land in order to understand how the game is played on it. A regulation football field spans a little more than an acre—at 100 yards long and 53.5 yards wide—which I'm told makes for just the right wide shot on those rectangular wide-screen televisions. Unlike baseball or soccer, where field dimensions can change drastically from one venue to the next, these measurements are standard from middle school fields all the way up to the professional level.

Players don't run the length of the field every time the ball is in play. In fact, the most successful teams grind out yardage in a methodical way. With this approach, there's no need to cover a ton of ground on any single play, as long as you keep moving the ball forward, toward the goal line, and as long as you manage to hold on to the ball. (More on all this yardage business later.)

The look of each field is also fairly standard—except, of course, for the fancy designs, doodads, and team logos you'll often find spray-painted in the end zones and at midfield. (Lately, in what can only be a nod to fans at home, I've seen some college football stadiums experiment with colored turf that leaves me looking to adjust the tint on my television.)

At both ends of the field are white lines to mark the end zones, which extend on each side of the field another 10 yards to the back line. A thick white line borders the entire field, including the end zones, to indicate the boundaries.

Anatomy of a Football Field

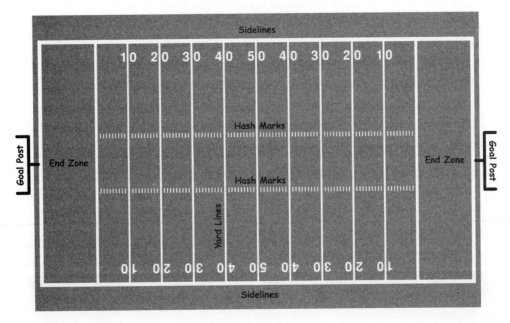

There are other white lines, running parallel to the end zone lines, and crossing the field at 5-yard intervals with the 50-yard line in the center. These lines, in turn, are crisscrossed by two rows of dashes known as hash marks that run parallel to the sidelines. Before each play, officials place the ball between these rows of hash marks where it has come to rest on the previous play—or, if play was stopped outside the hash marks, on the row of hash marks closest to where the previous play ended. Goalposts constructed with a 10-foot vertical pole topped by an 18.5-foot horizontal crossbar sit in the middle of each end line, at the back of each end zone. Vertical uprights extend from either end of the crossbar to provide a target for kickers attempting a field goal or an extra-point conversion.

The Ball

Official NFL footballs are made of a rubber bladder encased in leather (originally pigskin, today cowhide or a synthetic material) and inflated to between

HISTORY OF THE GAME

TAKING SHAPE

The first egg-shaped American football was patented in 1867. Football historians aren't too clear on how the football got its shape, but it seems to have happened almost accidentally. Early games were played with a perfectly round ball, but it was difficult to inflate the bladder of the ball to the proper dimensions. If you read through some of the accounts of the day, you'd find that what usually happened was that the players took turns blowing up the ball, until they eventually tired of the ordeal and went back to the game—with a somewhat lopsided ball. Over time, the players came to favor the odd shape for the way it permitted a better grip on the narrow end, helping them cradle and protect the ball when they ran with it, and for the uncertain bounce it took when it hit the ground, making it difficult for opponents to collect a loose ball. In short, it made things interesting.

12.5 and 13.5 pounds. Regulation balls are shaped like an extended spheroid, 28.5 inches around the long axis and 21.25 inches around the short axis. Every ball must weigh between 14 and 15 ounces. And here's a little-known fact that I couldn't have guessed if I hadn't been poring over the NFL rule book in preparing this text: Home teams are required to provide league officials with 36 regulation balls prior to the start of games in open-air stadiums, or 24 regulation balls prior to the start of games in domed stadiums—along with a pump so game officials can make any on-field adjustments they deem necessary. I'll bet your man didn't know that!

The Game Clock

NFL games consist of 60 minutes of playing time, divided into four quarters of 15 minutes each. (Whatever you do, don't make the mistake of calling these quarters periods, because that will just get your man all kinds of crazy. Periods are what you have in hockey, when the same 60-minute clock is divided into three 20-minute intervals. And for all you hockey fans out there, don't go calling those intervals quarters, because, well . . . that just doesn't add up.) A 12-minute halftime takes place at the game's midpoint, during which the teams return to their locker rooms and following which they defend the opposite end zone.

The official game clock is stopped at the end of each quarter and at each change of possession. The clock is also stopped whenever the ball is run out of bounds, when a team throws an incomplete pass, or when the referee signals a "2-minute warning" before the end of each half. Game officials may stop the clock for a variety of additional reasons, such as to call a penalty or to allow a coach to review a play.

Each team is awarded three time-outs per half, during which the clock is stopped. They can elect to use them at any time between plays or not at all, although unused time-outs cannot be carried over from the first half to the second.

A regular-season game that results in a tie at the end of regulation play extends to a 15-minute overtime period, also known as sudden death, during which the first team to score is declared the winner. If no team scores within the overtime period, the game ends in a tie. In a play-off game, where a winner must be declared so that one team can advance to the next round, overtime periods will continue until a team manages to score. (After the fuss I made earlier, careful readers will note that these 15-minute overtime intervals are called periods and not quarters, probably on the internal logic that you can only have four quarters in a game and we've plum run out—so try to keep things straight.)

There's also a 40-second play clock that kicks in after each play is whistled dead. This clock requires the offense to start each play within 40 seconds, else

HISTORY OF THE GAME

EARLY RULES CHANGES

The first widely adopted rules came from Princeton University in 1867. One of the major mandates of these rules was to set a limit of 25 players per side. Just up the road, at Rutgers University, there was another set of rules in play, and a natural rivalry developed between the two schools, leading to what many football scholars now refer to as the first intercollegiate football game. Held in New Brunswick, New Jersey, on November 6, 1869, Rutgers won by a score of 6-4.

By 1873, the standard number of players for each side was reduced to 20; by 1876, it was down to 15. Each change appeared to open up the game, and to highlight individual skills. The changes also reduced congestion around the ball and allowed for more exciting breakaway runs and open-field tackles. That same year (1876), Harvard challenged Yale to a game played under a strange hybrid of accepted rugby and soccer rules, beginning a storied rivalry that continues to this day. The two schools joined with Princeton and Columbia to form the Intercollegiate Football Association—the game's first real governing body. Among the many new regulations set by this new association was the size of the field. Up until this time, games had been played on whatever open spaces were available, but now fixed field dimensions of 140 by 70 yards were established—unless of course there was a row of trees or hedges or some other natural boundary to require some last-minute adjustments.

the game clock is stopped, a flag is thrown, and the offense is penalized for a "delay of game."

The Teams

NFL teams dress 53 "active" players for each game. Additional players might be considered part of the team, such as "taxi" (practice-squad) players, and players on the injured reserve list, even though they might be ineligible for a particular game. Of these active players, 11 are deployed on the field at any given time. I'll discuss the different offensive and defensive positions in chapter 3, and also look closely at common positional alignments, but for now I'll just offer the short course.

On an offensive unit, players are commonly divided into two distinct groups: linemen and backs. The linemen play on the line of scrimmage (that imaginary line running through the position of the ball); the backs (such as the quarterback and running backs) take up their positions behind the linemen. In most systems, receivers are considered part of the backfield, although they usually line up wide (to the left or right) of the rest of the formation on the line of scrimmage. There's a row of linemen on the defensive team as well, a row of linebackers, and a group of defensive backs, also known as the secondary.

The Officials

Professional football games are presided over by a referee, an umpire, a linesman, a field judge, a back judge, a line judge, and a side judge. That's seven officials in all, with the referee having the last word on virtually everything. Known derisively as "zebras" for the vertically striped black-and-white jerseys they wear, these men are charged with maintaining the integrity of the game—or throwing it into question, as the case may be. All officials carry a yellow penalty flag, which they can toss on the field to indicate a rules violation of some kind, which stops the game clock in the process. While I'm on it, I should

THE OFFICIAL WORD

The 12 signals below are probably the most common you'll see from the officials in an NFL game. Penalties for these infractions range from loss of yardage to the loss of a down; a player can even be ejected from the game for a flagrant violation.

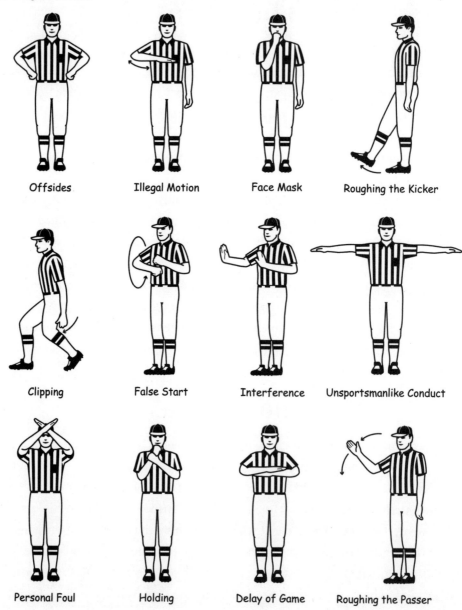

Offsides

Illegal Motion

Face Mask

Roughing the Kicker

Clipping

False Start

Interference

Unsportsmanlike Conduct

Personal Foul

Holding

Delay of Game

Roughing the Passer

put in my two cents on these flags. I really wish the officials would just drop them on the ground instead of needlessly throwing them toward the players at the spot of the foul. Those bad boys are anchored with sand and hurt like heck if you get hit with one. I've seen some serious and unnecessary injuries happen this way. Just a thought.

Officials also carry a whistle that they sound to indicate a dead ball, or the end of a play, or the ability of an offensive team to resume play after a stoppage of some kind. Each one of these guys has a specific job: The linesman marks the position of the ball; the umpire rules on matters concerning player conduct, equipment, and positioning; the field judge monitors the game clock. And so on. The referee is like an on-field supervisor, able to overrule any of the six other officials if he disagrees with a call, or to settle the matter in the event there are conflicting calls from two officials.

A word or two on instant replay, which in recent years has assisted officials in making calls they might miss with the naked eye. A lot of football folk object to using cameras to call the game on the field, but my feeling is, Why not? There's so much riding on some of these big games that it's incumbent on the league to keep the playing field as level as possible. If that means giving the officials the ability to second-guess themselves or to build more time into the game to free them from making snap judgments, then I'm all for it. There is nothing more frustrating—to players, coaches, and fans—than losing a game based on a bad call, especially when we have the technology to make double-sure that the calls are correct.

The Scoreboard

Scoring in football is a complicated affair, with point values that at first glance appear to have been randomly assigned to different objectives (field goals, touchdowns, etc.).

A touchdown is the point of the whole damn enterprise and is achieved whenever the ball is successfully run into the end zone or caught within it. So it makes sense that a touchdown is assigned the highest value of any game objective: six points. Many rookie fans assume a touchdown is actually worth seven points, because it leads directly to a point-after-touchdown conversion—an opportunity to score an extra one or two points. This conversion does not cause additional time to elapse from the clock, and there's no chance that the defensive team might block or otherwise interfere with the attempt and result in a score or in strong field position for the other guys. It's like a bonus—the cherry on top of a dramatic score.

In an extra-point conversion, the offensive team lines up at the 2-yard line and attempts to kick the ball through the uprights, as in a field goal. From such a short distance, the extra-point attempt is virtually assured; and last I checked, placekickers were successful in more than 95 percent of their extra-point tries. Beginning in 1994, however, the NFL added a two-point conversion option, which allowed offensive teams to run or pass the ball into the end zone from the same 2 yards out. Unlike the extra-point kick, the two-point conversion is no gimme. But it has added a new wrinkle to the never-ending chess match that goes on between the opposing coaches. In most game situations, teams tend to opt for the easier extra-point conversion, but every weekend you'll see coaches looking to pile on points with two-point attempts, either to pad a lead or to chase a deficit.

If a team is facing fourth down and has not managed to cross the opponents' goal line, and they are in what's called "field-goal range" (typically 50 yards or less from the uprights), they will most likely attempt a field goal on their fourth-down play, hoping to kick the ball through the uprights at the back of the end zone for three points.

Regardless of the outcome of the conversion, the game is restarted after a field goal or a touchdown with a kickoff from the scoring team's 30-yard line—just as it is at the start of each half.

As indicated earlier, the defense can get in on the scoring by tackling an opponent in his own end zone for a safety, worth two points. Following a safety (and adding insult to injury), the offensive team is required to punt the ball to its opponents—returning the ball to them immediately following a score.

How the Game Is Played

POSSESSION AND KICKOFF: NFL games begin with a coin toss at midfield to determine possession of the ball. The visiting teams' captains are invited to call "heads" or "tails." (In neutral-site games, such as the Super Bowl, the referee designates which team calls the toss.) The team that wins the toss has several options for determining possession of the ball. They can elect to receive the ball at the start of play or to kick off and begin the game with their defensive unit on the field. (A kickoff, as the term implies, is when a team concedes possession of the ball to its opponents, kicking it downfield in hopes of pushing the other guys deep into their own territory.) Or they can choose which end zone to defend, thereby allowing the other team to determine initial possession.

When deciding possession, teams consider a range of factors. For example, a team with a particularly strong defense and a mediocre offense may find it effective to begin the game without the ball, on the theory that a quick and effective defensive series can yield enough momentum to jump-start a nothing-special offensive attack. In an open-ended stadium with a spiraling wind, it might be more of an advantage to begin the game with the wind at your back than to start out with possession of the ball.

At the beginning of the second half, the opening kickoff scenario is reversed, leaving open the possibility that a team could score on the last play of the first half and receive the ball on the ensuing kickoff to start the second half.

Since 1994, the ball has been placed on the kicking team's 30-yard line for each kickoff; prior to that, it had been placed on the 35-yard line, and prior to that on the 40-yard line. It was moved back over the years to compensate for the increased leg strength of professional place kickers, and to give the receiving team a little more room to mount an effective return.

MOVING THE BALL: Any player on the receiving team is eligible to catch, pick up, or otherwise gain possession of the ball on a kickoff, after which he can advance it towards the opponents' goal line until he is tackled or run out of bounds. A player is considered tackled, or "downed," when one knee touches the ground. A player is considered out of bounds when a finger, toe, elbow, or any other body part touches the white boundary line bordering the field.

Each team is given four downs (plays, attempts) to move the ball 10 yards down the field. So if you advance 3 or 4 yards on each play, you'd be in good shape over the course of the game. If a team achieves those 10 yards in four plays or less, it is awarded another four attempts—"a new set of downs" in football parlance—to cover the next 10 yards. And so on. When there are no longer 10 yards left to gain, it usually means an offensive team has run across the opponents' goal line and scored a touchdown, accomplishing their primary objective—unless of course a player has taken a few too many hits to the head and has run in the wrong direction, which, believe it or not, has been known to happen.

If after four downs an offensive team has been unable to gain those 10 yards or score a touchdown, it must give up possession of the ball to the defending team, whereupon the action on the field shifts direction. In this way, I guess, the game is a great model for teaching our preschool kids how to share—each side gets a turn and no one gets to hog the ball without earning the right to hog it.

Once the ball shifts possession, the team that is now on offense must try to advance it toward their opponents' goal line; the team now on defense must try to keep them from doing so. It's in this back-and-forth that the game is played. (Talk about playing fair! Playing nice, however, doesn't seem to be in the game's lesson plan.)

Typically, a team will punt (kick) the ball on its fourth attempt if it hasn't gained the necessary first-down yardage, sending it downfield and pushing the opponent further away from its own goal line before giving up possession. However, if they're in field-goal range, they might go for the three points as a kind of consolation prize.

A play is considered stopped when the ballcarrier is tackled; when a ballcarrier is considered to be "in the grasp" of a defender and his forward progress has been clearly halted; when a forward pass hits the ground or lands out-of-bounds without being caught; when a ball is dropped (or "fumbled") and lands out-of-bounds or in the arms of a downed player; or when a kicked ball leaves the field of play. However, the game clock continues to tick during most of these scenarios.

PLAY CALLING (OR DECIDING WHAT TO DO): Between plays you'll usually notice each team gathered in a tight circle on its designated side of the field, where players will go over strategies and formations for the next play. These tight circles are known as huddles, and I've always thought they were one of the cutest aspects of the game. You don't usually hear words like cute tossed around regarding football players, but what can I say? Ever since I was a kid, I thought it was adorable the way these brutes lined up and circled their wagons to discuss their next moves. (In some college programs, players even hold hands in their huddles—I mean, how cute is that?!)

The offensive team will form its huddle about 10 yards from the ball, where for about 10 to 15 seconds the quarterback will bark out a play and offer general words of encouragement (or constructive criticism that may or may not include a few carefully chosen expletives) to his teammates. Frequently, the play will be decided by a coach on the sidelines or up in a box who will send in his call through a series of hand signals, a set of hollered codes—or, these days, via radio transmission from a headset to an earpiece strategically placed inside the quarterback's helmet.

At the same time, the defensive team will form its own huddle, just beyond the ball on its side of the field—as close as possible to the goings-on of their opponents. (Ah, the better to possibly hear what's going on in the enemy camp.) Here, too, a defensive captain will communicate to his teammates how the coaches want them to approach the next play.

In some situations, most notably toward the end of each game when time is running out and trailing teams move into "hurry-up" mode, teams might deploy a no-huddle offense. This means that plays are called at the line of scrimmage when players are already in formation, instead of in the huddle. This also means, logically, that defensive teams must go without a huddle as well, because the quarterback can start the play whenever he wants.

Actually, let me amend the "whenever he wants" part of this last statement. The quarterback can't actually start the play until his offensive unit has lined up in formation and until the defensive unit has retreated to its side of the ball. Plus, there's the 40-second play clock within which the offense must start each play to avoid being penalized for a "delay of game."

In any case, play resumes after the ball is spotted (placed down) by the linesman and the two teams break from their huddles and line up in formation on either side of the ball, which becomes known as "the line of scrimmage."

Typically, one of the offensive linemen (the center) will line up in a crouch over the ball and snap it between his legs to the quarterback on an agreed-upon signal. The quarterback can then hand it off or make a forward or lateral pass to an eligible back or receiver, or run it himself. A forward pass may only be made from a position behind the line of scrimmage, and only during a play run from scrimmage. (That is, a forward pass cannot be attempted on a kickoff or punt return, or following an interception or fumble recovery.) A lateral pass (a backwards throw from the QB to a running back or wide receiver) may be made at any time, from anywhere on the field. Similarly, a handoff may be made at any time, from anywhere on the field, provided that the initial ballcarrier hands the ball off to a receiving ballcarrier from a position away from the downfield side of his body. During a play run from scrimmage, the initial ball-carrier can hand the ball off from either side of his body, provided he has not yet crossed the line of scrimmage.

Nine-Tenths of the Game

Football is a possession game, really. It's a matter of control, which is why when we women finally come to it and understand it, we're all over it. We like to be in charge, wouldn't you agree? Indeed, when things are going well on the football field, the dominant team can really call the shots, dictate the flow of play, and control the tempo of the game. For one example, a team with a strong running game can eat up those all-important yards on a slow, purposeful drive down the field; and in so doing, eat up those all-important minutes on the clock, thereby leaving their opponents with less time to counterattack. For another example, a team with a strong passing attack can open up the game in such a way that it becomes doubly difficult for its opponents to guard against them. And a team with a strong running game and a strong passing game can mix things up and really leave the defense on its heels. Conversely, a defensive team with a strong pass rush or excellent pass coverage can really shut down a team that relies on its passing game, while a top-notch defensive line can sometimes put the brakes on even the best running attack.

A lot of folks talk about football as a kind of war. In fact, the language of the game is steeped in military tradition. A team is said to march into an opponents' "territory." A game can be a "hard-fought battle." A player who takes a good deal of punishment while continuing to dish it out is said to be a "warrior"—or, more to the point, a "gladiator." The line of scrimmage, where the action tends to be the fiercest and most brutal, is sometimes known as "the trenches." Announcers refer to a player's equipment and uniform as a "suit of armor." Most fans embrace the endless analogy, and home crowds have been known to unleash the kinds of rallying cries that were once heard on the fields of battle.

Possession, territory, field generals, lines of attack . . . these are the terms of engagement on the field, and we beginning fans will do well to understand them in context and then set them aside. You see, as a fan, I've always appreciated the strategy behind the game. I've always thought of it as more of a chess match than a war. Ask a guy like my husband Rodney, who has spent most of his adolescence and adult life on and around a football field, and he'll tell you it's a war down there—he describes the line of scrimmage as "the point of battle." And for most guys I know, the real thrills come only in those hard, unexpected hits across the middle of the line.

But a war is less interesting to me than a chess match. Decide for yourself where you check in on this, but for my money there's less subtlety to a war, less room for grace and artistry. Warfare suggests more a match of brute strength and will than a thinking-man's contest. To me, some of football's most exciting moments come in those perfectly executed plays where no one gets hurt.

———————

I'm happy to report that once you commit this stuff to that place in the back of your head where you don't have to think about it anymore, and once you watch enough games to attach a mental picture to your rote memory, you'll be good to go. What will take considerably longer, I'm afraid, is taking your "game" to the next level, to where you can talk the talk at the busiest sports bar in town, sucking back suds in front of a Monday Night Football game. For that you'll need some serious game-watching experience, same as those guys on the field. It's only fitting, don't you think? After all, these guys don't reach the pinnacle of their sport without logging their time in the trenches.

10

ALL-TIME GREATS OF THE GAME (POST-1970)

Picking up where we left off on the previous Cheat Sheet, here are 10 standout players every beginning fan should know. Listed once again in no particular order, these Hall of Famers are of more recent vintage. All are currently retired, although some of these guys played recently enough that Rodney had the honor to play against or alongside them, which has given me a firsthand (by marriage!) perspective on what it takes to make a lasting impact in the game of football.

I have to mention that it's rough to leave off greats like Terry Bradshaw, Roger Staubach, and even the freshly retired Emmitt Smith. But whenever you limit yourself to ten, many "greats" get left off.

BOB LILLY (1961–1974): This guy straddles our two "eras", but he certainly deserves mention as one of the best defensive tackles ever to play the game, and he is slotted here because he was still an impact player into the early 1970s . . . "Mr. Cowboy," so named because he was the first draft pick in franchise history, the first All-Pro, the first Pro Bowl selection, and the first player who spent his entire career with the Cowboys to be inducted into the Hall of Fame . . . incredibly quick for his size, he was a mainstay of Dallas's notorious "Doomsday Defense" and a staunch competitor . . . I remember watching him play when I was a kid and being struck by what a nice guy he appeared to be; but now that I know a bit more about the game, I realize he was a tenacious force . . . among his most notable accomplishments: he never missed a regular-season game in his 14 NFL seasons . . .

JOE MONTANA (1979–1994): A tremendous "big-game" quarterback, quite possibly the biggest gamer in football history . . . Montana boasted an average arm, average speed, and average overall athletic ability, and yet he put it all together in a package that was off the charts . . . flourished under coach Bill Walsh's trailblazing "West Coast" offense, which featured high-percentage, short-yardage passes and played neatly into

Montana's innate ability to read defenses and anticipate plays . . . really, this guy was un-canny . . . teamed with wide receiver Jerry Rice to form the most successful passing combi-nation the game has ever seen . . . an effective scrambler early in his career, rushing for 1,676 yards and 20 touchdowns over the course of his career . . . compiled a stellar 92.3 career passer rating, amassing over 40,000 passing yards (plus another 5,772 in the post season) . . . best remembered in San Francisco for leading the 49ers to four Super Bowl victories, grabbing three Super Bowl MVP trophies along the way, and establishing his reputation as the best post-season quarterback in anyone's memory . . . also known as a pressure player, Montana engineered 31 fourth-quarter comeback victories in his Hall of Fame career . . .

LAWRENCE TAYLOR (1981-1993): "L.T." . . . overcame some serious off-field turmoil to become one of the most ferociously intimidating defenders ever, giving new meaning to the term "driving force" . . . named NFL Defensive Player of the Year in 1981, his rookie season, serving notice that the game had changed for the foreseeable future, and vaulting the New York Giants from second-division status to perennial championship con-tenders . . . transformed the role of middle linebacker to where it was his responsibility to rush the passer, stop the run, and guard against the pass, all at once . . . made his presence known on virtually every play from scrimmage . . . played with a passion that appeared to be equal parts anger and hunger . . . notched double-digit single season sack totals for a record seven consecutive seasons, encompassing his career year of 1986, when he recorded 20½ sacks and led the Giants to their first Super Bowl title . . . that same year, Taylor was named NFL Player of the Year, the only defensive player in league history to win the award since 1971 . . . retired with 10 Pro Bowl appearances, two Super Bowl rings, and 132½ sacks in his 13-year career . . .

WALTER PAYTON (1975-1987): "Sweetness" . . . one of the strongest, best-conditioned athletes who ever played the game, Payton was the complete-package running back, able to run, catch, and block like nobody's business . . . he wasn't especially fast, but he had an explosive first step that was enough to help him skate past would-be tack-lers into open territory . . . he wasn't especially "sweet" either—at least not on the field—pun-ishing defenders with blocks that belied his relatively small size, but the name stuck because of his soft-spoken demeanor off the field . . . Payton piled on more yardage after contact than any runner in recent memory, helped by a bruising stiff-arm, tremendous leg strength, and

a refusal to go down without a fight . . . a nine-time Pro Bowl selection who missed only one game, during his rookie year, and then went on to play for 13 consecutive NFL seasons . . . Payton put together a remarkable 77 100-yard rushing games in his career, including a then-record 275 yards in a 1977 game against Minnesota . . . Emmitt Smith has since surpassed Payton's 16,726 career rushing yards, but his 21,264 combined rushing/receiving yards remain a benchmark . . . began his career on a series of mediocre Bears teams, but hung on long enough to help Chicago win its first Super Bowl in 1985 . . . died in 1999, at the too-young age of 45, of a cancer complicated by a rare liver disease . . .

BARRY SANDERS (1989-1998): Lightning-quick Detroit Lions running back, arguably the premier player at his position throughout the 1990s . . . the former Heisman Trophy winner was thought to be too small to play in the NFL when he graduated from Oklahoma State in 1989; but the Lions took a chance and Sanders came up big, rushing for 1,470 yards in his rookie season, beginning a record-setting string of 10 consecutive 1,000-yard seasons, including 2,053 yards in 1997 . . . Sanders had more moves than the Dallas Cowboy Cheerleaders, stutter-stepping and juking his way past tacklers and into the record books . . . some weeks he seemed to show up in every other halftime highlight, that's how consistently dazzling he was, game in and game out . . . amassed 15,269 career rushing yards, which put him just a season or so behind Walter Payton for the top spot on the all-time list, when he abruptly announced his retirement just before the 1999 season . . . named to the Pro Bowl in every one of his 10 NFL seasons, a testament to his steady excellence . . . named also to our list of all-time favorite teammates, since Rodney says he never played with a more talented, grounded, or humble athlete in all his years in the game . . .

JOE GREENE (1969-1981): "Mean Joe" . . . an anchor of Pittsburgh's famed "Steel Curtain" defense, and a central figure in the Steelers' run to four Super Bowl championships . . . that run was made all the more remarkable when set against the previous four decades in franchise history, when winning seasons were scarce and marquee players almost always turned up in an opponents' uniform . . . 10 Pro Bowl selections in 13 seasons secured his reputation as one of the all-time greats, but it was the fear he struck in opposing offensive linemen that set Greene apart . . . considered one of the strongest, quickest linemen of his generation . . . he wore his nickname like it mattered, grunting and snorting his way to a reputation as one of the nastiest players of his generation, but he was said to be a pussycat when the game ended . . . became a pop culture idol in a landmark Coca-Cola commercial, in which he offered his sweat-soaked game jersey to a little kid in a locker room tunnel in exchange for a bottle of Coke and a smile . . .

RONNIE LOTT (1981-1994):
Our great pal, and Rodney's fellow USC Trojan, Ronnie Lott was one of the best safeties ever to roam a defensive backfield . . . a fixture on those great 49er teams of the 1980s, with four Super Bowl rings to his great credit, Ronnie was known for his vision and instincts as well as for his punishing blows . . . he was already a Pro Bowl cornerback when he switched positions in 1985, becoming a free safety—and, later, a strong safety, where he pretty much thrived . . . collected 63 career "picks," putting him fifth on the all-time list, but his ball-hawking skills could not be measured by statistics . . . he was one of those tenacious defenders who cause opposing quarterbacks to rethink their game plans—and opposing receivers to rethink their career choices . . . finished his career with the Los Angeles Raiders and the New York Jets, but will be best remembered for his 10 standout seasons with San Francisco . . .

ANTHONY MUNOZ (1980-1992):
One of those under-the-radar-type players who quietly put together a glorious career at one of the game's most unheralded positions . . . Munoz was widely regarded as the best offensive tackle in the game throughout his 13 NFL seasons, although he played in relative obscurity for the Cincinnati Bengals . . . despite two Super Bowl appearances (both losses to Joe Montana's San Francisco 49ers), Munoz's Bengals were rarely featured on nationally televised games, and he ended up doing his thing without great fanfare—that is, from folks outside the game . . . to his teammates and coaches, and to opposing players and coaches, Munoz was the consummate lineman, protecting his quarterback and creating holes for his runners with an aggressive approach that rivaled his fiercest defenders . . . selected to 11 Pro Bowl squads, the man could flat out level you . . . ask any quarterback of the 1980s who they wanted on their offensive line and Munoz would have been at the top of every list . . . heck, Rodney and his buddies still talk about this guy, and he's been retired since 1992, so you know he was the real deal . . .

DAN MARINO (1983-1999): Got to make room for this guy, who as of this writing owns pretty much every major career and season passing record on the books . . . (of course, as of this writing, Indianapolis's Peyton Manning is doing what he can to rewrite some of those season marks, but that's for another edition) . . . owned one of the quickest arms the game has ever seen . . . look in the dictionary under "pure passer" and you'll likely come across a picture of Marino, who could launch a perfect bomb or loft a soft floater with precision accuracy . . . pro scouts didn't make much of his chances, and he was the sixth quarterback taken in the 1983 college draft, after a standout career at the University of Pittsburgh . . . made his mark in his second year, passing for a season-record 5,084 yards and 48 touchdowns (also a season mark, until Manning got his hands on it) . . . established career marks in passing yards, completions, and touchdown passes that may never be broken . . . a fiery competitor with tremendous field vision, Marino never won a championship, but he was a true champion in virtually every other respect . . .

O. J. SIMPSON (1969-1979): "The Juice" . . . say what you will about this controversial fallen icon, but Orenthal James Simpson was the best running back of his generation, and he rates a mention here for his on-field accomplishments . . . one of the most heralded running backs ever to play at the college level, on his way to winning the Heisman Trophy, O.J. set all kinds of NCAA records at Rodney's alma mater, USC. . . . almost single-handedly lifted the Buffalo Bills to respectability in the early 1970s, with six Pro Bowl seasons and a threshold-shattering 1973 campaign during which he became the first running back to rush for more than 2,000 yards in a single season . . . he also established the records for most rushing yards in a single game, and most touchdowns scored in a season . . . after nine great years for the Bills, he hung on for a couple more with the San Francisco 49ers, before easing into a retirement that included acting, sports commentating, and golfing . . . one of his best-known gigs was in a popular television commercial for Hertz rental cars, where he could be seen leaping over luggage in a crowded airport, rushing to catch a flight . . .

3

Assume the Position

Who Are These Guys?

If you're like most rookie fans, you undoubtedly wonder about all those players running out onto the field between plays. I've been watching football since just about forever, and to me it still looks like a whole lot of chaos out there each time they switch things up. First time I ever paid close attention to a game, it seemed fairly random, the way the players ran onto the field and into position—like a mad scramble for no good reason. Even today, as a veteran fan, I look at all that activity between plays and it's hard to imagine that every single one of these guys has their assignment straight. Really, it's a wonder they don't run into each other in the middle of all that confusion. They're scurrying about, getting into position, lining up in a variety of schemes and formations— and from the top row of the stadium, it can look like some strangely choreographed dance. And from the standard camera angles on most television broadcasts, it looks pretty much the same way.

OH, PIONEERS!

Among legendary football names to remember, Walter Camp should be at the top of the list. A former Yale coach, Camp is widely known as the father of American football for the way he combined the roughshod elements of rugby and soccer with new rules resulting in a more orderly, more disciplined game that allowed players' true athleticism to rise above brute strength. He reduced the size of the field to 110 by 53 yards, confining the action to a more manageable area, and lowered the number of players per side from 15 to 11, giving each player a more central role. Another of Camp's innovations was placing the ball down and out of play at the end of each advance, for what he termed a "scrimmage," after which both teams lined up on either side of the ball before it was put back into play. And it was Camp who came up with the system of downs, or attempts to move the ball over a set distance. In the beginning, teams were given three opportunities in which to advance the ball 5 yards before giving up possession to the other team, but when this proved too easy, the required yardage was increased to 10. A fourth down was added in the early 1900s.

Here's another name you should add to your list: John William Heisman, the legendary college football coach from Auburn and Georgia Tech who once ran up the score to 222-0 in a Tech victory over a hapless squad from Cumberland. It was Heisman who dreamed up the snap from center and the forward pass, which wasn't legalized until 1906—and his offensive-minded teams took full advantage of the new rule. Also, it was Heisman who first uttered the memorable line, "When in doubt, punt," which has now seeped into everyday conversations having nothing to do with football and everything to do with cutting your losses.

When Heisman retired from coaching, he established the Downtown Athletic Club, the noted organization of sportswriters and officials that annually awards college football's most prestigious honor to the nation's best college player—the Heisman Trophy.

There's actually a regimented order to the game that begins and ends with each player's assignment. In most cases, you can tell what position a guy plays by just his size and shape. In certain cases you can even tell by how he carries himself off the field, as I'll explain. To start, you've got your thick-necked, big-bellied guys whose job is to block and tackle. Then you've got your somewhat less thick-necked, somewhat smaller-bellied guys whose job is to block and tackle. You've got your fleet-footed guys on offense whose job is to throw, run, or catch the ball, and your fleet-footed defensive counterparts whose job is to keep them from doing so.

Simple enough, right? And it gets simpler, once we break things down by position.

The Offense

The offensive unit is on the field when its team has the ball. The centerpiece of the offense is the quarterback; he's part of the *offensive backfield,* which also includes *running backs, fullbacks,* and *halfbacks.*

The unsung heroes of every offensive unit are the *offensive linemen*—the *center, guards, tackles,* and *tight end.* Sometimes you'll hear an announcer refer to a "weak-side" lineman or a "strong-side" lineman. When I first heard the term, I thought they were dissing the less-talented or less-celebrated players on that front line, referring to them by reputation—as in, "Why the hell did they run that play toward the weak side behind that lame-ass blocker, when they had that strong-side stud to lead the way?" Turns out it has nothing to do with strengths and weaknesses and everything to do with how many guys are on either side of the center. Here's the deal: Count up the number of linemen, including the tight end. The side of the field with the greater number of linemen (usually, it's the side with the tight end) is considered the strong side; the side with the lesser number of linemen is considered the weak side. A team always puts 11 players on the field, but coaches use so many different formations, for so many different situations, that a casual fan never quite knows what to expect at the start of each play.

Here's the position-by-position breakdown.

Offensive Backfield

Football is a team game, but if you had to pick out one guy on the field who is in the best position to determine his team's fortunes from one week to the next, it would be the *quarterback*. Think about it: Other than the center (see page 55), he's the only player on the offensive unit who touches the ball on every single down. It's such a key, central role that the term to describe it has even seeped into our everyday language. We talk about a leader as someone who can "quarterback" his team to victory, or success, or some other heady accomplishment. A "Monday morning quarterback" is someone who second-guesses something with the benefit of hindsight—be it the previous day's game or a business plan that somehow ran aground. The term quarterback has become part of the culture in such a way that folks who've never even seen a game of football will know what you're talking about when you use it in a sentence. Try telling someone you'll "tight-end" them to some goal or other and he'll either look at you funny or call the cops.

I'm not just saying all this because I'm married to a quarterback; Lord knows, as long as I have anything to say about it, Rodney doesn't call the shots anyplace *but* the field. It's the quarterback who calls the shots on the football field, and in a bygone era it was the quarterback who actually decided a team's next move. These days, most teams rely on the coaching staff to call the plays from the sidelines; however, the quarterback must read (that is, quickly analyze) the defense when he prepares to take the snap, and make a quick assessment about whether the play his coaches have called matches up with the defensive alignment he now sees on the line—and to shift gears, if necessary. Such a last-second adjustment is called an *audible*—so named, I'm guessing, because it's up to the rest of the offensive unit to listen in to the quarterback's call. Every once in a while, you'll see a quarterback signal for a time-out at the line when he doesn't like what he sees from the defense and can't get his teammates to make the necessary adjustments within the brief 40-second play clock. Coaches hate to burn a precious time-out over a miscommunication, which explains why you'll frequently see these guys scowling at such moments.

Some quarterbacks are gifted, all-around athletes, able to dodge opposing linemen and to shed would-be tacklers and turn busted plays into gains; some are merely blessed with golden arms that let them hurl footballs like bullets through tires hung from trees at distances of 50 yards. Most are smart, and fiery, and competitive—and deeply appreciative of their teammates' extra efforts. Each Christmas, they'll shower their offensive linemen with lavish gifts—diamond watches, MP3 players, cruise vacations—as a relatively small token for covering their cute little butts all season long. It's the least they can do. It took me a little time as a rookie NFL wife to see the value of these expensive gifts coming out of our household budget, but it soon became clear to me that it was about appreciation, respect, and (frankly) the well-being of my other half. So what if we had to sacrifice a family vacation here or there!

Running backs position themselves a couple steps behind the quarterback or off to his side, and their primary job is to run the football. On some plays, they're meant to block for the quarterback, and on others they're meant to head downfield for a pass, but the best of 'em carry the ball 20 to 30 times each game, usually through heavy traffic.

Running backs have a flashy swagger, but they take too much of a beating to worry about style points. Still, they make it look easy. I used to joke with Emmitt Smith—back when Rodney played with him during our season in Dallas—that I could run one play up the middle if I had the kind of blocking he was used to getting from the Cowboys' offensive line. And Emmitt used to joke back that I'd be in the hospital for a week . . . only I don't think he was really joking. The line on running backs is that they walk away from 15 car accidents per game; and as a result of all that punishment, they tend to have shorter careers than any other player. Last I checked, the average career of an NFL running back covered less than 5 years, so it clearly takes its toll. Although every now and then you'll come across a long-lasting, Energizer bunny–type like my buddy Emmitt or Hall of Famer Marcus Allen, who managed to keep it going season after season after season.

Most running backs I know are hard-charger types—fearless, durable, and determined, no matter what role they fill in the backfield. Within the category, there are *fullbacks*, who lead the way for the *halfbacks* (also known as tail-backs). A fullback is generally bigger and heavier than his backfield running mate, while a halfback is quicker and more explosive. Fullbacks are like offensive linemen—theirs is another one of those thankless positions on the field, throwing blocks and setting decoys. Most All Pro running backs give much love to their fullbacks for helping them look good—and they should! When Emmitt Smith finally retired at the end of the 2004 season, he singled out Darryl "Moose" Johnston, his longtime backfield partner, for helping him to pile on all those yards—a well-deserved nod, indeed.

Some offensive alignments call for only one running back on a particular play, while others require the more traditional two-man backfield. And running backs of every stripe are called on regularly to catch the ball as well as run with it, so they've got to have soft hands to go along with their hard heads.

Usually, teams will feature one primary running back throughout the game, although some teams present a more balanced attack spread across two or more featured runners. We had a really effective duo in Philly in 1996, when Ricky Watters and Charlie Garner teamed up to form the "Thunder and Lightning" backfield. The 2004 Steelers enjoyed great success with Duce Staley and one of my faves, Jerome Bettis, coming in on the goal line to punch it in—meaning, to power the ball past a swarm of defenders in a short-yardage situation. Personally, I've always loved teams with multifaceted running games; it's a great weapon for a coach to have such a versatile arsenal. Occasionally, you'll come across a three-pronged attack—most notably with the old Miami Dolphins of the early 1970s, under legendary coach Don Shula, when Larry Csonka, Jim Kiick, and Mercury Morris each put together a Pro Bowl–type season out of the same backfield.

Offensive Linemen

The *center* is one of the easiest players to spot on the field because he's the one who lines up over the ball and snaps it to his quarterback to start the play. (A snap, for those of you new to the term, is when the center hands-off, hikes, throws, or otherwise delivers the ball to the quarterback on a prearranged count or signal, usually through his legs from a forward-facing, crouched position that puts him at a huge disadvantage for blocking onrushing defenders.)

It's a tough, thankless, highly skilled position. Over the years, I've found centers to be among the sweetest, most easygoing players on the team. With few exceptions, the ones I've known have been kind, even-tempered, generous souls. Maybe it has something to do with the way centers have been smacked about the head their entire careers, play after play after play; or maybe it takes a certain self-effacing personality to play such a selfless, team-oriented position. But whenever I hear a center's wife refer to her husband as "that great, big bear of a man," I know exactly what she's talking about—and I'm always grateful that her great, big bear of a man has been charged with the safekeeping of my somewhat smaller bear of a husband.

While I'm on it, it's worth noting the special bond between the quarterback and his center, which extends in some ways to the quarterback's wife. (The easy joke on me, I'm afraid, is that it might also extend to the center's wife, but so far that hasn't been a problem—and never will be if Rodney knows what's good for him.) Many say that special bond has to do with the way the quarterback has his hands tucked beneath the center's butt at the start of each play—that he's got him, almost literally, "by the balls." But I really think it has more to do with the mutual respect these guys have for each other, the way they watch each other's backs, and the way they get their jobs done. Their timing together is crucial. Whatever they're asked. Whatever it takes. One of Rodney's favorite centers was a guy named Kevin Glover, who played with him on the Detroit Lions in the early 1990s. Rodney used to call him "Glove" because, as he so delicately put it, "his ass is like a glove." (Maybe it does have to do with their close anatomical relationship after all.)

THE OFFENSE

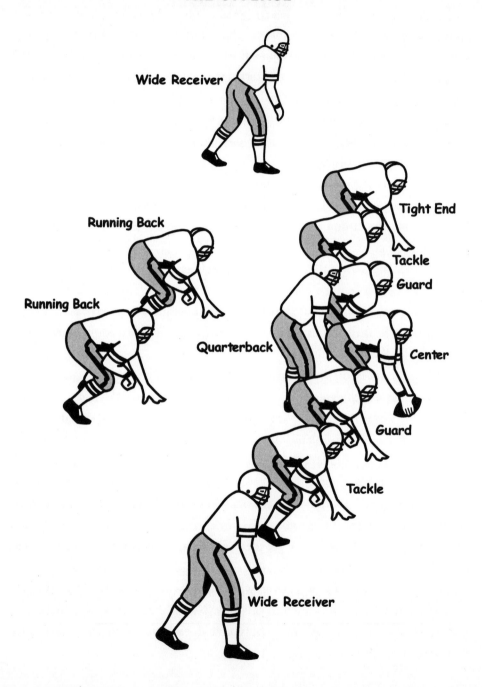

Wide Receiver

Running Back

Running Back

Quarterback

Tight End

Tackle

Guard

Center

Guard

Tackle

Wide Receiver

On each side of the center, you'll find a *guard,* appropriately named because, like the center, the guards protect their quarterback, and open up holes for their running backs by pushing defenders out of the way and clearing a path through which they might advance the ball.

In most offensive formations, a *tackle* is positioned outside each guard. They also protect their quarterback, and open up holes for their running backs, but their name doesn't fit their assignment the way it once did. Owing to a whole bunch of rule changes designed to level the playing field, they're no longer allowed to tackle the guys on the other team, per se—unless, of course, those guys have somehow managed to come up with the ball. Modern rules prohibit guards (or tackles and centers, for that matter) from grabbing their opponents in any way. They can drop low and take their legs out, or they can hit them high and hard and hope to knock them off balance, but they can't actually tackle them, so the name doesn't quite line up with what they're asked to do.

There is one *tight end* on the offensive line, usually located next to one of the tackles. Increasingly, teams utilize two tight ends, putting one on either side of the ball and opening up a whole mess of passing and blocking options. Many tight ends are built tough and low to the ground, in such a way that you can't always tell them apart from the other linemen. But they need to be quick and sure-footed, with soft hands and an offensive mindset. (*Soft hands,* as long as I'm on it, refers to a player's ability to catch a pass, as in when a receiver is able to catch anything that comes his way, no matter how the ball is thrown. Conversely, a player who can't seem to catch the ball is sometimes said to have bricks for hands, for the way the ball is always bounding from his grasp.)

Like the center, guards, and tackles, the tight end's job is to block for his quarterback, give him time to throw the ball while the play develops, and open up holes for his running backs. As the only eligible receiver on the offensive line, he is also called upon to catch a pass from time to time and to run downfield with it. Under some coaches, "from time to time" can also mean "more often than not," so it's not unusual to see a tight end lead his team in receptions over the course of a season. He can be a real weapon when featured prominently in an offensive attack.

Here again, the position takes its name from its spot on the field: Tight ends line up at the end of the offensive line, and tight to that line. Line them up any place else and, well, they wouldn't be tight ends. Slot them on the line between the guard and the tackle and they wouldn't be eligible to catch a pass, because the rules state that they must be lined up at the end of the line to be considered a receiver. (Note: Any player on the line can catch a deflected ball; it's just that the center, guards, and tackles cannot be the intended target of a pass.)

Tight ends come in every shape and size, and about the only constant is that they're tremendously strong and versatile. Some are cut like basketball players—tall and lean and built for speed. Others are cut more like their counterparts on the offensive line—short and stocky and built for power. Some are better at catching passes and others are better at blocking defenders—strengths and weaknesses that are factored into a team's overall offensive strategy. And as part of that strategy, as indicated earlier, some teams deploy two tight ends at a time, giving them a mess of options on the line, and making them doubly difficult to defend.

As a group, tight ends are some of the most reliable guys you'd want to meet, but they're not as sweet or good-natured as centers. There's something slippery about them, the way they pretend to block and then roll out to catch the ball. Along with the quarterback, they're probably the best actors on the team, always trying to deceive their opponents into thinking one way and then sneaking in some surprise move or other. These days, the Kansas City Chiefs' Tony Gonzalez—at 6'5" and 250 pounds—is probably one of the most feared tight ends in the game because of his ability to catch anything that comes his way, and to strong-arm his way past any defender who presumes to challenge him. He's also extremely easy on the eyes.

Moving off the offensive line, you'll find the *wide receivers*, so named because they line up wide of the other offensive players and are eligible to receive the ball. Realize, only seven players are allowed to line up *on* the line of scrimmage, and most coaches run out five offensive linemen (the center, two guards, and two tackles, let's say). That leaves room for a tight end and one other player, usually a wide receiver who'll toe the line of scrimmage on the weak side of the field. A second wide receiver, sometimes known as the flanker, will line up wide of the linemen a step or two off the line of scrimmage, on the strong side of the field.

Wide receivers are probably the best all-around athletes on the field. I know some defensive backs and running backs who will argue the point, and some middle linebackers who might fight you for it, but these guys are fast, agile, wiry, and fast. (Have I mentioned fast?) They're also great jumpers, with incredible hands, and the kind of precise body control you might expect to find from a dancer. (As a matter of fact, there have been several wide receivers whose off-season training has included ballet—most notably, the appropriately named Hall of Famer Lynn Swann of the Pittsburgh Steelers, one of the more graceful athletes to ever man the position.)

Wide receivers also have more personality than you can pack into a stereotype—colorful, and about as arrogant as they come on a football field. This is a compliment if you can believe it, because receivers are so out there and on the line with every big play that they have to be a little bit cocky to do their jobs well. (Run a polite, mild-mannered mama's boy on a pass pattern across the middle of the field with defenders coming full speed from either side of him and see if he gets close to the ball.) Receivers are good actors, too, because the ball only comes their way a half-dozen or so times each game—maybe more for a real go-to guy—and yet every snap from center they're sprinting down the field and cutting this way and that way and going through the motions at full-tilt, like their number has been called. They've got to sell the play, even when they're nowhere near the play, to lure defenders away from the ball.

For my money, the Philadelphia Eagles' Terrell Owens is the poster boy for today's crop of wide receivers. He's supremely talented, blessed with speed, flair, and bluster, and about as uninhibited as it gets in terms of letting it all hang out. (He's also got it going on in some other areas, as you'll see on page 169.) If you've followed the game at all over the past few seasons, you might remember it was T.O. who thought to hide a Sharpie marking pen in the pads surrounding the goal post before a game. He retrieved it following a touchdown and used it to sign the football before tossing it into the crowd. As touchdown celebrations went, this one beat all for ingenuity and originality—although poor T.O. did have to pay a fine to the league for his unique brand of showmanship that some folks thought transcended the bounds of good sportsmanship. Oh, well. The fans in the cheap seats ate it up, and there were quite a few of us in the not-so-cheap seats who got a kick out of it, too.

Absolutely, these guys are the flashiest, sassiest players on the field—and off the field, as well. It's a total package. Generally speaking, they are football's divas, who will quickly remind you that you can't spell T-E-A-M without M-E. When Rodney played for a season in Dallas, he was teamed up with Michael Irvin, one of the Cowboys' all-time great receivers. One Sunday afternoon, following a game, I went to meet Rodney in the players' parking lot and saw Michael's tricked-out Mercedes pulling away, with the license plate "PLYMKR" riding the bumper. I thought to myself, "Man, what a narcissist! To be calling attention to himself like that! *Playmaker!*" But then I thought, "Holly, give this man some credit. You can't have the success he's had on the field without also having some of this big-time swagger running alongside of it." And at the end of the day, that's precisely what he does: He makes plays. Wide receivers . . . They've got it going on. They're all style *and* all substance—all the time.

The Defense

The defensive unit comes on to the field when the other team has possession of the ball. There are three layers of defensive players—defensive linemen, linebackers, and the secondary (also known as the defensive backfield). These players fill three distinct roles from three distinct spots on the field. Here's how it breaks down.

THE DEFENSE

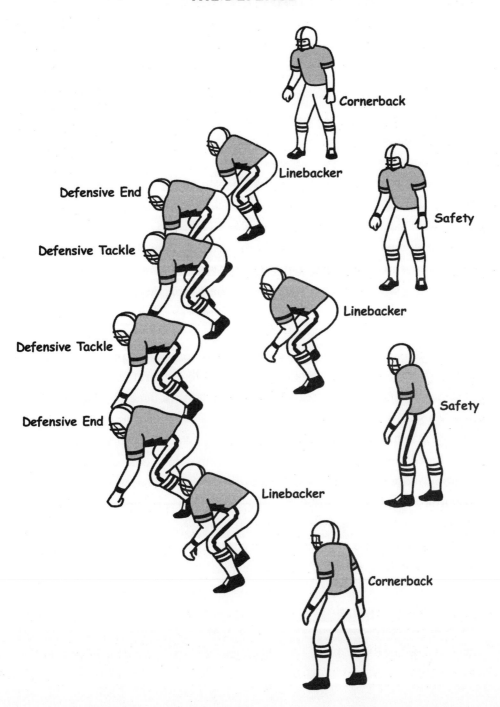

Cornerback

Linebacker

Defensive End

Safety

Defensive Tackle

Linebacker

Defensive Tackle

Defensive End

Safety

Linebacker

Cornerback

Defensive Linemen

These guys are the first line of defense, and they stand as mirror images to the offensive linemen. They're just as big and beefy and just as down and dirty, but they tend to be a little quicker and a little more athletic—which comes in handy when trying to chase down the opposing quarterback. Their basic job is to stop the other team's offensive players from running the ball and to rush, pressure, or otherwise charge at the quarterback so that he doesn't have too much time to look down the field for an open receiver.

Most teams line up four defensive linemen on the line of scrimmage—two *tackles,* who in this case *are* allowed to tackle opposing players (in fact, they damn well better, else they'll be out of a job!), and two *ends,* who line up on either side of the tackles, on the end of the defensive line. As such, you'll have a *right tackle* and a *left tackle,* and a *right defensive end* and a *left defensive end.* For certain plays in which a team lines up only three defensive linemen, you'll still have a *right defensive end* and a *left defensive end,* but the guy manning the middle is known as a *nose tackle.*

Defensive linemen can also be among the more colorful personalities in the game. The best of them are fan favorites, wildly celebrated for their accomplishments—and for their creative celebrations ("sack dances") that invariably follow a sack of the opposing quarterback or a punishing hit that stops a running back behind the line of scrimmage. I don't know about you, but I've always hated that little sack dance these guys do, which comes across to me as taunting and unsportsmanlike (another objective observation from the wife of a quarterback); but the fans and the media seem to eat it up.

When I was first learning the game, I discovered that many teams have distinct personalities and styles of play that can be traced to their defensive linemen. The Minnesota Vikings' defensive line was known throughout the 1970s as "The Purple People Eaters," for the color of their uniforms and their all-out ferocity. The Pittsburgh Steelers won four Super Bowls on the back of its "Steel Curtain" defense, led by Hall of Famer "Mean" Joe Greene. And the Los Angeles Rams of the late 1960s featured its "Fearsome Foursome," a defensive line that is still considered among the most formidable in NFL history, setting an NFL record for fewest yards allowed (in a 14-game season), behind Lamar Lundy, Rosey Grier, and Hall of Famers Deacon Jones and Merlin Olsen.

The great thing about a solid defensive line is the way the linemen can work together to accomplish their objective. The best are able to "stunt"—or switch positions to confuse the offensive linemen—and to "gang tackle" or "bull rush" the running back in such a way that he'll think twice before attempting to run the ball through the line a second time. It's a team effort.

Linebackers

This second layer of defenders lines up just behind the defensive linemen. Their job is to guard against the pass and the run, and to generally mix things up and make things happen—so they've got a whole lot of ground to cover. If there are four players on the line, a team will run out three linebackers; if there are three linemen, there'll be four linebackers. The *middle linebacker* is, in many respects, the quarterback of the defensive team. On most teams, he's the one barking out orders in the defensive huddle or shouting out a defensive audible at the line. (In a defensive set featuring four linebackers, *one* of the middle linebackers will usually fill this role.) The *outside linebackers* are positioned outside the guys in the middle—duh!—and just to keep up the symmetry, there are *weak-side linebackers* and *strong-side linebackers*; the *strong-side linebacker* lines up opposite the other team's tight end.

It used to be that linebackers were big, menacing brutes looming on the other side of the line like furious warriors moving in for the kill. Lately linebackers have gotten smaller as a general rule, yet if you ask anyone on the field, they hit just as hard as they ever did. Here again, quickness is key, because they've got to react to *every* imaginable scenario. For the most part, the middle linebackers focus on running plays, and the guys on the outside focus on passing plays—but they all focus on the ball.

The prototypical linebacker in today's game is a guy like Ray Lewis of the

Baltimore Ravens, who has such tremendous speed and quickness and an innate ability to read the offense and anticipate each play. Plus, one visit from him and you'll know what it's like to run into a brick wall—just ask Rodney. Ray Lewis is a modern cross between Ray Nitschke, who reinvented the middle linebacker position for the magnificent Green Bay Packers teams of the 1960s, and Lawrence Taylor, the great outside linebacker for the New York Giants of the 1980s and 1990s who transformed the position yet again, lifting the ideal to match his all-around athletic prowess.

Secondary

Also known as the *defensive backfield,* the secondary is actually the third layer of defense, reinforcing the defense from the back. If you've been keeping score, you'll note there are four defensive positions still unaccounted for. (Re-

HISTORY OF THE GAME

BUT WHO'S COUNTING?

One of the most curious things I found in looking back at the origins of the game was that a touchdown used to be worth only four points, while a field goal counted for as many as five. Apparently the kicking aspect of the game was once considered more difficult and possibly even more important than the running game—unlike the emphasis in today's game.

Over time, those point values shifted even further. In 1898, the touchdown was changed from four points to five; in 1912, it was changed from five points to six. In 1904, the field goal was dropped from five points to four; in 1909, it was dropped from four points to three. Nowadays, of course, teams must "settle" for a field goal after failing to score a touchdown or to advance the ball on downs, but back then I imagine it was the desired result of a long scoring drive—and, arguably, the more difficult test of a player's abilities. Plus, it put points on the board without taking additional time off the clock or subjecting your attacking team to any unnecessary punishment.

member, each team puts 11 players on the field at the start of each play.) Those final four spots are taken up in most formations by two *cornerbacks,* positioned behind the linebackers at either corner of the field, and the two *safeties,* who usually line up in the deepest part of the field to guard against the long pass.

Like wide receivers, cornerbacks and safeties are an arrogant bunch. Outrageously gifted with speed and keen athletic instincts, they've got to match the other team's receiving corps stride for stride. And they've got to match up in attitude, too. More than anyone else on the field, cornerbacks and safeties take tremendous pride in what they do, probably because they're exposed more than anyone else on the field. They're the last line of defense, and they mean business. And their butts are on the line every time the ball comes their way—or not, as the case may be. If a quarterback keeps throwing to one side of the field, it's because he doesn't think the defensive back assigned to that side of the field can cover his man; if he keeps throwing to the opposite side of the field, it's because he doesn't want to test a guy he knows to be at the top of his game. Plus, if a lineman or a linebacker misses his assignment, there are a half-dozen other guys playing behind or alongside him to help fill in the blanks. When a defensive back misses his mark, it usually means six points for the other guys, so this is a pressure-packed position.

If I had to generalize about the defensive backs in my acquaintance, I'd say they were a shade more ornery than their teammates—not quite as full of bravado as the wide receivers they're meant to mark, but close. And they can dish it out! Goodness, some of these guys are relatively small—especially when you stack them up against the linemen and linebackers—but they pack a serious wallop. They have to, I guess, because they do most of their tackling one-on-one, out in the open field. Our old pal Ronnie Lott, who for most of his career terrorized opposing receivers as a safety for the San Francisco 49ers, was arguably the most vicious tackler in any secondary in the league, putting his patented "wo-o-o-o hits" on poor opposing players—so named because these hits made the crowd say "Wo-o-o-o!" afterwards. Take a guy like Ronnie Lott away from the field, though, and he's a pussycat. (Okay, strike that; he's not exactly a pussycat, but he's as docile as a big cat on medication.)

Special Teams

As the term suggests, players on the special teams unit are on the field only for special circumstances. You'll want to know the difference between the punter and the placekicker (or kicker)—component parts that can mean the difference in any given game. The *punter* is the guy who lines up on fourth down to receive the long snap from center, and then kicks the ball downfield in a change-of-possession. A top-tier punter can keep opponents on their heels all game long, pushing them deep into their own territory with his booming kicks. The *placekicker* is the guy who kicks the field goal and point-after-touchdown attempts and who kicks off from a tee to start each half and following each score. A top-tier placekicker makes it possible for his team to put points on the board from midfield and to keep scores close.

In this era of super-specialization, some teams feature a long-yardage placekicker and a short-yardage placekicker. As you might imagine, the short-yardage guy is extremely proficient at kicking the ball through the uprights from up-close; the long-yardage guy is more of a hit-or-miss marksman, with much more carry to his ball. Or, you might have a scenario where one placekicker is better in wet weather, on a slippery field, while another excels on dry turf.

In the forties and fifties, most kickers pulled double-duty elsewhere on the field—as quarterbacks, running backs, defensive backs, or what have you. During the sixties and seventies, diminutive European-born soccer players began to turn up on NFL rosters and were widely touted for their placekicking abilities—even though they didn't know the first thing about American football and looked like they couldn't withstand a tackle from yours truly. Lately, teams have found American-born talent to fill these all-important roles, although placekickers still tend to be tiny compared to their teammates—a good thing, I suppose, because it makes it easier to lift them up on your shoulders to celebrate a game-winning field goal.

On the decidedly not-tiny side, there's also a *long-snapper,* whose incredibly difficult and precise job it is to send the ball backwards through his legs to the punter, while managing to block the rushers on the receiving team. From time to time, you'll see a team's center double as the long-snapper; but for the most part the role is filled by a specialist, who spends most of his time at practice rifling the ball between his legs, trying to hit his mark.

Two other special teams players of note are the *punt returner* and *kick-off returner,* who are assigned the task of receiving the opposing team's kick and securing possession of the ball before attempting to move it upfield. It's also one of the tougher assignments in the game. Typically, these guys are fast, with sure hands and an intrepid demeanor. A lot of times, teams will feature a wide receiver or a defensive back in this role. You have to be a little fearless to get under one of these booming kicks while 11 opponents thunder toward you like you have a bull's-eye on your jersey, yelling, "Drop it! Drop it!" along with other annoying things designed to distract you from catching the ball. I always feel bad for their wives—that's some major pressure on one player.

———————

So there you have it—a thumbnail description of every position on the field, which at least lets you know where these guys are meant to stand and what they're meant to accomplish on each play.

10

ALL-TIME GREAT FOOTBALL NAMES

My dad was a great collector of great football names: fun names, original names, out-there names, ethnic names . . . you name it. A football player with a cool, memorable name was everything to him, and over the years I've found I inherited the habit. I miss my dad the most whenever I'm watching a game and hear the guys in the booth announce a name I know would have made him light up. He loved clever, evocative nicknames—William "The Refrigerator" Perry, Elroy "Crazy Legs" Hirsch, and "Mean" Joe Greene—but he also dug real birth certificate-type names that seemed perfectly suited to a player's particular abilities or to his persona.

One of our favorites was Sam "Bam" Cunningham, the Philadelphia Eagles running back who was always called on to punch the ball into the end zone in goal-line situations. We loved this name for the way it matched so neatly with the way this guy played the game. I'm sure it wasn't quite what poor Mrs. Cunningham had in mind when she christened her child, but who else would you give the ball to in a short-yardage situation?

Below is a collection of some of my father's favorite names, mixed with some of my own that I know he would have loved.

DICK BUTKUS: This is one of those tough names to wear as a kid, a name that could have gotten your "butt" "kussed" if you were any kind of nerd or wallflower, but if you were a big, bruising brute like Dick, it's one of the best names ever.

DAVID "DEACON" JONES: My dad got a tremendous kick out of the fact that there was a "Deacon" playing in the NFL. And, when The Monkees ruled the airwaves, there was a Davy Jones playing in the NFL. Something for everybody.

I. M. HIPP: I remember when this running back was at Nebraska and my dad called to report that he had stumbled across the next noteworthy name in the NFL draft. Ole I.M. had a short pro career—he played only one game for the Oakland Raiders, in 1980—but we never forgot him in the Robinson household.

LAWYER MILLOY: No one could "object" to this one. Daddy couldn't wait to hear the announcers call out his name. Whenever Milloy, a Pro Bowl defensive back for the New England Patriots, crossed to the sidelines to consult with one of his coaches, my father would refer to it as a sidebar.

PLAXICO BURRESS: I just flip for this name. He might be one of the great receivers in the league, but every time I hear his first name, it sounds like some new medication awaiting FDA approval.

KABEER GBAJA-BIAMILA, ANTWAAN RANDLE-EL, AZ-ZAHIR HAKIM: Islamic names are always cool, even if they have to be continued on the front of the jersey. And the great side benefit, of course, is listening to the guys in the booth struggle to pronounce them.

TEDY BRUSCHI: The perfect marriage of a name to a profession. I mean, what goes better with football than a "bruschi"?

PRIEST HOLMES: We always loved Priest's name for the way it completed a set. My father used to say that any league with a Deacon, a Lawyer, and a Priest was all right by him—and it was all right by me, too.

PEERLESS PRICE: Peerless is fearless, when the Price is right!

MERCURY MORRIS: Another favorite in the Robinson household, and all kinds of fitting. After all, anyone named after the fastest god was destined to be one heck of a running back.

4

Three Teams in One

Finding Order in the Chaos

Okay, so we've established that three distinct units make up a single professional football team—offense, defense, and special teams. But it's clear to even a first-time fan that these guys aren't running around the field willy-nilly or pell-mell looking for someone to tackle or block or shuck. (By the way, you will never find the phrases "willy-nilly" and "pell-mell" in an NFL playbook, and chances are you won't hear them on any sideline or in any broadcast booth or locker room, and you'll do well to avoid them in every football-related situation except this one right here. Also: "loosey-goosey," "herky-jerky," "freaky-deaky," and any other hyphenated rhyming couplet intended to suggest frantic, frenetic, or frazzled movements of any kind . . . so steer clear.)

Remember those old Esther Williams synchronized swimming productions, filmed from above the pool in such a way that the swimmers appeared to form a hexagon or a letter or a flower? Well, that's how it sometimes looks, the way these players move about when they're getting into position. I half-expected my husband Rodney's teammates to form the Panther logo right there in midfield, like each play was about to burst from these comings and goings into a beautifully choreographed halftime show.

Just how do these guys know when to take their positions, when to take a knee, and when to switch gears all over again? There's most definitely a logic to these sudden shifts in personnel. It's basic, and if you don't catch on to it early, you'll be scrambling. You'll be stuck on that unfortunate Esther Williams metaphor and never fully grasp one of the game's most basic truths: Football is a team game.

The Sum of a Team's Parts

When I set that last line to paper, I thought to myself, Duh. Good job stating the obvious, Holly. But the reality is that most new fans don't really appreciate how intricate the team concept can be—and how essential it is to the sport of football. They see a bunch of guys dressed in one uniform, and a bunch of guys dressed in another uniform, and figure the two groups will just have at each other until they produce a winner or until time runs out on the clock. But it's not every-man-for-himself out there. No way. It's every-man-for-his-*teammates*. Or, it's every-role-for-the-appropriate-game-situation. What's that old cliché you always hear about the theater? *There are no small parts, only small actors.* Well, it's pretty much the same on a football team. There are all kinds of roles. Some guys might get all the glory, but there are no small jobs. Every role is essential, even if a coach doesn't need to call on each player in each role in every single game. Think of it like a game of Jenga: Each game piece supports the ones next to it; pull any block from the mix, and the whole structure might crumble; add a block that doesn't belong, and the whole structure appears out of whack.

So how are we fans supposed to keep track of all these "game pieces" on the field? Well, it's easy enough to count that there are 11 players on either side of the ball every time it's put into play (at least there should be, else the referee is likely to call a penalty for an extra man on the field). But there are far too many players roaming those sidelines and shuttling in and out of the game for most fans to keep track of everyone. For one thing, the players won't stand still long enough for you to do your counting. For another, they all look alike with their pads and helmets on—unless of course you're looking at someone like the momentarily retired Ricky Williams, the great Miami Dolphins running back whose Bob Marley-esque dreadlocks beneath his helmet used to flap in the breeze as he ran. (Believe it or not, an opponent once brought Ricky to the ground yanking on those bad boys. . . . Is that a penalty? *Dreadlock drop . . . 10 yards . . . first down!)*

Of the 53 players carried on every NFL active roster, each has a specific job to do and, typically, each player fills a meaningful role on only one unit. It used to be, back when my father watched the game as a kid, that some players had a role on the offensive and defensive units ("both sides of the ball"). In fact, in the early days of the game, substitution rules prohibited a player from leaving the field at all. But for as long as I've been watching the game, there haven't been too many "two-way" players, outside of trick plays, special circumstances, and rare exceptions. (Think Deion Sanders or Warren Sapp.)

Who's on each of these units? Let's review. There are offensive players who do most of the ball-handling (quarterback, receivers, and backs) and offensive players whose jobs are to block or clear a path for their ball-handling team-mates (tackles, guards, centers). There are defensive players meant to sidestep or muscle past those blocks and to otherwise stall the other team's progress (tackles, ends, linebackers), and other defensive players who must shadow their opposite numbers on long sprints and pass patterns and deny them the opportunity to catch any ball thrown their way (cornerbacks, safeties). There's even one guy (the kicker) whose principle job is to kick the ball soccer-style through the goalposts at either end of the field, and another guy (the holder) who holds the ball at just the right angle, laces pointed forward, as the kicker approaches.

There are specialists and versatile utility players who are particularly good at crashing through a line of blockers and getting enough of their hands on a kicked ball to change its course. They take their places on the special teams unit. Each player is an essential part of a coach's arsenal, even if they don't get into every game.

The main thing you have to realize is that all of these players don't take the field at one time, because they're only called upon to do their jobs in specific

HISTORY OF THE GAME

A GOOD SHOW

Most early football games were played by hale-and-hearty college athletes looking for a break from their studies. Probably, they were also looking to blow off some steam, but as the game spread from the hallowed, Ivy-covered campuses of the Northeast, it grew even more violent. Many of the rules changes that took place around the turn of the century made the game safer—protective equipment was refined to take the hard hits opposing players dished out; restrictions on tackling were put in place; a no-contact zone, about the width of a football, was established to more clearly separate the offensive and defensive lines before the start of each play—the area of the field we now know as "the line of scrimmage."

Despite these adjustments, the game continued to be rough and dangerous. In fact, several college presidents and trustees tried to eliminate the game from their campuses. Almost every game resulted in some type of serious injury, and there were even a dozen or so reported deaths. In 1906 no less an authority than President Theodore Roosevelt stepped in to help tone things down by establishing the American Football Rules Committee.

The professional game was another matter, and Roosevelt held a little less authority over the sometimes shady businessmen who looked to make big bucks on the back of the game. Team owners and game promoters knew that to sell tickets, they'd have to allow their players to beat the tar out of each other. So on the pro level there was less emphasis on making the game safer and protecting the players and greater emphasis on giving spectators a good show.

game situations. For instance, a team's quarterback and its cornerback would never be on the field at the same time. The quarterback is to offense as the cornerback is to defense. Similarly, a wide receiver would never be on the field at the same time as one of his team's linebackers. And so on. Taking it one step further, it's important to note that each player in each position has developed a very specific set of skills to carry out his responsibilities. Let's take the quarterback, for example, whose job is vital to the offense's goal of scoring. He's got the throwing arm, the ability to read defenses and find open receivers—and, in recent years, the ability to run and/or scramble to advance the ball himself. Put it this way: You wouldn't ask your quarterback to block the other team's 300-pound defensive lineman because he'd probably get hurt.

There can be some back and forth between the offensive and special teams units, or the defensive and special teams units. From time to time, for example, you'll come across a speedy wide receiver who moonlights as a punt returner, thus occupying a spot on the offensive and special teams units. Or you may find a speedy defensive back who covers ground in the kind of hurry coaches want to see on their punt return teams. But you'll have to look long and hard to find a contemporary player who's a regular on offense and defense. Why? Well, conventional wisdom suggests that a player puts too much wear and tear on his body as it is, and that if he never left the field to make way for the next unit, he'd burn out by the second week of the season. So, in most cases you won't find an offensive player pulling double-duty with the defensive squad.

Making Sense of It All

So, how does the rookie fan determine which unit is on the field at any given time? It is possible, with a practiced eye, to identify certain players by their uniform number, their size and shape, or where they line up on the field relative to the ball. (More on this later.) Want a simpler way? Just locate the quarterback. (Sorry . . . I can't help myself.) Go ahead, see if you can spot him. He should be pretty easy to pick out—he's the guy with his hands between a pair of butt cheeks, preparing to receive the ball from the center—and once you've spotted him, it's easy to place everyone else. Every player on the quarterback's team is on his team's offensive unit, and every player on the opposing team is on his team's defensive unit. Easy enough, right? And if there's no quarterback lining up to take the snap, then each team has put one of its special teams units on the field—to attempt or block a field goal or to give or take possession of the ball with a punt or a kickoff.

In most offensive formations at the professional level, the quarterback will stand directly behind the center like in a wheelbarrow race at a company picnic. Sometimes he'll have his hand on the guy's butt, or he'll stand a couple steps back in what's known as a *shotgun* formation. (If you're married to either a quarterback or a center, you'll probably take a lot of kidding for this hand-on-the-butt business, and if you happen to be pregnant when the quarterback steps back into the shotgun, you'll of course hear a couple jokes about that as well.) If you can keep your eye on the quarterback—and, baby, I *always* keep my eye on *my* quarterback—you'll get a good read on whatever it is that's about to happen on the field. And you won't be the only one watching him closely. The 11 guys on the defensive side of the ball will all have their eyes on him as well.

The center, usually one of the bigger-necked guys on the field, is the one with his hands on the ball as it rests on the ground before the start of each play. He snaps it back between his legs to the quarterback while somehow managing to block his onrushing opponents. Incidentally, I was always glad that I wasn't the wife of a center; it seems like such an impossibly tough and endlessly thankless job, but more than that it looks dangerous; it's tough enough being married to a quarterback, but I'd have my heart in my throat on every play if my husband was a center.

Here's another great trick to help you keep track of all those players on the field. Check out their jersey numbers. In other sports, there's usually no rhyme or reason why certain players wear certain numbers. Everybody's got a lucky number, or a birth date, or a street address, or a favorite player they want to honor, and players request their uniform numbers accordingly. In football, though, it's all circumscribed. The NFL has pretty strict guidelines in place, re-quiring that uniform numbers correspond in some way to a player's normal po-sition on the field. It's one of the ways referees have to quickly determine whether or not a player is eligible to receive a pass or to line up in a certain po-sition—and the bonus for the rookie fan is that the numbers also signal those of us in the stands or watching at home and tell us who will be involved in the upcoming play and what we can likely expect from that player.

According to the NFL Rule Book, all quarterbacks, punters, and place-kickers must wear uniform numbers between 1 and 19. Wide receivers and tight ends must wear numbers between 80 and 89, although the numbers between 10 and 19 are also acceptable if the higher numbers are unavailable. Running backs and defensive backs carry numbers between 20 and 49. Centers must wear a number between 50 and 59, although numbers between 60 and 79 are allowed if the lower numbers are otherwise assigned. Offensive guards and tackles are given numbers between 60 and 79, as are defensive linemen; if these numbers are taken, or retired, or otherwise out of circulation, players manning these positions can also wear numbers between 90 and 99. If a special play or circumstance calls for a player to line up out of position—say, an offensive guard who intends to line up as a tight end—he'll need to check in with one of the officials to report his new position immediately before the start of the play.

It can get a little confusing, and you'll need a scorecard to get a good handle on everything, but eventually you'll be able to spot these guys with a quick look at the backs of their jerseys. And, over time, their body types will also give them away. Offensive guards and tackles, and defensive linemen tend to be big and burly and beefy, with a low center of gravity and tremendous upper-body strength. Centers are even more so—they've got those great big huggable necks I alluded to earlier! Wide receivers are tall and sometimes wiry. And place-kickers are usually the shortest, least athletic-looking players on the field. Nothing against these guys, it's just that their specific skill sets don't require them to be all that fast, big, or muscular, as long as they have a strong-enough leg to kick the ball, and kick it with accuracy.

Of course, uniform numbers and body types won't tell the whole story, because if you've been paying attention, you'll have noticed that offensive and defensive linemen wear numbers in the same range and tilt the scales at about the same weight. This takes us back to the quarterback (I really can't help myself) and where he is in relation to the ball at the start of each play.

It's a lot to consider, all at once, but the great thing about football is that you don't have to consider everything all at once. No ma'am. There's a whole mess of opportunities for you to study the game because there's a whole mess of games to learn from over the course of a long season. Plus, there are great technical innovations like instant replay, VCRs, and TiVo that allow you to watch the same plays over and over again until you understand what you're watching. I tell my friends all the time that if they have a pretty good idea what

HISTORY OF THE GAME

GOING PRO

In the early days of the professional game, before there was an organized league, promoters dug deep to hire established local college stars to fill out their volunteer ranks, hoping to draw a crowd on the backs of certain hometown heroes. The Pro Football Hall of Fame credits former Yale All-American William "Pudge" Heffelfinger as the game's first professional player. Heffelfinger, who once played guard for Walter Camp at Yale, was paid $500 to play for the Allegheny Athletic Association in a single game against the Pittsburgh Athletic Club on November 12, 1892, a game in which Heffelfinger tallied the lone score on a fumble return for a touchdown.

The very first professional game in which *all* players were paid for their services was played in 1895, in Latrobe, Pennsylvania, although each man earned a fraction of the astronomical fee paid out to Heffelfinger. (That $500 fee, incidentally, represented about half the average annual income in Latrobe at that time.) The game pit the Latrobe YMCA against a thrown-together outfit from nearby Jeannette, Pennsylvania, but it took another 25 years for a viable professional league to emerge from the loosely affiliated professional teams of the period.

they're looking for, they'll have a pretty good chance of spotting it on the field. Absolutely, it pays to know the situation. Know the score. Know your coach's tendencies. For example, most teams will send in one of their kicking units when it's fourth down and they need to move the ball more than 2 or 3 yards for a first down. (In football shorthand, this is known as "fourth and long.") In this situation, they'll either attempt a field goal—or, if they're beyond their kicker's field goal range, they'll line up to punt. When a team needs to move the ball less than a yard for a first down or a touchdown, they'll typically "go for it" or line up for a running play, hoping to gain the required yardage by sheer force. The more you watch, the more you'll begin to anticipate which of these alignments you're about to see on the field—and if you ask me, it follows that the more you know going into each game situation, the more you'll take from the game as it progresses.

It really is like a dance, don't you think? It's an elaborate routine, rehearsed into the ground, the way all these players manage to alight on their predetermined spots, at the predetermined time, to go through their predetermined motions. All that's missing is the music.

A Special Note on Special Teams

I've never been able to get a good explanation as to why players and coaches referred to the special teams unit in the plural, as opposed to a special team unit. After all, there's just one unit on the field at any one time. It made no sense, but there it was, and every time I asked my husband, Rodney, about it, he just shrugged and said, "I don't know, honey. That's just the way it is."

Isn't that typical? These guys, they grow up around the game, it becomes a part of them, to where they'd never think to question a small detail like this. But the knowing is in the details, right? When you come to the game late, as most women do, or when you're always trying to prove yourself as a fan to the men alongside you on the couch or in the stands, as many women are, these small details loom pretty damn large. I've thought about this one a lot, and I've asked a whole lot of people for their explanations, and about the best I can come up with has to do with how the special teams unit is constructed. As I mentioned earlier, there are actually six different alignments within a typical special teams unit: a group for attempting a field goal and another for blocking a field goal; a group for punting the ball and another for receiving a punt; and there's a group for the kicking team on a kickoff to restart the game after a score or at the start of each half and an opposing group lined up to return that kick. So, yeah, there are those half-dozen special *teams* lineups, waiting to be deployed by their coaches as their relevant situations warrant, and there are those millions of American women, wondering what that extra *"s"* is doing there, and how it is that their American men can't manage a decent explanation for it.

10

ALL-TIME GREAT COACHES OF THE GAME

More than any other team sport, football is a coach's game. Players live and die by the whims and insights of their head coaches—and in this era of super-specialization, by the whims and insights of an army of assistants and coordinators and scouts and advisers. Franchises also live and die by the direction and leadership of the men in charge. General managers will tell you that the decision to hire this or that coach is perhaps the most important personnel move they're likely to make, which is why it wasn't all that surprising a couple years back when the New England Patriots agreed to part with a whole mess of draft choices and a future Hall of Fame running back in Curtis Martin for the right to hire coach Bill Parcells from the New York Jets.

Let's face it, outside of football you don't see too many trades of players and prospects for coaches. But in football it can sometimes make sense, because the right coach can mean everything, while the wrong coach can be a disaster. Talk to Rodney or any of his buddies and you'll get that they'll run through a wall for some coaches and that they wouldn't cross the street for others. It all comes down to respect—that is, a coach's ability to command it from his players, from his opponents, and from the fans. Of course, anyone can demand respect, but only a special few actually deserve it, and here I offer a short course on the best coaches of all time. Once again, I've limited my discussion to the professional game, which leaves out Knute Rockne, who in 12 years at Notre Dame led the Fighting Irish to an all-time winning precentage of .818—still the standard for both college and professional coaches. Even at the professional level, there are dozens more who have built Hall of Fame–type careers and left their stamp on a team or a Hall of Fame–type player, but these guys set the standard.

In alphabetical order, they are . . .

PAUL BROWN: Founding coach of the Cleveland Browns in 1946, and perhaps the game's greatest innovator . . . the first professional coach to work with a full-time coaching staff on a year-round basis, and the first to scout college talent in any kind of systematic way . . . also, the first to use notebooks and films and charts in a classroom-type setting, and the first to insist that his players room together in a hotel the night before home games as well as away games . . . (that's a lot of *firsts*) . . . developed the practice of shuttling in players to deliver plays from the sideline, and organized passing schemes to exploit specific holes in the defenses of each opponent . . . Brown's post-war Browns, quarterbacked by Otto Graham, were a true football dynasty, running the table in the old AAFC and then switching to the NFL and running the table all over again . . . in 17 seasons with Cleveland, posted a 167-53-8 record, with four AAFC championships, three NFL championships, and only one losing season . . . after a brief retirement, returned to the NFL as the founding coach and general manager of the expansion Cincinnati Bengals . . .

JOE GIBBS: A fixture on the Washington Redskins sidelines throughout the 1980s . . . known for his ability to adapt to changes on the field, especially in his own ranks . . . the only coach in NFL history to win three Super Bowls with three different quarterbacks—Joe Theismann, Doug Williams, and Mark Rypien—which I've always thought was the greatest tribute to his system and style . . . in 12 seasons, Gibbs' Redskins put together a 124-60 regular season record, and a 16-5 postseason record, for a combined winning percentage of .683, good for third all-time . . . his Redskins posted only one losing season, on their way to winning four NFC Eastern Division titles, four NFC championships, and three Super Bowls . . . retired after the 1992 season, but returned to coach his beloved Redskins in 2004, at the urging of new Redskins owner Dan Snyder . . . it struck sportswriters and football analysts as all kinds of unusual, to hand over the reins to a guy who hadn't coached in over a decade, but many thought Gibbs's fluid demeanor would help get him past the long layoff . . .

GEORGE HALAS: "Papa Bear" . . . the public face of the Chicago Bears from the team's inception in 1920 until his death in 1983, as a player, coach, owner, and promoter . . . coached the Bears for 40 seasons . . . his 318 regular-season wins were a long-time standard . . . under Halas, the Bears won six NFL championships and three additional divisional titles . . . his teams finished in second-place 15 times . . . like Brown, Halas was also an innovator, holding daily practice sessions, utilizing opponents' game films, and perfecting a T-formation offensive attack . . . in the 1940 NFL Championship game against Washington, Halas famously deployed his man-in-motion T system to full effect as his Bears romped to a 73-0 victory . . . a strict disciplinarian, Halas ruled the Bears with the strength of his personality—and, in later years, with the force of his own legend . . . a formative influence around the league, Halas was named president of the National Football Conference in 1970, following the NFL-AFL merger, a public nod to his lasting role as one of the league's founding fathers . . . retired from coaching following the 1969 season, but was an active part of the Bears' front office at the time of his death . . .

EARL "CURLY" LAMBEAU: Another founding father figure, Lambeau helped to launch the Green Bay Packers in 1919 as a player-coach and to establish the team as a viable small-market franchise with enormous community support . . . his early teams reflected Lambeau's talents as a passer, in an era not yet known for the forward pass . . . throughout the 1920s and 1930s, Green Bay was famous for its passing attack while other teams scrambled to keep up . . . football historians credit Lambeau with opening up the game and creating passing opportunities on any play from scrimmage . . . scouted and signed future Hall of Fame receiver Don Hutson in 1935, who under Lambeau became a prototypical player at the position . . . upon his own retirement as a player, recruited future Hall of Fame quarterback Arnie Herber to help continue the Packers' passing attack . . . left the Packers following the 1949 season, but continued to coach in the NFL with brief stints for the Chicago Cardinals and Washington Redskins . . . when he retired, his 229 career victories ranked second to Halas . . . his name and legacy live on in Green Bay, most notably at Lambeau Field, where the Packers continue to play before die-hard, sold-out crowds . . .

TOM LANDRY: Inaugural coach of the expansion Cowboys in 1960, who remained on the Dallas sidelines for the next 29 years—the longest consecutive head coaching tenure with any one club in NFL history (surpassing even Halas, who stepped down from the Bears job on three occasions during his 40-year career) . . . Landry was said to be an inspirational leader, although you could never tell from his stoic sideline demeanor beneath his trademark hat . . . (The man never seemed to smile!) . . . the Cowboys flourished under Landry, becoming "America's Team," with 20 consecutive winning seasons, 13 divisional championships, five NFC titles, and two Super Bowl victories . . . his 270 career wins (including post-season) rank third on the all-time list . . . a great student of the game, Landry pioneered the "flex defense" in the 1960s and put the "shotgun" formation to wide and effective use in the 1970s . . . his dismissal following the 1988 season after a change in Cowboys ownership was met with disapproval among the Dallas faithful, who continue to regard him as the soul of the franchise . . .

VINCE LOMBARDI: This man was in a class by himself—just as his Green Bay Packers of the 1960s were in a class by themselves . . . a former player and assistant coach of the New York Giants, Lombardi was tapped to revive a struggling Packers franchise in 1959 . . . known as a creative offensive coordinator and all-around perfectionist, and it was felt in Green Bay that he could help the team rebound from a dismal 1-10-1 1958 season . . . a tremendous motivator, Lombardi took Green Bay by storm, leading the Packers to a surprising 7-5 turnaround season in 1959, and then on to six divisional titles and five NFL championships in the next 9 years—not to mention victories in Super Bowls I and II . . . his constant pursuit of excellence was passed on to his players—and, soon, to Green Bay fans, who came to expect nothing but the best from their Packers . . . according to legend, Lombardi was the most single-minded coach in the game, famous for tossing off such inspirational lines as "Winning isn't everything, it's the only thing" . . . retired as Packers coach following the 1968 season, only to return to the game the following year to revive the flagging Washington Redskins, posting another strong turnaround in his first season, but Lombardi's "comeback" and his brilliant coaching career were cut short by cancer . . .

EARLE "GREASY" NEALE: Longtime Philadelphia Eagles coach, beginning in 1941, widely credited with improving George Halas's original T-formation and showcasing it to championship effect . . . also credited with developing the 4-3 defensive formation, an alignment still deployed by many of today's teams . . . a former end for Jim Thorpe's Canton Bulldogs (and a former outfielder for the Cincinnati Reds), Neale was a shrewd judge of talent and helped to build an intimidating Eagles roster that was marked by future Hall of Famers Pete Pihos and Steve Van Buren . . . coached the Eagles to back-to-back championships in 1948 and 1949, with 7-0 and 14-0 victories over the Chicago Cardinals and Los Angeles Rams, marking the first time a team had won consecutive titles by shutting out their opponents—a credit to his swarming "Eagles Defense" . . .

CHUCK NOLL: What I love about this guy was the way he made something out of nothing . . . resurrected a lowly Pittsburgh Steelers franchise that had never won a blessed thing before Noll signed on as head coach in 1969 . . . the team went 1-13 in his first season, but by 1972 Noll had turned things completely around, guiding the Steelers to an 11-3 record and the AFC Central Division title, beginning an impressive run of championship-type seasons unmatched in NFL history . . . his Steelers won four Super Bowls (IX, X, XIII, XIV) in a 6-year span and were widely regarded as one of the true dynasties in team sports . . . known as a shrewd judge of talent, Noll retired in 1993 with a 209-156-1 record in 23 seasons with the Steelers, including a 16-8 record in the post-season . . .

DON SHULA: The winningest coach in NFL history, with a career mark of 347-173-6 in 33 seasons . . . began his coaching career with the Baltimore Colts, leading them to seven consecutive winning seasons, before signing on for the next 26 years with the Miami Dolphins . . . his teams reached the post-season an astonishing 20 times in 33 years, including two Super Bowl victories . . . (Shula's six Super Bowl coaching appearances are also a record) . . . his greatest team was probably the 1972 Dolphins, who posted a perfect 14-0 regular season record and went on to win three post-season games (including a 14-7 victory over Washington in Super Bowl VII), completing the only perfect season in NFL history . . . Shula's teams invariably featured savvy, precision-oriented quarterbacks, like Johnny Unitas, Bob Griese, and Dan Marino, and classic, ball-control offenses, but he was a defensive player at heart and placed a special emphasis on team-oriented defensive schemes . . . the Dolphins' heralded "No-Name Defense" of the 1970s was a hallmark of this style of play . . .

BILL WALSH: Probably the most influential coach in today's game, even in retirement . . . widely credited with the development of the "West Coast offense" in current favor around the league . . . felt strongly that teams could run a dynamic, ball-control offense with a quick-set, quick-drop, high-percentage, short-yardage passing game . . . as an assistant coach with the Cincinnati Bengals and San Diego Chargers, he developed a reputation as a quarterback specialist, which he displayed to full effect when he was named head coach and general manager of the San Francisco 49ers in 1979 . . . in just 3 years, turned a hapless franchise into national champions, largely on the strength of his quarterback, Joe Montana, and his highly efficient passing game . . . in his 10 seasons in San Francisco, Walsh posted a 102-63-1 mark, with six NFC Western Division championships and three Super Bowl championships . . . named NFL Coach of the Year in 1981 and NFC Coach of the Year in 1984, but he might have won a few more of these if his 49ers weren't expected to finish at the top of the heap every darn season . . .

5

Play-by-Play

Getting Beyond Xs and Os

Ihad always been a casual football fan, along for the ride with my
dad, but I didn't become a diehard until I realized that the whole
operation was practiced and choreographed and rehearsed into the
ground. That realization changed everything for me. For whatever
reason, I just loved that these big, beefy guys would take the time to
learn all of these moves and plays, and that they would do it as a
group—because if any one of them dropped the ball, the whole enterprise would crumble. I loved that there was a game plan, which I
guessed was a whole lot like a script—which I suppose appealed to the
budding performer in me.

Of course, I had known this in theory for a long time, but it took
hanging around Rodney and learning the game from the sidelines for me
to realize it in a fundamental way. Despite appearances to the contrary,

the game of football wasn't just a group of guys wearing skin-tight jerseys and hugging each other and patting each other on the butt and running around like chickens with their heads cut off—which would have been interesting enough. Nope. There was so much more going on out there—a whole damn strategy!— and the more I realized how much was happening out there, the more I wanted to know about it.

The Game Script

As a little girl, I used to wonder why the Philadelphia Eagles running back kept barreling through the line, straight up the middle, even though he never managed to gain more than a couple yards on each play. I would look on and think, Why did that fool barrel straight up the middle again? I'd wonder, What in the world is that man thinking? It never occurred to me that this running back was told to keep pounding up the middle, again and again and again, and that there were other players whose job it was to clear a path for him, again and again and again; and the reason the running back never seemed to get anywhere was because these other guys kept missing their blocks and their assignments, or the defense was somehow able to anticipate our plays—also, again and again and again. This was fascinating to me, and I've never lost that fascination over the years.

It turns out there's very little room for improvisation on a football field, unless you're talking about a busted play, or one that has been successfully executed to allow a runner to blast through the line and dance his way across an open field. It's all scripted and plotted and thought through. Rodney's played for coaches who have the first 20 or 30 plays set down on paper before the game even begins, taking into account this and that circumstance and every possible outcome—a prospect that was inconceivable to me as a young fan. There are plays for third down and long yardage, second down and short yardage, and fourth down and inches.

The closer I got to the game, the more I realized how smart these players were, and how smart these coaches were, and how difficult it was to actually play the game at the professional level. The players have so much committed to muscle memory and instinct that they make it look easy, and so we lose sight of what it really means to play the game. It requires all kinds of mental preparation, mental toughness, and mental agility. And hours and hours of practice. And patience. And stamina. And on and on.

Rodney is forever giving me grief for the way I mix up the terms of what he does for a living with the terms of what I do for a living. I'm always saying, "What time do you get out of rehearsal?" And he's always saying, "It's *practice,* Holly." Call it what you will, but these guys are out there rehearsing plays, the same way I have to go in and rehearse a new episode of a sitcom. I learn my lines; they learn their assignments. Really, when it comes down to it, we have such parallel lives, Rodney and me. I work all week long rehearsing a show; he works all week long rehearsing his game plan. We start by talking about it; and as the week moves along, we get it on its feet, and go through the motions and simulate the real deal. A show, a game . . . it amounts to the same thing; and at the other end of all that preparation, we're both out there strutting our stuff in front of an audience. We're performers, after all, and his stage is the football field. The only real difference is that we actors aren't competing with anybody on our stage. We might compete with other shows in the ratings, and we might compete with other actors on auditions, but we don't go head-to-head and duke it out the way football players do when it's their version of showtime. And you'd never, *ever* say "Break a leg" to a football player before a game!

All of which takes me the long way back to my point: The game of football is scripted to an unbelievable degree. The play's the thing, as I mentioned in the introduction, bending that line from Shakespeare. It's not the same in other sports. Basketball, hockey, soccer . . . even baseball. They've all got their plays and signals and set pieces for given situations. They have their rehearsals—uh, practices. But none of these sports compare in complexity to football. In Rodney's playbook—at any given time—there are at least 50 different plays that he and his teammates need to know in their sleep, and usually there'll be 11 distinct assignments on each one of them. And I'm not talking about variations or permutations on the same play, either. I'm talking about 50 *different* plays, from 11 different angles; and from one game to the next, the coaching staff might toss out a couple dozen plays that didn't work the week before and install a couple dozen new ones in their place. There are specific plays designed to go up against specific teams, in specific situations—all in an attempt to exploit one team's strength against another team's weakness. There are wet-weather plays, and cold-weather plays; and I wouldn't be surprised to learn that some team,

HISTORY OF THE GAME

A LEAGUE OF THEIR OWN

The American Professional Football Association formed in 1920. Franchises were awarded for the whopping sum of $100 per team, and from one year to the next there were as many as 22 teams playing out the league schedule. Teams went in and out of business for a variety of reasons: Owners ran out of money or lost interest; fans couldn't be bothered; players bounced to "stronger" franchises, looking to cut their best deals. Typically, local business owners thought a team bearing the company name and promoting the company's product or service would be good for business—and in success, it usually was. Trouble was, it was tough enough to get paying fans to turn out for the games, and tougher still to draw them to a losing team, so success was a little too long in coming for some owners.

The game found its warmest reception in Ohio, where it quickly rivaled baseball as the state's most popular game. In fact, the very first APFA organizational meeting was held in an automobile showroom in Canton, which is now the site of the Pro Football Hall of Fame. Jim Thorpe, the fabled Olympian who many regard as the most influential athlete in American history, was named president of the new league, while continuing as a player-coach for its Canton franchise.

The APFA formed the basis for the National Football League we know today—and over the years, it managed to survive challenges from no less than three upstart professional leagues looking to cover some of the same ground in the same cities, all of them oddly christened the American Football League.

somewhere, has been working on a play for when it's 72 degrees with a slight northwesterly breeze.

Rodney has been on six different teams over the years, and I've seen a whole lot of playbooks; and let me tell you, it's not easy to learn all of that stuff. The intricacies, the timing, the synchronicity . . . all choreographed and mix-mastered into one seamless play. What the quarterback has to do, what the running back has to do, what the receivers have to do, who has to block, who doesn't have to block . . . and there's a lot of acting involved, too. One guy feints this way, another guy feints that way, a wide receiver makes a decoy run down the sideline to stretch the defense. Plus, the language is so weird. *Texas scat. Dallas one. Outback slant.* A lot of these plays sound like steakhouses—which, come to think of it, is probably where a bunch of them were drawn up.

Running vs. Passing

What is a play, really, other than a single piece of an overall game plan or approach? To understand any isolated play, I suppose it's necessary first to understand the bigger picture. Let's start with one of the game's most basic strategies. A team's **running game**—an offensive strategy based on running the ball down the field to gain yardage—is important because, when successful, it allows you the freedom to go to your passing game. Similarly, if you can establish your **passing game**—an offensive strategy that relies on throwing the ball down the field to gain yardage—early on in a contest, it loosens things up on the line of scrimmage for your running game. So, the two very clearly go hand in hand. Teams that rely exclusively on one or the other tend not to do as well over the long haul. Why? Well, not to simplify things too much, but the answer is that it's too easily figured out. Pull the same moves every time, and you might as well not have any moves at all—that's what it comes down to.

If I were a coach and could choose between a ridiculous running game or an okay passing game, I'd take the ridiculous running game any day. (Ridiculous as in crazy, off the hook, or really, really good.) And I think most coaches would probably choose the same because it's so much easier to build a strong team around a powerful offensive line and a talented workhorse running back. Put those weapons to good and effective use, and it opens up your passing game because the defenders are focused on the workhorse back who keeps running down their throats all game long. It's like an elaborate sleight of hand: Get your opponents to look one way, and blindside them from another.

Matchups are key. If you're going up against a team with one of the best defensive backs in the league (say, Deion Sanders in his prime), you'll typically design a game plan where most of the action goes to the opposite side of the field—effectively taking the all-star defensive back out of the game by refusing to engage him. If you're facing a team that features an explosive kick returner, you'll probably instruct your kicking team to send the ball short, end over end, to where it will most likely be picked up by a bigger, slower, less explosive player whose principal job is to block for his quicker, more explosive teammate.

The Play's Very Definitely the Thing

Let's look at some of the more common terms that define and describe both the passing game and the running game. They indicate plays, formations, and strategies on both sides of the ball, so you can learn what to look and listen for when you're watching a game. (See page 107 for the key to abbreviations.)

Passing Game Terminology

There are as many ways to move a football through the air as there are quarterbacks to throw one. Some plays are designed so that the ball is lofted over a defender's outstretched arms and into the receiver's hands, and some work only if the ball is thrown like a bullet. But for a pass play to work, the quarterback has to find his target; overthrow your man or screw up the timing, and even the best-run pass pattern will be ineffective. And keep in mind, some rule changes over the years have made it a little easier for the receiver to chart a clear path to the ball. Nowadays, a defender can't touch a receiver once the receiver's gone 5 yards downfield from the line of scrimmage. Within those first 5 yards, all bets are off; and if you fix your eyes on these matchups, you'll see all kinds of interesting contact in that confined space. It's the defender's first (and, technically, last) opportunity to slow down the receiver; and at the same time, it's the receiver's first and best chance to fake out the guy who's supposed to guard him and gain an all-important extra step. Virtually every pass pattern—long or short—succeeds or fails in those first 5 yards, where you'll see receivers juke and dance and stutter-step their way clear, and defenders reach into their own bag of tricks to contain the guy on the other side of the line.

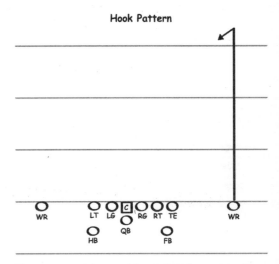

Hook Pattern

The receiver sprints toward the goal and then curls back toward the line of scrimmage.

PASS PATTERN: Refers to the route the receiver takes across the field on a pass play. Conveniently, most traditional pass patterns carry names that describe the pattern itself. A *slash*, for example, is a pass pattern that takes a receiver across the field in a slashing, diagonal route. A *down and out* refers to a route run by the receiver that takes him directly downfield, with a sharp cut to the outside of the field. A *hook* calls for him to sprint toward the goal and then to curl back towards the line of scrimmage. A *post* pattern is a beeline toward the goal post, while a *flag* pattern calls for the receiver to angle toward the corner of the field where the goal line meets the sideline.

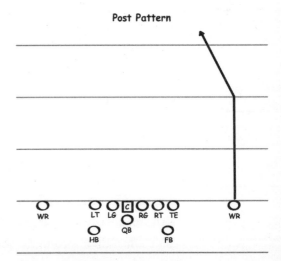

Post Pattern

The receiver beelines toward the goal post.

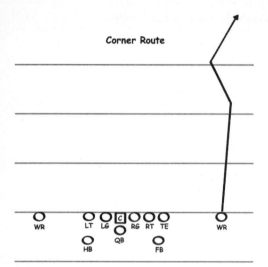

Corner Route

A pass pattern in which the receiver runs downfield then slants toward the corner.

(This last gets its name in a throwback sort of way, because in the "golden" days there used to be a flag positioned in that corner, instead of those bright orange pylons they use today. These days this play is also referred to as a *corner route*.)

PLAY ACTION: This refers to one of the most common sleights of hand in a quarterback's arsenal and to any passing play designed to look like a running play. Typically, the offensive linemen push forward the way they would if they were blocking for a run, while the quarterback pretends to hand off the ball to one of his running backs. The running back then bobs and weaves toward the line as if he has the ball. The idea is to throw off the defenders for a beat or two, allowing the quarterback to drop back and find an open receiver.

PUMP FAKE: Another common tactic to fool the defense. On occasion, you'll notice the quarterback fake a throw prior to releasing the ball. This is usually done by design, in an effort to get the defenders to hesitate or otherwise react and to give the receivers a chance to gain an all-important advantage. It is sometimes done on the fly, when a quarterback cocks back to release the ball and suddenly realizes his man is no longer open.

THROWING IT AWAY: The practice of deliberately throwing the ball out-of-bounds or over the head of the nearest eligible receiver. This is usually a desperation move when a quarterback can't find an open receiver or when he's in danger of being tackled behind the line of scrimmage. And, since the game clock is stopped with every incomplete pass, it's also an effective way to pause the game when time is running out.

INTENTIONAL GROUNDING: As above, although if one of the officials determines that there is no eligible receiver in the vicinity of the thrown ball—or, according to the NFL Rule Book, if the ball is thrown "without a realistic chance of completion"—a 10-yard, loss-of-down penalty can be called. This always struck me as one of the most arbitrary rules on the books. Don't you think a team should be entitled to throw the ball away and give up a chance to advance it any time it chooses? Plus, a quarterback is permitted to "spike" the ball (drive it into the ground directly in front of him), which essentially accomplishes the same thing—as long as he does so in a continuous motion upon taking the snap from center. The distinction—once again according to the official rules—is that a spike is purely a clock-stopping maneuver, a strategic move, while intentional grounding can result from a busted play or a strong pass rush; but it's a silly, meaningless distinction. (See, this is why they don't let players' wives rewrite the rule book!)

SCRAMBLE: A passing play that turns into a running play despite itself. Some quarterbacks are especially quick and creative on their feet (think Michael Vick, for present-day fans; think Fran Tarkenton, for fans who go back a few years). Others aren't able to move much at all, especially late in their careers (think Joe Namath). And yet invariably there are times when a primary *and* a secondary receiver are unable to get open downfield, or when an offensive lineman misses his block, or a passing play otherwise unravels and a quarterback is left to improvise—or *scramble* his way to safety. Some of the most exciting plays occur when a quarterback is scrambling to outrun a fast-approaching defender, while continuing to look down or across the field for a suddenly open receiver who, for his part, has been doing some scrambling of his own. If the quarterback manages to buy himself enough time to release the ball, you're left with a passing play that has a few more zigs and zags to it than the coaches intended. If the quarterback manages to get past the line of scrimmage before being tackled or run out of bounds, it's considered a running play, and the yardage gained is recorded in the team's rushing statistics. If he's tackled behind the line of scrimmage, it's considered a sack, and the loss of yardage goes against the team's passing line—as in the team stat.

INTERCEPTION: A quarterback's greatest fear (as opposed to a sack, which is the greatest fear of the quarterback's wife). An interception refers to a ball caught by a defender, intended for a receiver on the offensive team. Also known as a "pick" or an "INT," an interception can turn the game around in a heartbeat, canceling out a sustained drive or killing an all-but-certain opportunity to score.

THE BOMB: My favorite pass play because, when it works, there's nothing quite like it. Simply put, it's a long pass (about 30-plus yards) to one of the wide receivers. It's used sparingly because it's difficult to execute and easy enough to defend against, but it's a great way to stretch out the field and tell your opponents that you're willing to air it out and see what happens. If you can pull it off, it's also the quickest way I know to put six points on the board and suck some of the life out of your opponents.

**Screen Pass Left
to Halfback**

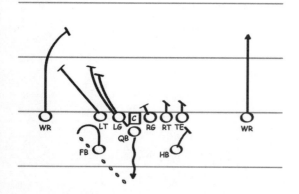

The quarterback tries to invite the defense to rush him, then throws the football to the halfback. The halfback pretends to block, then slips out to the open spot. The center, left offensive guard, and left offensive tackle block for 2 seconds, then run left to block for the halfback.

THE SCREEN: A bait-and-switch deception play intended to dupe the defensive linemen into thinking they have a shot at sacking the quarterback, when in reality they are being lured out of position for a short pass play to the running back. Here's how it works: The quarterback backpedals into the pocket while his offensive linemen backpedal with him, allowing the defensive linemen to move toward the ball. At the same time, the running back begins to move toward one side of the field, behind a wall that has now been formed by the backpedaling linemen. As the defenders inch closer to the quarterback, he lofts the ball softly to his running back, who is now free to advance behind the protection of the offensive linemen, who have begun to move toward the same side of the field as the running back. Sound complicated? It is. But it can be an effective way to eke out short yardage in a must-gain situation; done right, it can be an effective way to break the game open with a big-time gain.

SHOTGUN FORMATION: A passing formation that essentially tells the defense what the offense is about to do, because the quarterback lines up 5 or 6 yards behind the center to receive the snap. Indeed, the shotgun quarterback is so far behind the line that it's unlikely he'll hand the ball off to one of his running backs. On the face of it, you'd think this might hurt a team's chances because it allows the defense to expect the pass, but there are so many advantages for the quarterback that it can be a good trade-off. From his perspective deep in the pocket, the quarterback has more time to study the defense and direct his pass; presumably, it also gives the receivers more time to run their routes and get into position to make a catch. In recent years, the shotgun has become more and more popular with coaches—and, accordingly, with fans, for the way it opens up the passing game. Used selectively, it can be an important part of a team's offensive strategy.

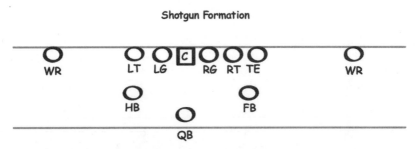

Shotgun Formation

A passing formation in which the quarterback lines up 5 or 6 yards behind the center to receive the snap.

SHOVEL PASS: A running play disguised as a passing play, usually run from the shotgun formation. In a typical shovel pass play, the running back is slotted a couple of steps ahead of the quarterback to receive a ball that is pushed (actually shoved) more than it is thrown. The play works best when the quarterback tricks the defense into believing he is looking downfield for an open receiver.

BUMP-AND-RUN: A type of pass defense (or coverage) having to do with the 5-yards-from-scrimmage restrictions I wrote about earlier (see page 93). Remember, it's legal for a defender to *bump* the receiver within those first 5 yards; if done effectively, it can upset a carefully timed passing pattern. Trouble is, if it's done ineffectively, and the receiver is able to skate past the defender, he can break free for a potentially huge gain. Okay, so that explains the *bump* part of the term, but what about the *run*? Well, following the bump at the line, the defender will have to match the receiver stride-for-stride down the field, so he'd better be able to run—and fast.

MAN-TO-MAN COVERAGE: Any pass defense that assigns a specific receiver to be covered by a specific defender.

Man-to-Man Coverage with Full Blitz

In a full blitz, there is no free safety in the middle of the field. All secondary defenders (free safety, strong safety, and both cornerbacks) cover receivers, tight ends, and running backs. The linebackers who are not covering are rushing the passer (blitzing).

DOUBLE COVERAGE: Another kind of pass defense, in which two defenders are assigned to cover the same receiver; it's usually deployed as part of a larger man-to-man scheme when there is a particularly dangerous receiver who needs to be contained.

ZONE COVERAGE: A pass defense that requires defenders to cover a specific area of the field, and any receivers who might roam within that area.

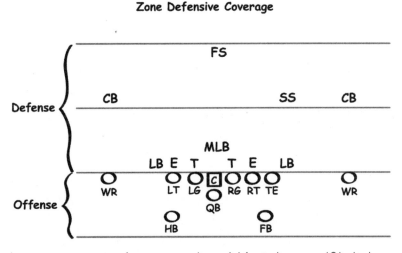

Zone Defensive Coverage

This is the most common version of zone coverage. It uses 4 defensive linemen and 3 linebackers, each covering one third of the field.

BLITZ: A roll-the-dice defensive play that calls for more defenders to rush the passer than there are offensive linemen to block them. Typically, a defensive unit will rush three or four linemen on a pass play. Occasionally, they'll also send a linebacker or two into the fray, increasing the pressure on the quarterback. But sometimes, when a defensive coordinator has a certain hunch that the offense is looking to pass, he'll pull from his secondary to send a sixth and seventh defender to the line in a surprise attack. A successful blitz can drop the quarterback for a substantial loss or force him to hurry his throw, resulting in an interception. However, if a quarterback is able to read the blitz and see it

HISTORY OF THE GAME

COLLEGE TRIES

In the 1920s, professional team owners recognized the value of the college game in supplying players with local followings and fully developed talent, and agreed not to sign any college students before graduation. It's not clear whether these folks were actually interested in the education of these young men, or if they simply didn't want to bite the hand that fed them. After all, it made no sense to dip into the talent pool until the talent was fully developed, right? When it was determined that players could continue their intercollegiate athletic careers beyond their graduation under certain circumstances, owners agreed not to sign them until they had run through their college eligibility. They also agreed not to tamper with each other's players, modeling their player contracts after the established "reserve clause" standards of Major League Baseball.

The professional leagues struggled for a long time because football fans regarded the college game as the better showcase. And I guess it was. Players couldn't afford to make a full-time career in the low-paying American Professional Football Association, so they treated it like a part-time job. They would work factory shifts or construction jobs and were available for practices only in the evenings, only a couple times each week. Not exactly a winning formula for a league looking to establish itself as a showcase for top athletes. The "pros" probably appeared a little older, a little slower, and a little more beaten down than their collegiate counterparts, who were constantly available to their coaches, especially in pre-season, and were therefore better conditioned and better equipped to execute their set-plays and formations.

The college game continued to flourish and fans continued to regard the professional game as a second tier until the early 1930s, when the NFL coaches began to look more thoughtfully at the game as a contest of tactics and strategy and finesse as much as a test of will and strength and athleticism. A 1934 exhibition of the Chicago Bears against a team of collegiate all-stars ended in a scoreless tie in front of nearly 80,000 fans at Chicago's Soldiers Field, giving the professionals at least some measure of bragging rights against the amateurs and offering further proof that fan interest was on the rise. By the end of the decade, the league had broadcast its first televised game—to approximately 1,000 homes in the New York City area—and crossed one million in total season attendance for the first time in league history.

coming, the defense is vulnerable—provided the offense can make some quick adjustments on the line of scrimmage.

Running Game Terminology

For generations, the best running attacks have relied on a grind-it-out approach. Three yards here, 4 yards there, those final few inches for a first down. For many teams, the ideal is a ball-control offense that allows for a variety of plays on the ground and in the air. But the mix works only if the running game is sound. As we learned earlier, football was well past its infancy before the forward pass was made a part of the game, so the running game is football at its most basic. It's time-tested and little changed—I guess on the theory that if it ain't broke, there's no reason to fix it. And so despite all the innovations we've seen in different passing attacks and defensive alignments over the past several years, today's running plays look a whole lot like yesterday's running plays. And today's running backs are still trying to find a hole or a couple inches of daylight at the line, and to pound their way up the field for a small gain. Yet even at its most basic, there is all kinds of room for variety and creativity in a sustained running attack. Here are some of the more common terms associated with this old-style approach to the game.

HAND-OFF: The most basic method of transferring the ball from the quarterback to the running back. It looks and sounds easy, but it's a complicated maneuver that takes hours and hours of practice to accomplish smoothly. While certain plays call for the quarterback to gently (and obviously) place the ball into the arms of his running back, others require a bit of deception and shift-on-the-fly dexterity. A botched hand-off can be one of the most frustrating situations in all of football—for fans, players, and coaches alike—because it's one of those moves we all expect to be executed to perfection, every time.

PITCH: Another way to get the ball from the quarterback to the running back, but with a slightly higher margin of error. In this play, the quarterback makes a short, underhanded pass to his back, sometimes using both hands for greater accuracy.

LATERAL: A backward pass. In a designed play, it's usually thrown by the quarterback (overhanded or underhanded) to a running back or a wide receiver, who can then run with it or try to pass it off himself. Behind the line of scrimmage, the ball can be thrown in a forward pass a second or subsequent time, provided the ball has not yet crossed the line of scrimmage on the same play. In an open-field play, where the ballcarrier has crossed the line of scrimmage and is in danger of being tackled, he can lateral the ball to a teammate, who might be in a better position to continue to advance with it. Teammates can lateral a ball to each other at any time—during a play run from scrimmage, on a kick-off or punt return, or following an interception or fumble recovery.

TRAP: A blocking play following a quick hand-off on a run up the middle, designed to trick the defensive lineman into thinking he might have a clear path to the ball. When this happens, there is an immediate "switch" in blocking assignments, and the defender is blocked at an angle—or "trapped"—by an opposing lineman.

QUARTERBACK SNEAK: Not to be confused with a quarterback scramble, this is a play designed for the quarterback to lower his shoulder and barrel through the line, or to lunge through a hole created by his linemen, or to leap over a bed of downed linemen. There's usually an element of surprise to it, which I guess accounts for the name. Typically used in a short-yardage situation, when every inch of real estate is precious, and offensive coaches (also known as "coordinators") don't want to give up any ground by dropping back and handing off the ball to a running back.

SWEEP: A running play that takes the ball wide, toward the sidelines. Popularized (and, some fans say, perfected) by the Green Bay Packers teams of the 1960s and their legendary coach Vince Lombardi, the traditional sweep takes longer to develop than a running play up the middle; but if the linemen can con-

Strong Sweep Right

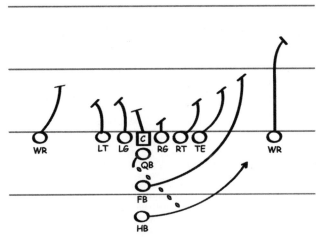

In this version of a sweep, the offensive line, tight end, fullback, and wide receiver on the strong side create an alley for the halfback to run in.

tain the defense and push them toward the inside of the field, and a fleet-footed running back can "turn the corner," there's the potential for big gains.

DRAW: Another running play designed to look like a passing play at the outset and intended to "draw" the defenders into rushing the quarterback. The idea here is for the quarterback to drop back into the pocket alongside a running back who appears to be in blocking position to protect the passer. As the defensive line approaches, the quarterback slips the ball with an afterthought-type hand-off to his back, who manages to dart past the line to daylight. One variation on the play is the *quarterback draw,* which is essentially a quarterback sneak run in a passing situation from the shotgun formation.

DIVE: A short-yardage play, usually run when a team is up against the goal line or a first-down marker. This play takes its name from the action it describes. The quarterback hands the ball off immediately to his running back, who hurls himself forward into, over, or otherwise past the sea of linemen at his feet.

END-AROUND: A running play that calls for a receiver or tight end to ultimately carry the ball from his position wide of the line of scrimmage. It's considered a trick play, but I've seen this play run so often by some teams that it seems like business as usual. The quarterback takes the snap and hands it off to one of his running backs, who proceeds to roll out in the direction of the wide receiver, as in a straightforward sweep. The wide receiver, for his part, is meant to nonchalantly double back toward the running back; and when the two men pass each other, the running back slips the ball to the wide receiver. The play is designed to mislead the defense into thinking the running back is going to advance in one direction, but the wide receiver actually collects the ball and catches the defenders short by using his momentum to shift the action in the other direction. One popular variation calls for the quarterback to roll out directly toward the wide receiver, and to make the unexpected hand-off himself.

NORTH/SOUTH RUNNERS: A term used to describe a runner who tends to cut a clean path toward his goal line. As opposed to *east/west runners*, who spend a lot of time traversing the field from sideline to sideline, avoiding contact in the center of the field, the *north/south runner* is not afraid to do his thing in heavy traffic and suffer the consequences.

BACKFIELD IN MOTION: Does anybody but me remember that great R&B song of the same name by Mel and Tim from too many years ago? To this day, I hear the term and set my toe to tapping—and I hear the term a lot, because the convention these days is for offensive units to move around a whole lot before the snap. Like everything else these guys do on the line, such movement is intended to confuse or confound the defense. Keep in mind, there is also the dreaded call of *illegal motion,* which prohibits 10 offensive players from moving a muscle, once they take their positions on the offensive line before the start of each play. That 11th player must be playing in a backfield position; and according to the rule book, he may be in motion "provided he is moving parallel to, obliquely backward from, or directly backward from the line of scrimmage. . . ."

I don't know about you, but I'm still trying to figure out what they mean by *obliquely backward from*. I'd ask Rodney about it, but he's liable to look at me like I'm insane—which I guess I would be if I thought to ask. You see, Rodney is like most true football fans in that he knows this stuff deep down. He can't quote the rule book, but show him someone running *obliquely backward from* anyone or anything, and he'll recognize it.

Watching the Game

Don't even try to remember everything you just read about dives and sweeps and blitzes and bumps. It'll come in time, and you'll start knowing what to look for on game day. And don't let the guys on TV confuse matters. The so-called experts—scouts, coaches, former players, sportswriters, broadcast booth guys—will tell you that they watch the line of scrimmage on each play, because that's where the action is. We garden-variety fans tend to follow the ball. There's nothing right or wrong about either approach; it's just how it is. A guy like John Madden is so tuned in to the personnel, the matchups on the field, and the offensive and defensive schemes he's likely to encounter in any given game, that he sees the field a little differently than the rest of us. Good for him. And good for us, because we get the benefit of his insight and experience when we turn up the sound on his *Monday Night Football* broadcasts. Or, if we don't want the benefit of his insight and experience, we can turn off the sound and bring our own expectations and analysis to each play. It's all good.

You see, every fan brings a different perspective when watching a match-up. Football is like anything else—we see what we want to see—only here there's *so much* to see at any one time. It can be overwhelming if you don't know where to look, or what you're looking for. Being a quarterback's wife, I've always watched my husband when he's in the game, but a lot of the team wives I sit with in the stands have also got their eye on the quarterback. (I can't say I blame them, either!) That's where our eyes go when we're first learning the game, because that's where the ball goes. It's elementary.

When you watch a game on television, it's hard to take in all the action from the single, wide shot you tend to see at the start of each play. Yes, it's a game that sometimes seems tailor-made for the medium, the way that rectangular field fits itself neatly in that rectangular screen; but it's not the same as being in the stadium, watching each play unfold. Of course, there are replays on television, and different camera angles, and by the time the teams are lined up for the next play, you've had a chance to see the previous one from every imaginable perspective. But it's not the same as taking it all in from the upper deck at the stadium, all at once, when you don't know what's about to happen. Even on television, I try to take in the formation before the ball is snapped, so that even if my eye naturally shifts to the quarterback, I'll know in the back of my mind that there are two receivers slotted wide right, and a third in motion and headed that way—so I am already thinking about a pass play in that direction.

Lately, like the guys on TV, I've begun to focus on the line of scrimmage a little more—that is, if Rodney's not in the game and I don't have to worry about him getting hit. I'll look at that battle in the trenches and figure out who's got his position, who's manhandling who, who's missing his blocks, who's pretty much a turnstile. (A *turnstile* refers to an offensive or defensive lineman who is consistently beaten by his opposite number, for the way the other guy just runs right through him; trust me on this, you don't want the quarterback's wife thinking your offensive lineman husband is any kind of turnstile, because that's just a cat fight waiting to happen.) It doesn't always matter where the ball is at any given moment; the line of scrimmage is where the game begins and ends.

I'm in awe of some of those broadcast booth guys, who are able to break down the action on the fly. But the truth is, as expert as these guys are, they've got all week long to prepare for a game, to learn all the players, to figure out who's playing well, who's nursing an injury, and whose wife is about to give birth. Plus, they've got a team of production assistants and interns handing them all kinds of statistics and other relevant information, and cueing them to a dozen different camera angles and slow-motion replays that the fans in the stadium don't get to see. So don't be intimidated by their intricate knowledge

KEY TO ABBREVIATIONS

LB = Linebacker

MLB = Middle linebacker

E = Defensive end

T = Defensive tackle

CB = Cornerback

SS = Strong safety

FS = Free safety

N = Nose tackle

WR = Wide receiver

RT-LT = Offensive tackle

RG-LG = Offensive guard

C = Center

TE = Tight end

HB = Halfback

FB = Fullback

QB = Quarterback

of the game or by the fact that they keep seeing things you keep missing, because they have a little help. I've been in the Fox Sports control booth during games, and there are a gazillion television monitors and another gazillion football geeks just cranking out material. (I may be overstating things, just to prove my point, but you get the idea.) So, yeah, these football analysts know their stuff, but they have a lot of help—and if you had that kind of help and if it was your full-time job to know your stuff, you could be right up there with them. (Hey, if Dennis Miller and Rush Limbaugh could be propped up as football analysts, then it's anybody's game!)

10

ALL-TIME GREAT SUPER BOWLS

Despite the hype and the hoopla, the Super Bowl doesn't always live up to its name. Most years, it seems, the game itself runs a distant second to all the buildup and pregame excitement, with one-sided contests that are frequently decided in the first quarter of play. Every now and then, though, the game justifies its billing, and we fans are treated to a true classic. Below, in chronological order, is a brief description of some of the most memorable games in Super Bowl history—culminating, of course, in Rodney's first trip to the big dance at the end of the 2003 season.

SUPER BOWL III
New York Jets 16–Baltimore Colts 7
Orange Bowl . . . Miami, Florida . . . January 12, 1969 . . .
ATTENDANCE: 75,389

After two "ho-hum" Super Bowls that saw Vince Lombardi's dominant Green Bay Packers make mincemeat of their AFL rivals, football fans were thirsting for an upset, and Jets quarterback Joe Namath guaranteed one just 3 days before the big game. And— wouldn't you know it!—the Jets delivered. Big time. New York's swarming defense intercepted Colts quarterback Earl Morrall three times in the first half, while Namath led a steady, ball-control offense that dominated much of the game. Jets running back Matt Snell rushed for 121 yards, but Namath was named the game's MVP—probably as much for his brash pregame prediction as for his on-field performance (17 of 28, for 206 yards). Legendary Colts quarterback Johnny Unitas, who had missed most of the 1968 season with elbow trouble, entered the game late in the fourth quarter and managed to lead his team to its lone touchdown, but the game was never in doubt.

SUPER BOWL XIII
Pittsburgh Steelers 35–Dallas Cowboys 31
Orange Bowl . . . Miami, Florida . . . January 21, 1979 . . .
ATTENDANCE: 79,484

The second Super Bowl showdown between these two rivals, widely regarded as the top teams in their respective conferences for most of the 1970s. Steelers quarterback and game MVP Terry Bradshaw passed for a record four touchdowns as Pittsburgh became the first team to record three Super Bowl victories. (They would go on to win a fourth the following season, with a 31-19 trouncing of the Los Angeles Rams.) The Steelers led all the way, but Cowboys quarterback Roger Staubach kept nipping at their heels, bringing Dallas to within two scores with just 2:23 left in the game. In one of the most exciting turns in postseason history, the Cowboys recovered an onside kick, and Staubach worked the clock and marched his team to a touchdown with just 22 seconds left, making the score 35-31. A second onside kick failed and the Steelers held on for the win, cementing their reputation as a true football dynasty under coach Chuck Knoll.

SUPER BOWL XVI
San Francisco 49ers 26–Cincinnati Bengals 21
Pontiac Silverdome . . . Detroit, Michigan . . . January 24, 1982 . . .
ATTENDANCE: 81,270

Bill Walsh's 49ers were the NFL's next great dynasty, led by Hall of Fame quarterback Joe Montana. San Francisco charged out to a 20-0 halftime lead, the most one-sided halftime score in Super Bowl history at the time and a sure sign that the Bengals were in deep trouble. But Cincinnati quarterback Ken Anderson, one of the most precise passers in the game, managed to bring his team back with two unanswered touchdown drives, along the way establishing Super Bowl records for completions (25) and completion percentage (73.5). The Bengals even managed to outgain the 49ers in yardage on the field, compiling 356 yards to San Francisco's 275 yards, but game MVP Montana was able to put together two clock-eating field goal drives to seal the victory.

SUPER BOWL XVIII
Los Angeles Raiders 38–Washington Redskins 9
Tampa Stadium . . . Tampa, Florida . . . January 22, 1984 . . .
ATTENDANCE: 72,920

Not exactly a nail-biter, but this lopsided Raiders victory rates a mention here for the killer performance of game MVP Marcus Allen, now in the Hall of Fame, who rushed for a Super Bowl record 191 yards on just 20 carries—including an outrageous 73-yard touchdown run. The game was never in doubt, but it was never boring watching Marcus and his mates. There was even a blocked Redskins punt to start the game and set the tone. At the end of the day, the Raiders' 38 points marked the highest total by a Super Bowl team, eclipsing Green Bay's 35 points in Super Bowl I.

SUPER BOWL XXII
Washington Redskins 42–Denver Broncos 10
Jack Murphy Stadium . . . San Diego, California . . . January 31, 1988 . . .
ATTENDANCE: 73,302

Another high-scoring rout, notable for the record-shattering performances of several Redskins players, led by quarterback Doug Williams, the game MVP (and the first black quarterback to ever win a Super Bowl), who set a Super Bowl passing record with 340 yards. His primary target for the day, wide receiver Ricky Sanders, set his own record, notching 193 yards on nine catches. And rookie running back Timmy Smith galloped into the record books, with 204 yards on 22 carries. Washington's six touchdowns and 602 total yards gained also set Super Bowl records. The most amazing aspect of this game was that most of the Washington onslaught came in the second quarter, which saw the Redskins pile on five touchdowns in just 18 plays, with a total time of possession of less than 6 minutes. Other than that one quarter, I guess you could say the game was pretty close, right?

SUPER BOWL XXV
New York Giants 20–Buffalo Bills 19
Tampa Stadium . . . Tampa, Florida . . . January 27, 1991 . . .
ATTENDANCE: 73,813

One of the great squeakers in Super Bowl history. A ball-control game all the way, with the Giants doing most of the ball-controlling. Buffalo took an early 12-3 lead, but the Giants closed the gap to 12-10 with a touchdown drive just before halftime and then took the lead with a methodical 75-yard drive to open the second half. (That 14-play drive ate up an astonishing 9:29 of the game clock—a Super Bowl record.) The Bills recaptured the lead on the opening play of the fourth quarter, with a 31-yard touchdown run by Pro Bowler Thurman Thomas, pushing the score to 19-17, but the Giants answered with a Matt Bahr field goal. With time running out, Buffalo's Scott Norwood attempted a 47-yard field goal, but the ball sailed wide right.

SUPER BOWL XXXII
Denver Broncos 31–Green Bay Packers 24
Qualcomm Stadium . . . San Diego, California . . . January 25, 1998 . . .
ATTENDANCE: 68,912

Certainly one of the more exciting back-and-forth contests in recent Super Bowl history. Quarterback Brett Favre led the defending Super Bowl champion Packers on a 76-yard touchdown drive to open the game, after which the Broncos and quarterback John Elway answered with a 56-yard drive of their own. After another Broncos touchdown and field goal, Favre marched his Packers another 95 yards downfield for a second touchdown as time ran out in the first half. The two teams traded momentum throughout the second half. The Packers tied the game with a field goal. The Broncos reclaimed the lead with a touchdown. The Packers responded with a touchdown of their own. And on and on, and back and forth, and this way and that way. Down by one touchdown, Favre orchestrated one final drive, taking his Packers to the Denver 35 with just over a minute left in the game, but his fourth-down pass to Mark Chmura was deflected by John Mobley, and the Broncos held on to win.

SUPER BOWL XXXIV
St. Louis Rams 23–Tennessee Titans 16
Georgia Dome . . . Atlanta, Georgia . . . January 30, 2000 . . .
ATTENDANCE: 72,625

Folks will talk about this one for generations, mostly for the way it ended, but what a lot of folks forget is the way it started. Rams quarterback Kurt Warner took his team inside the Titans' 20-yard line on each of its first six possessions, but St. Louis could manage only three field goals and a touchdown for a not-insurmountable 16-0 lead. The score certainly didn't scare the boots off the Titans, and they bounced back in the second half with two strong touchdown drives led by quarterback Steve McNair, to bring the score to 16-13 after a missed two-point conversion. Here's where things got interesting. The Titans denied the Rams a first down on their next drive, and managed a game-tying field goal on their next possession. Now it was Warner's turn. On the next play from scrimmage, he connected with wide receiver Isaac Bruce on a 73-yard touchdown pass, for a 23-16 lead with 1:54 left on the clock. McNair and the Titans took over and managed to push the ball to the Rams' 10-yard line. With no time-outs and just 6 seconds remaining, McNair threw a quick slant pass to Kevin Dyson, who was tackled just inches from the goal line as time expired. Whew!

SUPER BOWL XXXVI
New England Patriots 20–St. Louis Rams 17
Louisiana Superdome . . . New Orleans, Louisiana . . . February 3, 2002 . . .
ATTENDANCE: 72,922

The first "walk-off" field goal in Super Bowl history capped a workmanlike effort from the surprising Patriots, and signaled the emergence of quarterback Tom Brady, the game's MVP, as a bona fide star. New England controlled the scoreboard for much of the game, while St. Louis controlled the plays, but three turnovers seemed to do the Rams in. Rams quarterback Kurt Warner staged a stirring comeback in the game's waning minutes, leading his team to two unanswered touchdowns to tie the game with only 1:30 remaining. That's where Brady took charge, operating without any time-outs, and taking the Patriots into field goal range. Adam Vinatieri's 48-yard field goal split the uprights on the final play of the game, giving the Patriots a victory for the ages.

SUPER BOWL XXXVIII
New England Patriots 32–Carolina Panthers 29
Reliant Stadium . . . Houston, Texas . . . February 1, 2004 . . .
ATTENDANCE: 71,525

Darn that Adam Vinatieri, who once again kicked the game-winning field goal, this time with just 4 seconds left on the clock and sending Rodney and his Carolina Panthers home empty-handed. This was one of the wildest seesaw battles in postseason history, and yet for the first 27 minutes neither team could put points on the board. Really, the game started out like one giant snore. At some point during the elaborate halftime festivities, it seemed that Janet Jackson's "wardrobe malfunction" at the hands of Justin Timberlake might overshadow the game itself; but the players kicked things up a notch after the slowest start in Super Bowl history. The Patriots scored first. Then the Panthers took the lead. Then the Patriots went ahead. Then the Panthers tied it up again. This particular NFL wife had never seen a more thrilling game. Panthers QB Jake Delhomme had a great game, passing for 323 yards and keeping us in contention against the Patriots, once again led by quarterback Tom Brady, who grabbed his second Super Bowl MVP trophy. And then there was Vinatieri, who launched a picture-perfect field goal from 41 yards out, right through the uprights, sending a dagger across the Carolina sidelines and into our section of the stands—but nevertheless sealing his legacy as one of the great clutch performers in the game.

6

Don't Touch My Remote

We Fans and Our Routines

I have my little routines.

During football season, I have my whole week set up so that I'm good to go on Sundays. These days, the NFL sneaks us a treat every once in a while on a Thursday, and late in the season—after the college schedule winds down—there'll be a game or two on Saturdays, and of course there are those single, marquee games on Sunday nights and Monday nights. But it's the full slate of games on Sunday afternoons that I look forward to. And now, with TiVo and the NFL Sunday Ticket package you can get on DirecTV, it's like I've died and gone to Pigskin Heaven.

Man, it's just wall-to-wall football, coast-to-coast, all damn day if I want it. I've gotten to where I can understand what my girlfriends are talking about when they tell me they feel like they're encroaching on their man's private time if they try to watch the games with them. These days, we have a decked-out media room with a big-screen TV and five smaller sets, and they're all going at once. Now, on Sundays, I'm in true heaven, with all those games raining down on me (not to mention a TiVo box on each TV in case I miss anything). The only snag in my routine is when Rodney's team has a bye (an off week) and he's home on a Sunday—because the only thing we ever argue about is which game is designated the "A" game, earning the coveted spot on the big screen!

All week long I'm looking forward to Sundays; and on the West Coast we've got those games coming at us beginning at 10 o'clock in the morning. It's a great perk of the Pacific time zone; and I make a special point of getting up early, getting the house in order, and often transporting the kids to my mom's so I can watch without distraction—and avoid the kids quoting my potty mouth at school the next day. Forgive me, but no sailor has anything on me during games! (I'm not proud of that reality, but that's how I get when I'm passionate about a game.)

The one drawback to the early start on the West Coast is that it cuts into other Sunday routines. I hear this from my girlfriends, because Rodney's not around on Sundays during the season anyway, but they all find that their "honey-do" lists are necessarily shorter because, really, you can't expect your man to clean the garage, fix the sink, wash the car, *and* cut the grass before 10 o'clock in the morning. East Coast husbands can do their full slate of chores and errands before game time; but here in California, we wake up and get on with things.

For this fan, the Sunday Ticket package is the only way to go. Oh, I love the spectacle of being at the stadium for a big game, don't misunderstand, but there's nothing like the intimacy and the drama of watching the games on television. *All* the games on television—or, at least, as many as I can cram into an afternoon. Let me tell you, I am a certifiable maniac with that TiVo remote! The game-day producers have all these story lines that the sideline reporters follow throughout the game—whose wife is about to go into labor, who's coming back from an injury, who's on the outs with the coach, who planted what prop to use in the endzone for a hoped-for touchdown celebration—that it really adds an extra dimension to everything. But the best parts are all the different camera angles and slow-motion replays they throw at you. And you gotta love that yellow first down line! I mean, it's like *The Matrix* with all these high-tech special effects. You can't get any of that at the stadium. To be fair, most stadiums now offer instant and slow-motion replays on their Diamond Vision screens, but they won't show you any controversial calls (especially if they favor the visiting team), and they won't show you the plays from every imaginable angle. The only thing I hate about watching the games on television is that you really can't see the entire play develop as it happens. They'll break it down for you, and show a tight shot of the intended receiver after an incomplete pass, or a mad scramble for a loose ball. But I like to see the whole field all at once—the routes they're running, the commotion at the line, whether or not the QB took a hit after releasing the ball.

It's a trade-off, though—the comforts of home and the benefits of broadcast technology versus the sometimes ripping winds and general inconvenience of a stadium experience. There's no question, the best way to really *learn* the game is by watching it on television and listening to someone knowledgeable describe what you're seeing. The play-by-play announcers and the color commentators (the anecdote and analysis guys) break everything down so well and so thoroughly that it's impossible to miss a detail, even if they don't always speak in laywoman's terms. (My girlfriends tell me they sometimes feel as if they are expected to know so much already—not a good thing if you're expecting to be won over and called to the game.) At the stadium, a lot of the women I know get bored between plays—and there's a whole lot of time between plays! In a 60-minute game, with a game clock that is almost always running (unless there's a change of possession, an incomplete pass, a time-out, or the ball goes out of bounds), there's usually only about 10 to 12 minutes of action. That's it! Hard to believe we all make such a fuss over a measly 10 or 12 minutes, but we can pack a ton of sweat and effort and drama into that small amount of time, wouldn't you agree? And on television, the producers can fill all of that time between plays with the kind of insight and information a true fan craves.

I also look forward to the "Game of the Week" roundup—produced by NFL Films on the NFL Network—for the way they focus on key drives and plays and the way they edit and slick-package the whole thing. It really punches up the drama and excitement and cuts right to the good stuff. Plus, they've got their own camera angles and microphone feeds that let you see and hear things you'd never see or hear on a regular broadcast. And NFL Films' patented slo-mo technology and artful editing and narration are just so incredibly cool. You might catch a game live on the network feed, but you haven't really *seen* it until it's been filtered through the unique lens and sensibility of the "Game of the Week."

The other wives used to make fun of me when I first started dating Rodney because I would bring the technology with me to our home games. I'd have the radio going in my ear, the portable television in my lap, and the media guide open in my hands. I was so frantic trying to understand what was going on down on the field that I took a lot of ribbing for it. We lowly girlfriends were already treated like second-class citizens by the players' wives; and there I was making matters worse, looking like a football tourist. I had way too much going on, way too much "equipment," but I didn't care. Remember, I was a fan *before* I met Rodney, but once we started dating, and he had me watching game films and all, I realized that I didn't know the first thing about football. Well, maybe I knew the *first* thing, but I had some trouble with the second and third things, and everything after that. I didn't want to be the kind of girlfriend who peppered her man with a million annoying questions, so I figured the best way to get myself up to speed was to listen to everything I could about the game, to see every play from every possible angle, to really learn my stuff so I could keep up my end of the Monday-morning quarterbacking.

I've toned things down some over the years, and I've learned enough to get by without the color commentators whispering in my ear. Sometimes I even hit the "mute" button when they get too opinionated about coaching decisions, questionable calls, or players—especially if you know them personally or happen to be married to one. (Just tell me what happened on the field, keep me updated on injuries and other developments, and I will do the rest, thank you very much.) But I still read as much as I can to bring myself up to speed on each

HISTORY OF THE GAME

EARLY STARS

By the end of its first year, the upstart American Professional Football Association had grown to include 22 teams, including a team from Decatur, Illinois that would soon move their home games to Cubs Park in Chicago, at the urging of player-coach George Halas. The Decatur Staleys had been named for their original owner, A.E. Staley of the Staley Starch Company, but Halas reasoned that a new, fan-friendly nickname was in order, and since football players tended to be bigger than baseball players, and since he shared a field with the popular Chicago Cubs baseball team, he settled on the Bears. Halas became such a popular, influential figure in professional football, and such a beloved Chicago legend, that as the team and the game grew in stature, and as he himself took on in years, he assumed the fan-friendly nickname himself, becoming known as "Papa Bear."

Under Halas, the league took its next important step when the Bears signed Red Grange at the end of the 1925 college football season. The legendary "Galloping Ghost" was arguably the most popular college football player in the country—and the professional league, now known as the National Football League, was in desperate need of a star attraction. The All-American halfback out of the University of Illinois fit the bill. The largest crowd in pro football history—more than 36,000—filled Cubs Park on Thanksgiving Day for an exhibition against the cross-town Chicago Cardinals. The Bears then set off on a 2-week barnstorming tour of the Northeast, followed by another tour of the South and Southwest that culminated in a game against the Los Angeles Tigers before more than 75,000 football-mad fans, setting a new attendance record before the ink was dry on the first. For a brief, shining moment, Red Grange matched Babe Ruth as the most revered athlete in American sports, and the fledgling professional league received a tremendous shot in the arm.

The following year, the Duluth Eskimos signed another All-American, fullback Ernie Nevers out of Stanford, to give the league another top gate attraction, and the professional game was on its way. Grange and Nevers became the marquee players of their time, and fans turned out in record numbers whenever they took the field. In one heads-up contest, pitting Nevers's Chicago Cardinals against Grange's Chicago Bears, Nevers scored six rushing touchdowns and four extra points in a 40-6 victory to establish an NFL single-game scoring record that continues to stand. In fact, it's the oldest record on the books.

game I'm planning to watch, and I recommend this approach to anyone who wants to get full enjoyment out of a game. Men or women, it doesn't matter; we can all learn something from the experts who track the NFL for a living. Of course, sometimes the "experts" can be dead wrong, but you can disagree with them or challenge their opinions; and it always makes me feel good when I know something about a team that these guys haven't figured out. (Hey, we've been around the league a few times; and with the help of free agency, I've got friends on almost every team. And on top of that, there's all kinds of inside information I can squeeze out of Rodney . . . nothing beats pillow talk!)

For those of you just learning the game, it's a great idea to surf the Internet a day or two before the game, to learn some of the pregame matchups and tendencies, so you'll know what to look for on Sunday. The back-stories, I find, are all-important. If the New Orleans Saints are making a play-off push, it's helpful to understand the team history. (Did you know they used to be known around the league as the "Aint's," because they had never reached the postseason in franchise history?) If Drew Bledsoe is making his first start in Foxboro since leaving the Patriots for the Buffalo Bills, that's an important part of the pregame story; and if you know the ins and outs of his situation, you'll enjoy the game even more. If Deion Sanders is making his second or third comeback and hoping to be the same kind of impact player he once was, you'll need to know that as well.

I usually check out NFL.com and USAToday.com for their pregame reports; they've got some of the best, most comprehensive, up-to-the-minute coverage out there. Some sites will even rate the upcoming games for you, helping you decide which will be the most hotly contested, which will have play-off implications, which players are struggling, and which players are soaring. I might even print out a team roster or two, so I'll know who everyone is without waiting for the announcers to get around to telling me—the same way I'd follow along with a program at the stadium.

TiVo and DirecTV are probably the two most welcome inventions in my household. Almost overnight, it seems, they've changed everything about my Sunday football watching routines, and it's all good. It's gotten to where I can't imagine pro football without them. It used to be that you had one or two main national games on each network; and those matchups were chosen by the league at the beginning of the season, based on how the teams had fared the previous year. Then, if your home team managed to sell out its stadium, you'd get to watch the locals as well—but that was about it. Some weeks, when what had once looked like a great matchup turned sour because both teams had unexpectedly struggled, and when your home team was blacked out due to poor attendance, Sundays were a complete bust. But those days are long gone. Now I can watch every game—and I do! With TiVo, I can freeze the action and go into the other room to see about the kids, and come back and pick up right where I'd left off. I can go back and make my own replays if I want to see something again, or I can fast-forward to the next play if I'm already watching on a delay. It really is such an ingenious little device, the perfect tool for the mom (or dad) who doesn't want to miss a down. You can take in everything, in just about real time, without ruining the surprise. Or you can watch the entire game on a slight delay—1 minute, 1 hour, even 1 day—behind the rest of the country, whatever suits your schedule. Lately, I've become quite adept at speed-watching the games

HISTORY OF THE GAME

THE COLLEGE DRAFT

In an effort to keep teams from cornering the market on household-name players as they graduated from college, the league instituted a college disbursement draft in 1936, the first of its kind in the world of sports, awarding teams draft rights by the inverse order of finish. In other words, the last-place team at the end of the season would get first choice of all available players, on down to the first-place team, which would select last, before beginning another round of selections in the same order. In this way, it was hoped, teams would become more balanced over time, leading to an ongoing attempt at parity that continues to be a hallmark of the league. Ironically, the first player ever drafted (Jay Berwanger from the University of Chicago) decided not to play professional football at all.

I've put on delay, fast-forwarding to just before the snap, so it really maximizes the number of games I've got going. This drives my poor hubby nuts!

With the DirecTV Sunday Ticket package, I'm just a maniac in front of the television on game day. I'll have an A game going, and several B games, and a C and D game that I don't really care that much about, but that I'll monitor just to check out the coaches' play calling. They've even improved the package this season to allow you to run a quad screen, so there's this tremendous overload of pictures and information—and I just love the hell out of it. Really, I'm so in my element on Sundays that I'm out of control. And I can certainly understand how some of my girlfriends have grown a little timid about getting in their man's way in such a setting. Like I said, I can be a little crazy if Rodney gets in my way. A couple years back, when Rodney was without a team for a couple weeks at the beginning of the season, he found himself home on Sundays, and he was messing everything up. (This was before we put in our great new media room.) Rodney'd grab the remote and start flipping around, and I'd be hollering at him, "No, that's my A game! That's my B game! Don't make me miss that next play!" He had me so crazy I had to go upstairs and monitor the games on the Internet, and while I was online I started studying the rosters of every NFL team to see who might need a quarterback, because I certainly had one to spare. I had to get Rodney out of the house and back on to a team—so I could reclaim control of the television on Sunday afternoons.

I *had* to hook him up. You have to realize, from the time we first met, our football seasons had become our calendar. Every July, Rodney would be off to training camp and we'd slip into a different mode. Here it was September, and my honey was underfoot. Everything was all out of whack.

Around that time I happened to be at a golf fund-raiser with John Madden, the great color commentator, and Jon Gruden, who at that time was the coach of the Oakland Raiders. I found myself seated in between them. John Madden told me later that he had never seen a football wife as tenacious as I was on that day, because I was in Jon Gruden's ear the entire time. And why not? Jon had been the offensive coordinator in Philadelphia during Rodney's time with the Eagles. I was all over him for one particular game when he pulled Rodney from the lineup for no good reason that I could see. I wouldn't let it go. Here we were, in between teams, and I started in with him about how he owed us one, about how I'd checked his depth chart and determined that he needed a quarterback. "This guy is not a leader," I said. "This guy can't read defenses. You need experience. You need Rodney."

And sure enough, he did. He wound up signing Rodney that week—not *just* to shut me up (although I'm sure this was an attractive side benefit), but mostly because my honey could still play; and for me, the attractive side benefit was I got my Sundays back and our little routines—mine and Rodney's—were returned to normal. For the time being, anyway.

CHEATSHEET
10
ALL-TIME GREAT MOMENTS

One of the best things about football is the way die-hard fans can go over and over the same play, or scoring drive, or comeback effort and keep finding new aspects to explore, new arguments to make, new perspectives to consider. Really, we can talk some of these things into the ground. These days, with the proliferation of video highlights and instant Internet access, it's possible to review every conceivable play from every inconceivable angle, which I must admit takes some of the fun from the watery eye of memory.

Below are some of the most memorable games, drives, or single plays in NFL history—moments that will continue to be kicked around in sports bars across the country, and moments that every beginning fan should have on her radar. Some are impossible to believe. Others are just plain improbable. And don't just take my word for it. See if you can download video of some of the more recent games off the Internet and find out for yourself how legends are made.

In chronological order, these are the moments that football folk are *still* talking about . . .

"THE SNEAKERS GAME"
1934 NFL Championship
New York Giants 30–Chicago Bears 13

December 9, 1934 . . . A freezing rain left the Polo Grounds a virtual skating rink, and the heavily favored Bears closed out the first half with a 10–3 lead. Neither team was able to mount much of an attack in the difficult conditions, but Chicago had all kinds of momentum on its side, including a 17-game winning streak and 33-game unbeaten streak. During the halftime break, Giants coach Steve Owen dispatched his equipment manager in search of footwear more suitable to the frozen playing surface, and the guy came back with sneakers, which he thought might improve the players' traction. And, sure enough, they did. New York rolled to a 30-13 victory, ending Chicago's championship run and sending equipment managers around the league back to their drawing boards.

"THE ICE BOWL"
1967 NFL Championship
Green Bay Packers 21–Dallas Cowboys 17

December 31, 1967 . . . Frigid game-time temperatures of -16, with a wind-chill factor of -46, combined with a frozen underground heating system at Lambeau Field to create less-than-ideal conditions for what looked to be a classic matchup. The Packers grabbed an early 14–0 lead, but the weather soon took its toll, allowing the Cowboys to close the gap to 14–10 by halftime. Dallas took a 17–14 lead late in the fourth quarter on a halfback option pass, leaving Green Bay with one final drive. Packer quarterback Bart Starr took his team to the Dallas 1-yard line, with just 13 seconds remaining. Coach Vince Lombardi called for a quarterback sneak, and Starr crawled his way across the goal line behind a textbook block from Jerry Kramer, earning the Packers a trip to their second consecutive Super Bowl.

"THE HEIDI GAME"
1968 regular season game
Oakland Raiders 43–New York Jets 32

November 17, 1968 . . . A meaningful late-season contest between two of the AFL's top teams and most intense rivals. Each team brought a 7–2 win-loss record and hopes of a postseason run to this nationally televised game. The game itself did not disappoint. There were five lead changes, and an all-out air assault from opposing quarterbacks Joe Namath and Daryle Lamonica. Jets wide receiver Don Maynard hauled in 10 passes for an astonishing 228 yards. There was also an unusually high number of penalties—19, for 238 yards. Jets placekicker Jim Turner kicked a field goal with 1:05 left to play to give his team a 32-29 lead. NBC cut to a commercial . . . and never came back. Since the game had run long, the network switched to its regularly scheduled programming—a 7:00 P.M. premiere showing of the made-for-television movie *Heidi*, starring Jennifer Edwards as the pig-tailed, yodeling adolescent. Football fans were outraged, especially once they heard what happened in the final 65 seconds of the game: Lamonica threw a 43-yard touchdown pass to halfback Charlie Smith with just 42 seconds to play, giving Oakland a 36-32 lead. Next, the Raiders kickoff was mishandled by the Jets, and Raiders reserve fullback Preston Ridlehuber picked up the loose ball and scampered into the end zone. The game would mark the last time a network would switch to its regularly scheduled programming before the end of a game.

"THE KICK"
1970 Regular Season Game
New Orleans Saints 17–Detroit Lions 16

November 8, 1970 . . . A storybook ending to a storybook game. Saints coach J.D. Roberts was working his very first game as an NFL head coach, and with just seconds to play he was faced with the most important decision of his young career. His Saints were trailing 16-14, with the ball on their own 45-yard line. His options were to ask veteran quarterback Billy Kilmer to launch a desperation pass downfield and hope for the best, or to ask placekicker Tom Dempsey–who just happened to have been born with half a right foot–to send one through the uprights from an all-but-impossible distance. Dempsey, in his second NFL season, wore a special shoe with a flat front that had been approved by the league. Roberts went with Dempsey, who sent the ball through the uprights from 63 yards out, clearing the crossbar by several yards and sending the Tulane Stadium crowd into pandemonium. (Note: This mark was later tied by Denver Broncos placekicker Jason Elam in a 1998 game against Jacksonville, but it's Dempsey's kick that set the standard.)

"THE IMMACULATE RECEPTION"
1972 AFC Division Play-Off Game
Pittsburgh Steelers 13–Oakland Raiders 7

December 23, 1972 . . . It's been called the greatest play in NFL history, and it certainly wasn't completed by design. Pittsburgh was playing in its first play-off game in the team's 40-year history, and was edging Oakland in a defensive battle for the ages when Raiders quarterback Kenny Stabler scrambled 30 yards for a touchdown to give his team a 7-6 lead with just 1:13 left to play. With just 22 seconds left, the Steelers were up against it, on their own 40-yard line, fourth and 10. Quarterback Terry Bradshaw dropped back to pass, but faced immediate pressure from the Raiders. Still, he managed to send the ball about 25 yards downfield to running back Frenchy Fuqua. Raiders safety and self-styled "assassin" Jack Tatum arrived at about the same time as the ball, knocking Fuqua to the Three Rivers Stadium turf and sending the ball ricocheting through the air, where it was miraculously caught by Steelers rookie running back Franco Harris–on his shoelaces, at the Oakland 42-yard line. Some of the Raiders, including Tatum, had begun to celebrate their "victory" just after the pass to Fuqua had been broken up, but Harris had another idea. He ran the ball down the left side of the field, past a stunned Oakland secondary and into the end zone. Coaches and officials argued for a full 15 minutes whether Harris was eligible to receive the ball on a deflection from his own teammate, but it was ruled that Tatum had made contact with the ball between the two Steeler touches and the play was allowed to stand.

"THE HAIL MARY"
1975 NFC Divisional Play-Off Game
Dallas Cowboys 17–Minnesota Vikings 14

December 8, 1975 . . . The Doomsday Defense vs. the Purple People Eaters. A classic defensive battle that saw Vikings quarterback Fran Tarkenton engineer a late-game touchdown drive that put his team on top 14-10 with just 1:51 remaining. The home crowd began to celebrate what all thought would be a chance to return to the Super Bowl for the third consecutive season. Cowboys quarterback Roger Staubach took over on his own 15-yard line and moving Dallas to midfield in just nine plays. With no timeouts and less than 30 seconds left on the game clock, Staubach lined up in Dallas's trademark shotgun formation, pump-faked left and then unleashed a desperation bomb half the length of the field. Wide receiver Drew Pearson turned right to follow the flight of the ball. Cornerback Nate Wright followed, but lost his footing on the frozen field. Pearson seemed to catch the ball against his hip and galloped with it into the end zone, while Vikings safety Paul Krause cornered field judge Armen Terzian and demanded an offensive interference call. A Minnesota fan apparently agreed, tossing a whiskey bottle from the stands, which struck Terzian in the head. Staubach, who had been hit immediately upon releasing the ball, didn't even see the play unfold.

"THE SHOOT-OUT"
1981 AFC Divisional Play-Off Game
San Diego Chargers 41–Miami Dolphins 38

January 2, 1982 . . . The highest-scoring play-off game in NFL history at the time (and one of the longest), with the Chargers winning on Rolf Benirschke's 29-yard field goal with just 1:08 remaining in overtime. Benirschke had missed a 27-yard attempt earlier in the overtime period, while Miami's Uwe von Schamann's 35-yard attempt was blocked in the sudden death session. At the outset, it looked as if the Chargers would run away with the game, after opening a 24-0 lead in the first period, but Miami rallied to tie the game on its first possession of the third quarter. Chargers quarterback Dan Fouts set play-off records with 33 completions, 53 attempts, and 433 passing yards, while tight end Kellen Winslow established the standard for most receptions, catching 13 passes for 166 yards. The enduring image of this classic game was a shot of an exhausted Winslow being helped from the field by two teammates.

"THE CATCH"
1981 NFC Championship
San Francisco 49ers 28 Dallas Cowboys 27

January 10, 1982... The play that jump-started an NFL dynasty. Bill Walsh's 49ers were trailing the Cowboys by six points and the clock wasn't helping. Quarterback Joe Montana, who would become famous for his pressure-packed, come-from-behind drives to win big games, stood at his own 11-yard line and knew he had his work cut out for him. The Cowboys were the team of the '70s; the 49ers were about to become the team of the '80s. All that stood in their path were the 89 yards that separated them from the Dallas goal line. It took just 13 plays, and the last one was the charm—an anxiety-producing pass thrown under tremendous pressure toward the back of the Dallas end zone. From the flight of the ball, it looked for certain that it would sail out of bounds and hopelessly out of reach, but San Francisco wide receiver Dwight Clark extended his long arms and grabbed the ball by his fingertips. The play would be forever known in San Francisco lore as "The Catch," earning the 49ers a trip to Super Bowl XVI and earning Montana and Clark do-no-wrong status among Bay area sports fans.

"THE DRIVE"
1986 AFC Championship
Denver Broncos 23—Cleveland Browns 20

January 11, 1987... Denver quarterback John Elway orchestrated a classic 98-yard drive in the closing minutes of the season to cement his reputation as one of football's best clutch performers and to send his Broncos to the Super Bowl. The game was a hard-fought, defensive-minded affair when Cleveland took a late 20-13 lead. Denver muffed the ensuing kickoff and wound up with the ball on its own 2-yard line with 5:32 left to play. Elway took the field like there was no other place in the world he wanted to be but on that 2-yard line, and began a purposeful march against a Cleveland defense that appeared helpless against the Broncos' relentless attack. Fifteen plays later, after scrambling for 9 yards to the Cleveland 5-yard line and with just 39 seconds remaining, Elway threw the ball for the ninth time of the possession and hit Mark Jackson for the tying touchdown. Then, on Denver's first overtime possession, Elway marched his team another 60 yards on nine plays to put them in position for a game-ending 33-yard field goal. The first drive was christened, simply, "The Drive," and signaled the emergence of Elway onto the all-time stage; the second drive, in overtime, seemed merely inevitable.

"THE COMEBACK"
1992 AFC Wildcard Play-Off Game
Buffalo Bills 41–Houston Oilers 38

January 3, 1993 . . . The biggest comeback in postseason history? Well, that would have to be this stunning overtime victory by the Buffalo Bills, after being down by the seemingly impossible score of 35-3. And it wasn't just the 32-point deficit that stacked the odds all the way against Buffalo; it was Houston's all-out first-half dominance. Oilers quarterback Warren Moon just about *dissected* the Bills' secondary, throwing for four touchdowns in the first half. Then, on one of the first plays of the second half, Houston strong safety Bubba McDowell intercepted a Frank Reich pass and returned the ball 58 yards for another Oiler TD, causing many Bills fans to head for the exits. The Bills responded with a convincing touchdown drive, capped by a 1-yard run by Kenneth Davis. Now down 35-10, Buffalo attempted an onside kick, which was miraculously recovered by the Bills kicker, Steve Christie. Reich, who once led the University of Maryland Terrapins to the greatest comeback in college football history, then looked to make the same mark on the professional level, throwing for four straight second-half touchdowns to put the Bills ahead 38-35 with just under 3 minutes to play. The Oilers answered with an Al Del Greco field goal to tie the game and send it into overtime, but Buffalo defensive back Nate Odomes intercepted a Moon pass early in the extra period to set up Christie's game-winning 32-yard field goal. What a game!

7

DESPERATE HOUSEWIVES

What It's Like to Be Married to the Game

*C*atchy title for a chapter on NFL wives, eh?

To be fair, the desperate *is probably just a little off the mark, best I can tell—and* way off as far as my own life is concerned. And the housewife *part is probably off as well, because many of us have careers of our own, and most of us are out and about and active in our communities, working with local charities and schools and civic groups in such a way that we're hardly ever home. But you know us television types—always quick to latch on to someone else's high concept and make it our own. And so "desperate housewives" it is.*

In any case, I wanted to spend some time dishing with a few of my sisters in the NFL wives club, in part because we bring our own unique perspective to the game and to what our men go through on the field, but mostly because I thought it might be fun and interesting and maybe even a little enlightening to kick things around on our own turf, on our own terms. It's a take on the game most fans don't get to see. You have to realize, it's one thing to follow your favorite team through the ups and downs of a long season, but it's something else entirely when your husband's ass and career are on the line with every damn play. Even the most die-hard fan can set the game aside, but football has been such a constant in our lives for so long that it's difficult to imagine our days without it—and I suppose it must be equally difficult for the casual fan to imagine what our days are like within it.

Take Tuesdays, for example. Most folks outside the game don't know that Tuesdays are our Sundays during the season. That's our one day off, pretty much around the league, and in our house we filled it with as much family time as we could squeeze into a 24-hour period, before Rodney was called in to get ready for the next game. If he wasn't too sore, we'd go shopping at the mall, and then have lunch with the kids, maybe take in a movie.

But that's just us. Every NFL couple approaches things a little differently, and with this in mind I've asked Deanna Favre, Brenda Warner, and Sherice Brown to join me for a little girl-talk over these next few pages. Think of it like a mini talk-show segment, in book form. Anyway, that's the idea. (For those of you who don't recognize them by their names, Deanna is married to Green Bay Packer quarterback Brett Favre; Brenda is married to Arizona Cardinals quarterback Kurt Warner; and Sherice is married to former Oakland Raiders wide receiver Tim Brown.)

Rodney's been around the league so many times (he's played for six NFL teams), and he played for so long that I sometimes think I've had a chance to meet just about every NFL wife and girlfriend who ever roamed a sideline, but Deanna, Brenda, and Sherice are among my favorite friends in the game. We watch each other's backs, and when I told these girlfriends what I was up to with this book, they wanted to be a part of it.

So, here goes . . .

HOLLY: *People always ask me what I like best about our life in and around the game of football, and I never know where to start. It's all good, right? The easy answer, of course, is that most folks are beyond nice to you, because of who you are and whom you've married. Call me shallow, but I like that. You get great tables at great restaurants. You cut the line at amusement parks. You get to go to every game you want—usually in the best seats in the house. And there are perks every time you travel. Upgrades, freebies, what have you.*

In my case, I was recognized before I met Rodney, but there's such a tremendous difference in the way sports stars are treated compared to actors. Athletes are in a whole other category. They're fair game. Fans really think they own you and that you have to answer to them, which can certainly have its drawbacks. But when you're winning, they'll do absolutely anything for you. They'll cross the street just to congratulate you on a good game. That was the best feeling, when someone approached Rodney like that.

BRENDA WARNER: *Seeing my husband living his dream is truly the best part. For 26 years, Kurt was told over and over that he wasn't good enough to make it in the NFL. He warmed the bench in college, then played in the Arena Football League and then in Europe, just to keep his dream alive. He was a junior in college when we met, and all he wanted was to be an NFL quarterback. I was divorced, with two children, and all I wanted was to find a man who would be faithful to me until the day I died. We both got what we asked for.*

SHERICE BROWN: *I love the way we're always meeting new people and making new friends. There's always something exciting going on. Living in two different cities, shuttling back and forth, I never seem to get bored.*

DEANNA FAVRE: *The financial stability is a blessing. It's a lot less stressful knowing you can give your children a chance to go to college, or help out your parents or brothers and sisters in an emergency, not that they'd ever ask. And the ability to use Brett's name to help so many people. We have our Brett Favre Forward Foundation that helps disadvantaged and disabled children in*

Wisconsin and Mississippi, and it's opened so many doors. It's been a blessing, all around.

HRP: *But there's a downside to it, as well. Am I right? For every generous fan I've met when Rodney was winning, there have been dozens of mean-spirited fans who'd kick him when he was down. And the Eagles fans were just the worst. Hell, they wanted to kick me, too! Once, after a particularly tough loss in a 1996 Monday night game against Green Bay—thanks, Favre!—I was hassled by a cop as I was crossing the street, minding my own, and he pulled me aside. The first strike against me was that I wasn't crossing in the crosswalk. The second strike was when the cop looked at my license and recognized my name. "You're married to Rodney Peete?" he said, putting two and two together. "Yes," I answered cheerfully, thinking this just might get me out of a ticket. But the guy just kinda snarled at me and said, "Well, after the way he played last night, you deserve a ticket." And he wrote me up for jaywalking. Can you believe it? He just about hauled my butt off to jail, for the way I cussed him out but that's how some people are, I guess.*

SB: *That's just the worst, when that happens. I'm no jaywalker, Holly, but I get that all the time if Tim had a bad game, or if the Raiders are struggling. I get these people riding me, or criticizing Tim, or telling us we're no good. And then there are the people who look at you like you're only a trophy piece on his arm, like you're lucky to have him.*

DF: *I get that, too. People tend to stereotype us. They think we're all gold-diggers, or worse.*

SB: *And they think our husbands are out there chasing women on every road trip. That's the other stereotype. But people need to know that not all pro athletes are unfaithful to their wives. There are some great husbands in the pack, and we've got some of the best of them right here.*

BW: *It's all about perspective, isn't it? I'll tell you, I give interviews all the time, and people are always trying to get me to talk about how difficult it is to be rich* *and famous and in the public eye. But "difficult" was when I was a single mom of two on food stamps, living in low-income housing, not knowing if I could scrape together enough for a Happy Meal. So I try to keep things in perspective. People can think what they want about me. They can be quick to judge me and Kurt, but it doesn't matter. We know what matters.*

HRP: *It used to make me insane, the way folks would second-guess Rodney on this or that play, or this or that decision on the field. The constant negative media can just wear you out. But over the years, I've developed armadillo skin and I don't get nearly as bent out of shape anymore.*

BW: *So much time is devoted to reviewing and analyzing and predicting each play, each player, each team, each game. It's never-ending. These sports talk-show guys can just go on and on about nothing much at all. I listen to these guys and wonder if they ever played a game worth talking about, or what their wives would say if someone got on national television and said her husband was willfully bad. That's how they make it sound sometimes, like the player is not putting out his best effort on purpose. When our daughter was 10, she came home from school and asked if Daddy "sucked." The kids at school were all mimicking what they'd heard on television, and she was wondering if it was true.*

SB: *And what about all those crazies out there? Some of these fans are just way out. Usually, it's harmless, like the time some guy approached Tim, wanting to show him his tattoo. He pulled up his shirt, and there was a tattoo of Tim catching a pass. It started on this guy's stomach and reached all the way around to his back.*

HRP: *Security! Once, some guy followed me into the ladies' room, wanting to know if I could get his football card signed. That was a bit much.*

DF: *We don't get a lot of that in Green Bay. You've all been in big cities, but it's a lot quieter where we are. A lot more civil. I've got nothing against those big cities, but Green Bay is just a great place to raise kids. The schools are excellent, and everyone is so friendly. Sure, there are always those who are going to* *be mean or envious or whatever, but I try not to pay attention to them. They're always the minority, and it doesn't pay to get worked up about it. Most of the people we've met have been very friendly and helpful.*

HRP: *On an individual basis, I'd have to agree. Folks have been over-the-top nice. In Charlotte, especially. Even in Philadelphia, most people went out of their way for us. There were just those few rotten apples to spoil the whole deal. And those meanies on the sports radio station there. They have got to be the most ridiculously, needlessly cruel people. I have heard them talk about players' wives and kids, coaches' wives and kids. Nothing seems to be off-limits to them. Even when the Eagles are winning, they focus on the negative. After one awesome win in '96, they spent about an hour going on and on about why Rodney Peete smiles after he throws an interception. This was the topic. They actually took calls on it, and after a while I got so fed up, I disguised my voice and called in myself. I pretended I was a distant cousin of Rodney's and explained that he wasn't smiling, that he just had big teeth! Sometimes these guys just have no*

HISTORY OF THE GAME

THE WAR YEARS

World War Two took a big bite out of the NFL's momentum, as many teams folded or cut back their schedules. Rosters were depleted as players entered the service. In all, 638 former or active NFL players would serve in battle, and 21 would die in action—a sad fact of war that helped to establish players' reputations as true American heroes.

Slingin' Sammy Baugh, in one of the last great campaigns of the two-way player, managed to lead the league in passing, punting and interceptions in 1943. The fact that he did so against somewhat diluted competition in no way diminished his great season. But two-way players like Baugh were the last of a breed. In later years, a change in the league's substitution rules made it possible for coaches to more freely move players in and out of games, effectively ending the need for players to remain on the field in offensive *and* defensive positions, and leading to an era of increased specialization—both on the field, and among the coaching staff.

idea what they're talking about. They don't have the first clue what it's really like for our guys—the total focus on the game, the year-round dedication, the toll it takes on their bodies, the wear and tear. I think it should be mandatory that these sports critics should have had their butts on that field and taken some hits before they can rag on our men.

DF: *It's tough on the players, it really is. Brett struggles to get out of bed during the season. He has a really bad hip problem; it's bothered him since college, and there's nothing he can do about it. Plus, his feet have taken a beating and they'll never be the same. He has blisters buried beneath calluses, and it's just awful.*

SB: *For Tim, the mental toll is always far worse than the physical toll. It doesn't matter how banged up he is if they've won the game. If they've lost, that's just the worst.*

BW: *I always hate it when we go up against Warren Sapp. I sit there in the stands and I can see him across the field, warming up, and I can see him spit and blow snot. He reminds me of a bull who is looking to kill the matador, and the matador just happens to be my husband. I met Warren at the Pro Bowl one year, and he seemed so kind and loving with his children, and Kurt's always trying to convince me he's a good guy, but I look at him and all I see are horns.*

HRP: *He's a "QB Killa," Warren Sapp. And if he doesn't knock you out physically, he'll talk you to death!*

SB: *Junior Seau. He and Tim are good friends off the field, but he tries to hurt him anyway.*

DF: *There's someone like that on every team. All these defensive guys, they're always going after the quarterback. No matter who we play, I'm always extremely nervous. They're always gunning for our husbands.*

HRP: *Oh, it is no joke! And Rodney felt it. More and more, the older he got, the more he felt it. Monday mornings, even without any kind of serious injury, he was just plain sore. It's a wonder he could get out of bed. But miraculously* *by Wednesday he was ready to go again. And he never, ever complained. I'd have to go online to get an accurate injury report on him, because he'd only say "a little" when I'd ask him if it hurt.*

DF: *I know Brett's body can't take much more of this. He needs to retire soon, but I have mixed feelings about it. I know how much we'll miss the excitement of football season. It's been a blast to watch him play. I don't think football will be the same without him, and I know it won't be the same for us.*

HRP: *I won't miss the injuries and the aches and pains and all the politics and backstabbing and nonsense that can go along with professional football, but I'd be lying if I said I won't miss the excitement of game day. I'm like you, Deanna. That's been such a big part of our lives, for the longest time. Truthfully, though, I didn't think Rodney would ever retire. But I sure love him taking the kids to school every day.*

BW: *One thing's for sure, Kurt and I will not agree on when he should retire, but when it finally happens, I'll be thrilled. When we began dating, I already had two children, so we never really had that kind of time that couples have, when it's just the two of us. I look forward to raising the children and having plenty of time to enjoy each other.*

SB: *I'm looking at it from Tim's perspective, so I'm not looking forward to his retirement. Not at all. I know how much the game means to him, how he looks forward to it each off-season. He's going to truly miss it.*

HRP: *We have our lives back again, so that part is nice. We can actually make plans that don't revolve around the football season. That's more than 6 months out of each year, if you count training camp and a good run in the post-season. A lot of the wives I meet even plan their pregnancies around the football season. They're worried their husbands won't be able to get time off from the team to be with them in the delivery room, or that they'll go into labor while their husbands are on the road. Not me, though. Like I don't have enough to worry about without trying to schedule my pregnancies around the NFL* *season. Please! Three of our four children were born during the season, so there was all kinds of drama and logistical hassles to get Rodney there on time, including a police escort after an overtime game to get to the birth of our twins.*

SB: *Both of my pregnancies were a little complicated, mostly because I had to be on bed rest for several weeks, but our football schedule certainly didn't help. My first pregnancy, I delivered during training camp, and Tim managed to make it back. The second pregnancy, I delivered the same day as his first Super Bowl appearance. How's that for timing? But believe it or not, he made it back for that one, too. So it all has a way of working out.*

DF: *Brett was in the delivery room for both babies, but neither one of them was born during the season. That's just how it worked out. Although you're right, I meet a lot of women who plan it that way.*

BW: *I was pregnant when Kurt signed as the third-string quarterback with the Rams, in 1998. He called from training camp at the end of August to say he made the team, so I moved our entire household and two children to St. Louis immediately, and gave birth to our third child on September 29, just a few weeks into the season. Then I was pregnant with our fourth child when Kurt made it to the Pro Bowl one year, and by then we were doing well and we didn't want to miss out on an opportunity like the Pro Bowl, so 9 months pregnant, we flew out to Hawaii with my obstetrician, and as it turned out, I didn't deliver until 2 weeks after we returned home to St. Louis. Still, I don't think I could have made the trip without my doctor in tow. I wouldn't have had the same peace of mind.*

HRP: *What about the game itself? Were you a fan before you met your husband? I know in my case, I was a big-time fan. I had to have my Eagles fix. But once I met Rodney, I learned the game on a whole other level. I learned how to read his playbook, which can look like hieroglyphics. And even after all this time, I am still blown away remembering my hubby's poise under pressure on the field.*

BW: *Not me, Holly. I get that he's good at what he does, and that's a thrilling thing, but I really don't like sports at all. I don't get the grown men jumping,* *spitting, screaming, hurting each other, bleeding, analyzing, and getting paid more than teachers, nurses, and the President of the United States, all put together. It doesn't make any sense to me.*

HISTORY OF THE GAME

WINDS OF CHANGE

It's fascinating to look back and see how each generation of coaches adapted to each other, to each new development in the game, and to the new rules changes that came as a result. In the 1940s, for example, coaches began to borrow a page from Paul Brown, the pioneering coach of the Cleveland Browns team that carried his name, who was among the first to install a blocking system to protect the quarterback as he dropped back to pass. He arranged his linemen in the form of a cup, instructing them to push pass-rushers to the outside and create a kind of "pocket" for the quarterback. As a result of Brown's efforts, pass-blocking schemes became more sophisticated, and quarterbacks had more time to release the ball and to allow pass patterns to develop.

Over time, league officials would adopt rules changes to adjust to developments and trends on the field. For example, in the game's early days, the ball would be placed on the kicking team's 40-yard line before a kickoff, but as kickers grew stronger and kick-return coverage teams more proficient, placement was moved back to the 35-yard line—and, later, the 30-yard line. In the 1970s, for another example, when low-scoring defensive matches had become common, the hash marks—the "dotted" lines that run the length of the field—were brought in closer to the middle of the field to give quarterbacks more room to throw wide. Sure enough, the move increased scoring around the league, and generally made the game more exciting. It also made it easier on running backs, who suddenly had a lot more ground to cover on either side of the ball and began to pile on the yardage. For the first time in a 14-game season, 10 NFL runners gained more than 1,000 yards—generally considered the benchmark for a top running back. The following year, Buffalo Bills running back O.J. Simpson rushed for more than 2,000 yards, the first time a runner had ever crossed that threshold in a single season.

DF: *My mom has always been a football fan, so I grew up watching it. We only had one television, so I had no choice, but I learned to love it. I make it a point to go to all of the Packers' home games, and to about half of the away games, but it's tough to watch him play. I always want the Packers to win, but more important I want him to come home injury-free. I say a lot of prayers during the games.*

BW: *I pray too. Big time. Before the game, during the game, I'm praying. I try to keep my eye on Kurt. My favorite part is to watch him pass. I'm still in awe of his arm. When he throws one of those long, perfect passes, right to the receiver, I say to myself, "That's my man!"*

SB: *I didn't know much about football before I met Tim, and I still don't know too much about the game. I go to his home games, to support him, but it's hard for me to watch him play. I sit in the back of the luxury suite, so I can't see the field. I watch the game on television instead. If something good happens and I happen to miss it, I can see it again on the replay.*

HRP: *The longer we did this, the harder it was to justify going to the away games. It was an ordeal to pack up the kids and take them on the road, and as they got older, they had their own stuff going on over the weekends. Plus, most teams give you about 10 minutes with your man after the game before they whisk him off to the airport for the team flight home, and of course the wives can't travel with them, so it's just not worth it.*

DF: *My kids love to watch Brett play. Brittany actually cried after the Packers lost to Denver in Super Bowl XXXII.*

BW: *None of our kids watch Kurt's games. I used to take them to the stadium and put them in child care provided for the players' families, but getting through the crowd has become a challenge.*

HRP: *My kids loved watching their dad play . . . when we won. My daughter also cried her little eyes out when we lost the Super Bowl. She may be a tad too emotional to be the daughter of a QB. She took it so personally that the other team's fans were rooting against her dad. To make matters worse, there was even an obnoxious Patriots fan taunting her in the stands throughout the game. Can you believe it? She was 6 years old! I almost had to whoop his butt, but he apologized after the game. I'll never forget our coach's wife telling us that if we lost this Super Bowl, it would be the most expensive funeral we would ever pay for. Boy, was it ever.*

Okay, next subject. Tell us one thing about your husband that will surprise his fans. Something personal. I'll start. Not too shocking, but it's his taste in music that is so strange. He listens to '70s rock groups, like Journey. Hard-core hip-hop. Classical. Jazz. Blues. He listens to it all. When I drive his car, in his CD holder, he'll have Jay-Z followed by Sarah McLaughlin. He's not big into heavy metal, though. I count myself lucky for that.

SB: *Tim's into music, too. He plays the tambourine like a pro. And he's a very good singer.*

DF: *Brett's thing was poetry. When we were kids, anyway. We were high school sweethearts. We were both really athletic. I used to put on a face mask and shin guards and grab a catcher's mitt and catch him out in the yard. One day, his dad, Irvin, came out of the house and said, "Brett, don't throw that ball so hard at her." And Brett said, "She's catching 'em, isn't she?" But he had a soft side to him, too. He wrote a poem for me when we were juniors in high school. It was his way of making up after a short breakup. It went: "Roses are red/Violets are blue/You're my sweetheart/And I love you/I love your smile/I love your hair/Your presence is/Known with the gentle air/Your hair is black/Your eyes are green/And I still love you/Even when you're mean/You're a beautiful girl I must say/I like to be around you every day/To end this poem I want to say/That I love you now and will when the skies are gray." He really does have a sweet, soft side. He's not always so tough, although he might kill me when he sees this poem turn up in your book.*

BW: *I'll get you off the hook, Deanna. How about I tell everyone that Kurt paints his daughter's nails and tries to help her with her hair? That should certainly surprise some of his fans.*

HRP: *Yes, Brenda, it certainly should. And I wouldn't want to be in your shoes, Deanna, when Brett opens up this book and catches his cute little love poem in big, bold letters, although it really is sweet and doesn't surprise me. Brett is such a nice man. You have an awesome hubby. Really, we can all say that we scored in that department.*

Anyway, that's just a small taste of how things go in the wives' section on Sunday afternoons. We talk about our kids. We talk about our husbands. We talk about our futures. And in the middle of all this, we somehow find time to watch the game and cheer our guys on as if our lives (and lifestyles) depended on it—which, for a great many of us, they do.

10

ALL-TIME GREAT FOOTBALL MOVIES

There's nothing like a good movie to keep your popcorn company—and, for football fans, there's nothing like a good football movie to help fill the long space between seasons. For some reason, Hollywood producers have looked to the gridiron for all kinds of inspiration, because there's certainly no shortage of football movies on the shelves at your local video store. It's almost a genre unto itself.

For the beginning fan, some of these movies can be enormously helpful in bringing you close to the action by offering insight into the workings of the game, and shedding new and compelling light on the dramatic issues confronting professional football players and their families. And some of them are just a plain hoot.

I've put together a list of 10 movies Rodney and I have enjoyed together over the years. But keep in mind, this is a totally subjective list—I'm no Roger Ebert. What strikes me as funny might strike you as inane, and my idea of uplifting might be your idea of mind-numbing. But it's my book and I get to call the shots. To keep the list at 10, I've only included movies that have fared well over repeated viewings, or ones that have resonated over time, which is why you won't find the terrific but relatively new Billy Bob Thornton movie, *Friday Night Lights,* which really gets to the heart of this country's fascination with football, particularly in our small towns. Time will tell if this one still has something to say to me after I've seen it a few times. For the time being, then, here are my all-time favorite football movies, in no particular order.

Brian's Song: Rodney's hands-down favorite (and as he puts it, the only film he knows that is guaranteed to make any man cry). James Caan and Billy Dee Williams star in this 1970 made-for-television biopic based on the too-short life of Chicago Bears running back Brian Piccolo and his great friendship with the legendary Gale Sayers. It still turns up on late-night television from time to time, and if I come across it while channel surfing, I can't look away. It's soapy and sappy and a little bit dated, but I've yet to find a more moving portrayal of the real bond that can form between teammates, or a more emotional look at the way a personal tragedy can shape an entire team. Plus, there's nothing wrong with watching a young Billy Dee Williams dash up and down the football field in that old Chicago Bears uniform.

Heaven Can Wait: The 1978 remake of 1941's *Here Comes Mr. Jordan,* this all-time great features writer-director Warren Beatty as a golden boy L.A. Rams quarterback, killed ahead of his time in a car accident and returned (in spirit, at least) to earth in the body of an elderly millionaire. You'll need to make a couple leaps of faith in order to follow the complicated plot, and the football scenes aren't all that realistic, but it makes the list for the fine romance that blossoms between Beatty's character and the stunning Julie Christie. It's on my own all-time Top 10 list, football aside, because it's really more of a chick flick than a football flick, but since the game provides the setting, it rates on this list as well.

The Longest Yard: A weird little 1974 Burt Reynolds comedy about an NFL quarterback imprisoned for drunkenness and car theft, who somehow winds up coaching a rag-tag prison football team in a grudge match against the prison guards. All these years later, it seems a little predictable, but this was Burt at the top of his game, and it makes the list for the way it presents football as a release from our everyday concerns. A remake with Adam Sandler and Chris Rock came out in 2005, with Burt in a much-deserved cameo.

Any Given Sunday: Al Pacino stars in this hard-hitting, in-your-face Oliver Stone drama from 1999, with Cameron Diaz, Dennis Quaid, James Woods, and my buddy Lela Rochon (she introduced me to Rodney!), plus a star-making performance from Jamie Foxx. More than any other movie, this one cuts to the chase of what it means to play professional football, what it means to coach professional football, what it means to own and manage a professional football team, and what it means to live the game alongside your star-athlete husband. It works in our household for the way it explores the dilemma that dogs every athlete: how to know when your time has come, and how to know when your time is up. Great, down-and-dirty football scenes, but it's the behind-the-scenes stuff that makes this movie soar. There were a few scenes that struck me as a shade or two unrealistic (like the pet snake in the locker room shower, and the shot of the QB eating chips on the bench on the sidelines—come on!), but for the most part Stone got it right. A lot of players I know felt he took way too much dramatic license, but what do they know? The movie is fairly filled with great, gritty, and cleverly edited football scenes.

Rudy: One of the more uplifting movies you're likely to find, about football or anything else, this 1993 drama is based on a true story and features Sean Astin as Daniel "Rudy" Ruettiger, a Notre Dame student obsessed with the Fighting Irish and determined to play for his favorite team. Trouble is, he's been told he's too small to play college football, and he's out to prove everyone wrong. According to The Internet Movie Data Base, a great resource for information on your favorite movies and television shows, it's only the second movie ever shot on the Notre Dame campus. (The first: *Knute Rockne: All American,* the Ronald Reagan chestnut that gave us that great "win one for the Gipper" line.) But the storied campus isn't the only reason to catch this movie. The football scenes stand as a great backdrop to a moving story about a father and son, and a universal lesson on determination. And the ending will leave you cheering! Being a die-hard USC Trojan, it was difficult for Rodney to cheer on Notre Dame, even in a movie, and he was really hoping this movie didn't make my cut. (Those rivalries never die, do they?) But in the end, even my Trojan had to agree with me: As far as football films go, this one's a goodie.

Remember the Titans: Two words: Denzel Washington. I'd watch that man in anything, but he shines here as high school football coach Herman Boone, charged with helping his squad deal with issues of integration and tolerance in a racially charged environment, while at the same time managing to win a couple football games. In fact, Boone's Titans manage to string together an undefeated season as they march to the state championship. This 2000 drama is based on the true-life story of a suburban Virginia school that had been segregated until 1970, and the coach brought in to unify a divided program when the school was finally integrated. It's a powerful piece, with an important message, and the football scenes ring all kinds of true. The movie's still relatively new, but it's already regarded as a classic. A great movie to watch with the entire family. And Denzel always delivers.

Jerry Maguire: Two more words: Tom Cruise. I'll watch this guy in just about anything, too, and this 1996 drama is funny and smart and inside. One of the better takes on the backstabbing and politicking that goes into a successful football career *off* the field, and one of the better depictions of what really goes on between an athlete and his agent. Some of the football scenes fall short, especially compared to the edge-of-your-seat action in *Any Given Sunday* and *Remember the Titans,* but it's the whole package that reverberates. And it's not often that you find two lines from the same movie creep into the culture in such a defining way. When Tom Cruise returns to kiss and make up with Renee Zellweger and she tells him, "You had me at 'hello,'" she gives voice to a line that will likely repeat itself for eternity. And when Cuba Gooding Jr. celebrates his new contract by shouting, "Show me the money!" he ushers in a rallying cry for athletes and agents and anyone else hoping to cash in on sudden, well-deserved fame. The movie also features the best all-time football wife moment when Regina King, who plays Cuba's wife, watches him get hurt during a game;

she was so genuine that I was moved to tears. I was right with her . . . until Cuba got up and started doing gymnastics on the field. After what was supposed to have been a serious injury! I felt so let down by that moment, as did every other football wife I know. So many of our men have hobbled off or been carted off the field, to surgeries and months and months of rehab, that I found the kicker to this scene a little trite. Still, Regina had us going there.

North Dallas Forty: Nick Nolte and Mac Davis (goodness, remember Mac Davis?) lead the way in this gritty look at the seedy side of the game. It's ostensibly a comedy, but there's a lot of down-and-dirty to it as well. From the novel of the same name by former player Peter Gent, the 1979 movie is loosely based on the Dallas Cowboys, and there's some good game footage and locker-room scenes that get close to what it's like in the real trenches. One of Rodney's faves, although he's hard-pressed to remember what he loved so much about it.

Paper Lion: Alan Alda stars as George Plimpton in this true-life 1968 account of an unassuming journalist's attempt to suit up as an NFL quarterback for the ultimate insider's look at the game. A lot of the real-life Detroit Lions who played alongside the real-life George Plimpton are featured as themselves, and there are some great cameos from Alex Karras, Pat Studstill, and Lem Barney. There's even a bit with the legendary Vince Lombardi, playing himself. When I first saw this movie, I sparked to the story, but these days I'm loving the way it addresses a question that's dogged my man his entire career: No, you can't simply suit up in shoulder pads and helmet, take a couple snaps from center during a real NFL game, and expect to live to tell the tale. There's a lot more to it than that.

Wildcats: You'll have to forgive me for this one, but I'm a sucker for cute, and this 1986 movie has got it going on in the cute department. Goldie Hawn plays the daughter of a legendary gridiron star whose greatest desire is to coach a team of her own. Somehow, the chauvinistic powers that be assign her to an inner-city school team, and spunky Goldie clearly has her work cut out for her. Okay, so it's a little saccharine and contrived, but director Michael Ritchie does a great job mixing in the laughs, and the jokes are hilarious, and everyone involved seemed to be having a good old time. I think I mostly enjoyed watching Goldie mix it up with the guys and win our hearts. The great bonus here is the eclectic supporting cast, which included the up-and-comers Woody Harrelson and Wesley Snipes (who would later reteam and costar in *White Men Can't Jump*, which probably makes most folks' lists of all-time great basketball movies), and colorful supporting turns by Swoosie Kurtz and Nipsey Russell.

8

STANDARDS OF EXCELLENCE

What It Means to Succeed

Every team sport has a laundry list of statistical benchmarks that fans have used for generations to measure an individual player's relative value—big, fat, round numbers that serve to neatly compare players from different eras or settle bets during Happy Hour. Baseball has its .300 batting average and its 100 runs batted in for hitters, and its 200 strikeouts and 20-win seasons for pitchers. Basketball has its 20 points per game average and its 10 rebounds or assists per game. Hockey, when NHL owners and athletes can get it together to actually play out a full slate of games, has its 50-goal and 100-point seasons.

Football is no different. It's tough to admit, since football fanatics like to think our game stands apart from all the rest, but in this one respect at least we're much the same. We *love* our stats! (Oh, baby . . . do we love our stats!) Of course, a whole lot of football folk will tell you that the only milestone worth counting is the number of championship rings a player has on his fingers. After all, when the clock runs out and the postgame whirlpool shuts down for the night, winning is the point of the whole damn deal. Whatever you've managed to accomplish as an individual is what it took for you to win as a team. This is true enough, even if it sounds like a line from a movie, but it doesn't change the fact that we fans love to pore over statistics like they hold all the answers—as, indeed, they frequently do—or the fact that players trot out these numbers when it comes time to renegotiate their contracts.

Even coaches, general managers, and sports talk-show hosts have been known to get in on the game, and it's a good thing there are plenty of quantifiable numbers to go around—and enough certifiable number crunchers to keep things interesting. Some of the resulting statistics are meaningful, some frankly are meaningless, others are just plain tough to figure. You have to know what you're looking for to put the numbers into context and to have them inform what you're looking at on the field. See, on every single play, stat-keepers record every single nuance of virtually every single move by every single player. These numbers measure everything from yardage gained after each catch to the hang-time of a punter's kicks to passing efficiency on third-down plays. I can't say for sure, but there's probably somebody down there keeping track of the number of times the quarterback licks his fingertips between snaps or dries his hands on that cute little towel the center leaves hanging over his butt for just this purpose.

Obviously, it's difficult to chart or measure individual success from one play to the next, because anything can happen on any given snap from center. Even an unheralded running back can break a couple tackles and sprint the length of the field from time to time; and every once in a long while, a third-string quarterback can complete a Hail Mary pass for a game-winning touchdown. Realize, too, that it's impossible to measure intangibles like guts and drive and extra effort because, as the cliché tells us, such things don't show up in the box scores. But over the course of an entire game, or the run of a long season, or the arc of an entire career, it's possible to let history judge a player's performance—and to predict how certain players might perform in the future.

Like it or not, the numbers tell a whole bunch of stories.

HISTORY OF THE GAME

THE AMERICAN FOOTBALL LEAGUE

In 1959, as the game's popularity soared and television ratings increased, a Dallas-area entrepreneur named Lamar Hunt announced his intention to form a rival league, known as the American Football League, after lining up franchises in Dallas, Denver, Houston, Los Angeles, New York, Boston, and Oakland for its first season of play. The upstart owners looked to distinguish themselves from the senior National Football League in a variety of ways. Most significantly, they opened up new markets, playing in cities where there was no professional game.

Gradually, the AFL took hold and the two leagues were forced to coexist. League officials reached a verbal no-tampering agreement regarding players and negotiated separate broadcast deals with competing radio and television networks. Throughout the early 1960s, though, the NFL was generally regarded as the more competitive league. Top college athletes tended to sign with NFL teams, while second-tier players and journeyman NFL veterans tended to throw in on AFL squads.

AFL teams were also famous for signing local or regional college players to build a hometown fan base, even if those players might not make the grade on most NFL squads. That all changed in 1965, when the AFL New York Jets signed quarterback Joe Namath, the nation's top college prospect, for the then-stunning sum of $400,000. It was an astronomical figure, but Namath was regarded as a once-in-a-generation talent with the kind of golden arm and movie-star good looks to put fans in the seats. That he would now do so in New York, the grandest stage in the game, made the move even more remarkable. At last, the young league could boast a bona fide star—and top college players were persuaded to break from established practice and sign on to talent-hungry AFL teams.

What follows, then, is a short course on what it means when we say a player has had a great game, or a great season, or a great career—and what we fans have come to expect from these great players week after week after week. Sometimes, as you'll see, the space between greatness and pretty-darn-goodness can be measured in a single yard, and sometimes there are whole football fields separating the studs from the duds. I organized the stats in this chapter according to the specific type of player (quarterbacks, receivers, etc.) they measure. Pay attention over the next few pages, and you'll get what it takes for a player to be at the top of his game.

Running Backs

This one's easy. For generations, the *100-yard rushing game* has been the measuring stick for running backs in a single game. No one knows how we arrived at the century mark as the dividing line that separates greatness from the rest of the pack, but there it is. Maybe it has something to do with the fact that a football field is 100 yards long; and if you've managed to cover the whole field, you must have had a pretty good day. Clearly, this doesn't mean that a running back who manages to gain only 99 yards in a game has had a much lesser outing than a back who has run for 101 yards; but in round-number terms (and in terms of headlines and posterity and endorsement deals), that extra yard makes all the difference. Plain and simple, running backs are judged by the number of 100-yard games they put together over the course of a season, or a career. As benchmarks go, this one makes sense because if you've carried the ball enough times to collect 100 yards on the ground, it generally means you and your offensive line have controlled the game in a statistically significant way. Five or six 100-yard games in a season is considered a big deal; string five or six 100-yard games in a row, and you're really cooking; collect 50 or more in a career, and it's just about legendary.

Now, if 100 yards rushing marks a big game, how many yards mark a big season? Well, for the longest time, stretching from when the NFL inaugurated its 10-game season in 1943, through the years when it featured a 12- and later a 14-game schedule, and continuing up until the 16-game season was introduced in 1978, top running backs have counted 1,000 yards gained on the ground as the threshold for a strong season. That's the number on everyone's radar. Back in the day, during those 10- and 12-game seasons, it was a rare feat when a runner could amass more than 1,000 yards in a single campaign. In 1949, for example, the NFL featured just two 1,000-yard rushers in the same season for the first time (Steven Van Buren of Philadelphia and Tony Canadeo of Green Bay—go ahead, trot out *these* names if you want to impress the pants off your guy). More recently, in 2003, there were 18 1,000-yard rushers, led by Baltimore's Jamal Lewis with 2,066. Still, even though modern running backs have an extra couple games in which to reach the mark, 1,000 yards looms as a season-long goal for every featured running back, and most of the players I talk to don't regard it as a diluted stat just because of the longer schedule. In fact, a lot of them consider it an even greater accomplishment given they have to stay healthy over those extra couple games, and take the harder hits dished out by today's bigger and stronger defensive linemen and linebackers.

Coming out of that offensive backfield, it's all about the round numbers—and, to keep them round, think in multiples of 10. Running backs begin to think about Hall of Fame–type careers when they approach 10,000 *career-rushing yards*. To date, 17 NFL runners have reached that level, led by Rodney's old teammate and future Hall of Famer Emmitt Smith. Throughout my growing up, the standard was Jim Brown's 12,312 yards, set in just nine seasons for the Cleveland Browns—a mark that stood for over 20 years until it was surpassed by the late, great Walter Payton of the Chicago Bears. All three are considered icons of the game—and chances are good-to-great that all three will *always* be considered icons of the game.

Perhaps the most valuable measure of a running back's effectiveness over the long haul is *yards-per-carry*—a number that doesn't get the attention of the straight yardage stat, but one you'll do well to look for just the same. In a single game, you'll often see that number reach into the double-digits on the strength of a long run or two; but, over time, the numbers even out to where you can begin to make some judgments about specific players and their teams. The lower the number, the more you're likely to find a punishing, grind-it-out bruiser like Pittsburgh's Jerome "The Bus" Bettis, who's inclined to pound his way through the middle of the line and to scratch and claw his way across every available inch of real estate. The higher the number, the more likely you'll find a fleet-footed gazelle, able to shake tackles with the best of them while at the same time running to the outside and turning the corner for bigger gains—like Rodney's former teammate Barry Sanders, who was always so much fun to watch. In success, you're looking for a number somewhere between 3.0 and 4.0 yards per carry; 2.9 or less, and you're just not cutting it on any kind of leader-board; 4.1 or greater, and you're among the best in the business. (Note: If you're Jim Brown, who averaged an astounding 5.2 yards per carry *over his entire career*, you're virtually unstoppable.)

TOP THREE RUSHERS

Total Yards—Game
Jamal Lewis..................... 295 (September 14, 2003)
Corey Dillon .... 278 (October 22, 2000)
Walter Payton .... 275 (November 20, 1977)

Total Yards—Season
Eric Dickerson................ 2,105 (1984)
Jamal Lewis..................... 2,066 (2003)
Barry Sanders................. 2,053 (1997)

Total Yards—Career
Emmitt Smith 18,355 (1990–2004)
Walter Payton 16,726 (1975–1987)
Barry Sanders 15,269 (1989–1998)

Quarterbacks

This one's complicated. Quarterbacks are judged by the points they put on the board, the possession-drives they're able to engineer, and their ability to complete passes on a high-percentage basis. And yet none of these barometers are completely within the quarterback's control. Take *completion percentage,* for one obvious example. As the term suggests, completion percentage measures the ratio of completed passes to attempted passes—over time, a great indicator of a quarterback's accuracy and ability to read defenses. Still, a quarterback can throw a perfect pass to a wide-open receiver, who can somehow drop the ball; and when that happens, the miscue goes as a negative stat against the quarterback. Does that seem fair to you? (No need to answer. You know this QB spouse just had to ask.) Let me tell you, there have been some long, tense moments in the stands during Rodney's career, with me sitting next to the wife of some butter-fingered receiver who couldn't hold on to one of Rodney's passes. It was all I could do to hold my tongue—but I did because the very worst thing a QB wife can do is piss off her husband's receiving corps. I learned this wives' rule many years ago, the hard way, by telling one offensive lineman's wife that another lineman missed some blocks that resulted in Rodney running for his life, and way too many sacks. Well, that wife told the wife of another lineman, who told another lineman's wife, who eventually snitched to the wife of the actual lineman in question. By the time Rodney got to practice the next day, the whole line knew what had happened, and Rodney was told in no uncertain terms to control his wife's big mouth. (I went straight to the doghouse over this one.)

And here's another thing that always strikes me as unreasonable: If a quarterback needs to throw the ball away to stop the clock, or because none of his intended receivers have been able to get open for a pass, why should that incomplete pass get charged to the quarterback's personal ledger? It's really a team incompletion, wouldn't you agree? As long as we're on it, completion percentage is one of the first things coaches look for in assessing a quarterback, and it used to be that a QB who completed 50 percent of his passes was doing better than okay. However, that target number has increased over the years, season by season, as blocking schemes have become more sophisticated and short-yardage passes have become the order of the day, to where quarterbacks now look to complete about 55 to 60 percent of their passes. If they succeed at 60 percent or better over the course of a career, they'll count themselves among the all-time greats.

There's a lot going on in a quarterback's game—and as a result there are any number of ways to measure his effectiveness. One popular gauge is the *ratio of touchdown passes thrown to interceptions thrown,* which presumably gives you a measure of accuracy and effectiveness, and a vague read on a quarterback's composure in pressure situations. I was never crazy about this stat, but I suppose there's some merit to it over time; and if you're inclined to agree, you'll find success in about a two-to-one ratio, or better. Thirty-three touchdown passes in a single season is a tremendous accomplishment, but if it's underlined by 33 interceptions, it indicates a QB who takes a few too many risks, who makes a few too many miscalculations, who rushes his throws far too often.

Touchdown passes as a stand-alone stat are another key indicator of a quarterback's relative value—only here, too, there's a lot of room for interpretation, and quite a few contributing factors go into each score. A lot of it is out of the quarterback's hands—literally *and* figuratively—because once he throws that ball, it's up for grabs; and once it's caught, it's up to the receiver to run it in the rest of the way. It doesn't make sense to me that a soft dump-off pass to a running back who manages to sprint for a 50-yard touchdown is judged the same as a 50-yard strike that threads the needle between two defenders and finds the wide receiver's fingertips in the corner of the end zone—but that's how it goes. In some ways, I guess that makes up for the QB being charged for all those dropped passes!

Throw five touchdown passes in a game (as the Minnesota Vikings' Daunte Culpepper did three times in the first five games of the 2004 season) and you've really accomplished something; throw 30 in a season (and keep those interceptions at a minimum), and you'll probably earn a starting spot in the Pro Bowl; throw 49 in a season, as Peyton Manning of the Indianapolis Colts did during that same 2004 season, and folks will start checking the box scores to see how many "sixes" you put on the board this time; throw 200 in a career, and little kids (and grown men) will wear your replica jersey long after you retire; throw 400, and you won't exactly be in a class all by yourself, but you'll be sitting next to Dan Marino of the Miami Dolphins, who wrote his name all over the NFL record books before he retired in 1999.

For my money, the best measure of quarterback performance is *passing yardage,* because it takes into account all of these other stats and mix-masters them into one irrefutable, *understandable number.* Those italics highlighting this last statement will soon be made clear, as we look at the league's confounding quarterback rating system, another stat that combines all these other categories into a perplexing blend that few people comprehend. But for now we'll keep the focus on explicable measures like this one right here. Let's face it, if the object of the game is to move the ball down the field, we ought to simply and straightforwardly consider just how far down the field the quarterback has moved his team—and so as yardsticks go, passing yardage has got it going on. It factors in those long, seeing-eye bombs that miraculously find their targets, and those short, touch-passes that lead to long gains *after* the catch. Pass for 300 yards in a single game, and you'll be right up there with the best performances of the weekend; pass for 400 yards, and you might set the standard for that season; 500 yards, and they'll have a day in your honor (with a parade!) in your hometown. On a season-long basis, a quarterback can consider it a good year if he passes for 3,000 yards or more, and a great year if he eclipses 4,000 yards. Throw for 5,000 yards, and you'll be seated in that class-by-yourself alongside Mr. Marino.

All of which bumps me right into that strange, confusing stat, which is meant (I guess) to be the simplest—even though most quarterbacks I know don't have the foggiest idea how it works. The *quarterback rating system*—or passer rating, as it is more commonly known—measures completion percentage, yards per pass, interceptions, and the ratio of touchdown passes to passing attempts. I once asked Rodney about it, and from his response I got that he would rather talk about floral arrangements or soap operas. Really, the passer rating index has got to be the most arcane, obtuse statistic in all of sports, but for some reason it's survived because it produces an easy-to-understand number—even though there's nothing easy-to-understand about how the stat folks arrived at that number.

Here's how it works: If a quarterback aces all four of the above-mentioned categories, he'll receive a perfect passer rating of 158.3, which as far as anyone can determine has happened only once in the history of the game, over the course of an entire game—when Peyton Manning picked apart the Denver Broncos in an AFC play-off game in 2003. For that one game, Manning's completion percentage was better than the 77.5 formula standard; his ratio of touchdown passes to passing attempts was better than the 11.9 percent standard; he averaged better than 12.5 yards per passing attempt; and he threw no interceptions. Sound complicated? That's because it is. Sound like Peyton Manning had a great game? You better believe it—statistically speaking, he was perfect—and by this one weird measure, at least, it was arguably the best game of all time for a quarterback.

Think about it: In all of sports, perfection has never been measured by such an imperfect number. In baseball, a pitcher tosses a perfect game and doesn't allow a single base-runner: zero. In bowling, a perfect game carries a score of 300. In basketball, a free throw shooter can be a perfect 10 for 10 from the line, for a shooting percentage of 1.000. In golf, it's a hole-in-one. But 158.3? What stat geek came up with that?

Peyton Manning's *sick* 158.3 passer rating aside, a merely mortal 100.0 is considered a tremendous score for a single game—*that's* a number we mere mortals in the stands can get our heads around. We've all taken enough tests to get that 100 is a top score; so even though we might have no idea what the number represents in terms of "passer rating," we get that it represents excellence—like getting an A on a test. Anything better is like extra credit, or an A+. Season leaders usually check in with a passer rating somewhere in the 80s or 90s. Tennessee's Steve McNair bested all comers in 2003 with a league-leading 100.4, while Indianapolis's Manning set a new season standard in 2004, at 121.1. Career numbers can drop into the 70s and 80s for the all-time greats (Hall of Famer Joe Namath completed his career at what now looks like a middling 65.4); and you'll find that the top-rated quarterbacks are those who played most of their careers on low-risk, West Coast offenses, where short, quick, high-percentage passes dominated the playbook.

HISTORY OF THE GAME

THE TWO-POINT CONVERSION

American Football League organizers also made some significant rule changes they hoped would make the game more appealing to fans. They borrowed the two-point conversion from the college game, to allow more flexibility in scoring, and to add new levels of strategy. Previously, professional teams were allowed to attempt a point after touchdown following a touchdown drive. The ball would be placed on the opponents' 2-yard line, and the scoring team would attempt to kick it through the uprights of the goal post, as in a field goal. If they did so successfully, it was worth one point. From such a short distance, the point after touchdown was virtually automatic, to where most fans figured a touchdown was worth seven points instead of just six.

Under this new two-point conversion rule, teams could opt instead to run or throw the ball into the end zone from the same spot on the 2-yard line, and if they did so successfully, it would be worth two points. But even from this short distance, the two-point version was no sure thing, so all kinds of possibilities and probabilities would now come into play for teams tallying a six-point touchdown. Indeed, the two-point conversion proved so popular with fans, players, and league officials that the NFL adopted the rule in 1994.

TOP THREE PASSERS

Touchdowns–Season
Peyton Manning............. 49 (2004)
Dan Marino 48 (1984)
Dan Marino 44 (1986)

Touchdowns–Career
Dan Marino 420 (1983–1999)
Brett Favre 376 (1991–2004)
Fran Tarkenton 342 (1961–1978)

Total Yards–Game
Norm Van Brocklin........ 554 (September 28, 1951)
Warren Moon .... 527 (December 16, 1990)
Boomer Esiason............. 522 (November 10, 1996)

Total Yards–Season
Dan Marino 5,084 (1984)
Kurt Warner 4,830 (2001)
Dan Fouts 4,802 (1981)

Total Yards–Career
Dan Marino 61,361 (1983–1999)
John Elway..................... 51,475 (1983–1998)
Brett Favre 49,734 (1991–2004)

Quarterback Rating–Season
Peyton Manning............. 121.1 (2004)
Steve Young 112.8 (1994)
Joe Montana 112.4 (1989)

Quarterback Rating–Career minimum 2,500 attempts
Steve Young 96.8 (1985–1999)
Joe Montana 92.3 (1979–1994)
Peyton Manning............. 92.3 (1998–2004)

Receivers

We're back in logical territory in weighing the performances of receivers: number of catches, number of touchdown receptions, average yards per reception, total yards gained. Understand, when ranking receivers, league records don't distinguish among running backs, tight ends, and wide receivers. If you're eligible to catch a pass thrown from scrimmage, then you're lopped into the same category as everyone else, which explains why you'll occasionally see a running back atop the leader boards in rushing *and* receiving.

Here again, the numbers make sense. No odd formulas. No fancy equations. No PhD's needed to decipher the whole mess. Take *number of catches*, for instance. Catch 10 passes in a single game—and in one way or another, you've been in on every play. The ball might not have been thrown your way on every down, but you've been the focus of every defensive huddle. You've been a factor every time your team has had the ball. Collect 100 *receiving yards* as a receiver (the *total* yards gained on a pass play, measured from the line of scrimmage to the spot where the ball is whistled dead), and you have very likely changed the game as well. Multiply those figures by that same factor of 10 to get to 100 catches and 1,000 receiving yards, the magic numbers for any receiver in a single season—although, to be fair, some guys can be considered to have had *monster* seasons making 50 catches or amassing 700 or 800 yards, when you take into account the impact they have on their team's offensive attack. (Actually, the NFL continues to track consecutive 50-catch seasons, so 50 catches remains a significant milestone, even in football's pass-happy era.)

Career totals top out at 10,000 receiving yards or better for the all-time greats—and 20,000 and counting for the still-legendary Jerry Rice, who as of this writing is still active. (Incidentally, Rice saw one of the game's great record streaks come to an end early in the 2004 season, when he failed to catch a single pass in a game for the first time in 274 games—an unfathomable run that spanned 20 football seasons.)

The *number of touchdown receptions* in a career or a single season is another compelling indicator of a player's ability to get the job done, his flair for the dramatic, and his nose for the goal line. Also, and significantly, it's a reflection of his teammates' and coaches' faith in him as a go-to guy who gets things done. Average a touchdown per game for an entire season, and you'll be among the very best; get close, and you'll still be putting up big numbers. Grab 150 touchdown catches in your career, and your next pass pattern will take you all the way to Canton, Ohio. (Hint: That's the site of the Pro Football Hall of Fame.)

Personally, I love the *yards per catch* category, because it's a great reflection of a receiver's ability to break big plays and bust big tackles. It rewards two kinds of players: those deep threats who consistently manage to split the defenders and haul in long bombs *and* the short-yardage guys who manage to catch the ball and pile on the yardage after they've caught it. The best of the best might average better than 20 yards per catch over the course of a season—but even a legend like Jerry Rice will have a hard time repeating that performance, as teams begin to key on his deep-threat ability and look to double-team him the next time around the league. It's more common to see the league's best receivers consistently put up yards per catch numbers in the mid- to high-teens, although sometimes the most talented and feared receivers settle in at about 13 or 14 yards per catch by the end of each season because of their team's overall style of play or the number of other deep threats playing alongside them.

Rodney has always been partial to the stand-alone *yards after catch* statistic, because it reflects on a receiver's ability to break a big play, to run the ball down the field after he catches it, and to generally light things up in a way that owes as much to his individual efforts as to an overall team effort.

TOP THREE RECEIVERS

Total Catches—Season
Marvin Harrison 143 (2002)
Herman Moore 123 (1995)
Jerry Rice .... 122 (1995) [tie]
Cris Carter .... 122 (1994, 1995) [tie]

Total Catches—Career

Jerry Rice 1,549 (1985–2004)

Cris Carter 1,101 (1987–2002)

Tim Brown..................... 1,094 (1988–2004)

Touchdown Catches—Season

Jerry Rice 22 (1987)

Mark Clayton 18 (1984)

Sterling Sharpe 18 (1994)

Touchdown Catches—Career

Jerry Rice 197 (1985–2004)

Cris Carter 129 (1987–2002)

Steve Largent................. 100 (1976–1989) [tie]

Tim Brown..................... 100 (1988–2004) [tie]

Average Yards Per Catch—Season min. 20 receptions

Don Currivan................. 32.58 (1947)

Bucky Pope 31.44 (1964)

Bobby Duckworth.......... 28.60 (1984)

Average Yards Per Catch—Career min. 200 receptions

Homer Jones 22.26 (1964–1970)

Buddy Dial..................... 20.83 (1959–1966)

Harlon Hill 20.24 (1954–1962)

Total Yards—Season

Jerry Rice 1,848 (1995)

Isaac Bruce..................... 1,781 (1995)

Charley Hennigan........... 1,746 (1961)

Total Yards—Career

Jerry Rice 22,895 (1985–2004)

Tim Brown..................... 14,934 (1988–2004)

James Lofton................. 14,004 (1978–1993)

Defensive Players

The highest number you're likely to find on the defensive stat line is the number of *tackles* a player records. But I've never found this to illustrate anything but the type of defensive system a player plays under, the position he plays, the length of time he's on the field (which of course runs in direct proportion to the opponents' time of possession), and the number of plays run in a particular player's direction. Frequently, you'll find a talented individual on a weak team wrack up a mess of tackles just because his unit is on the field for so damn long the law of averages allows him to take down ballcarriers at a pretty good clip.

To my thinking, the most compelling defensive stats are sacks and interceptions. If you've been paying attention, you know that a *sack* is recorded when a defensive player tackles the quarterback behind the line of scrimmage. It's one of the most exciting plays a defensive unit can make, for the way it can pull the plug on a long offensive drive, or push a team beyond field goal range. It's a real momentum killer. Typically, defensive ends and outside linebackers are in the best position to record the greatest number of sacks in a season or career—but from one play to the next, any defender can get in on the action, even one of the defensive backs. (If two defenders assist on the same sack, each gets credit for half a sack.) Two or more sacks in a single game is big-time, 10 or more in a season is noteworthy, and the closer you get to a sack-a-game ratio the closer you get to defensive god status.

Interceptions are another great momentum killer—although there's a huge right-place-at-the-right-time factor you have to consider. A great many interceptions come as the result of dumb luck, or a quarterback miscue, or a deflected ball that should be more properly credited to the teammate doing the deflecting. But over time, the truly talented defensive backs find ways to snare passes meant for their opponents. Here again, two or more interceptions in a single game rates a mention; a half-dozen or more in a season ensures that opposing quarterbacks will be far less inclined to challenge you in coming seasons—and with fewer balls thrown your way, you'll likely never match that total again in your career.

TOP THREE PASS RUSHERS

Most Sacks—Season

Michael Strahan 22.5 (2001)

Mark Gastineau 22 (1984)

Reggie White .... 21 (1987) [tie]

Chris Doleman .... 21 (1989) [tie]

Most Sacks—Career

Bruce Smith 200 (1985–2003)

Reggie White 198 (1985–2000)

Kevin Greene 160 (1985–1999)

TOP THREE PASS DEFENDERS

Most Interceptions—Season

Dick Lane 14 (1952)

Dan Sandifer .... 13 (1948) [tie]

Spec Sanders .... 13 (1950) [tie]

Lester Hayes .... 13 (1980) [tie]

Most Interceptions—Career

Paul Krause 81 (1964–1979)

Emlen Tunnell 79 (1948–1961)

Dick Lane 68 (1952–1965)

Odds and Ends and Whatnot

There are all kinds of numbers we can look at, and all kinds of information we can glean from them, but for the purposes of this book, I wanted to hit the high notes. As you take more of an interest in the game, and as you begin to understand its complexities and nuances, you'll notice categories like *all-purpose yards* (the *total* number of yards gained by a versatile player, including rushing yards, receiving yards, and kick-return yards), and *field goal efficiency* (the number of successful field goal attempts divided by the number of attempts), and *hurries* (the number of times a defensive player rushes the quarterback and forces him to release the ball under pressure).

In the meantime, here are some additional indicators to help you get the most out of the game.

PUNTING AVERAGE: When I first learned the game, a 40.0-yard average would lead the league, but over the years we've inched towards a 45.0-yard average as the standard. What accounts for the bump? Well, for one thing, kickers have gotten stronger and more proficient. For another, teams have become more likely to go for it on fourth downs inside their opponents' 35-yard line (or, to attempt a long field goal), which cuts down on the number of short-yardage punts where the kicker tries to angle the ball out of bounds before it reaches the end zone, pinning the opponents deep in their own territory to start their next possession.

HANG TIME: This refers to the time elapsed from the moment the ball touches a punter's foot to the moment it hits the ground or is touched by an opponent. The league doesn't track this number as an official stat, but coaches and broadcasters pay all kinds of attention to it for the way it indicates how much time the kicking team has to run downfield to cover the return. The idea here is to keep the ball in the air for as long as possible in a great, booming arc while it travels as far as possible. This is different from a line drive–type kick that gets downfield quicker than your fastest coverage guy. Anything over 4.0 seconds is considered sufficient, although punters have been known to unleash kicks that hang for over 6.0 seconds. The key here is the average over time, and over all kinds of punting situations.

TOTAL POINTS: This hybrid category is dominated in some years by place-kickers and in others by running backs or wide receivers. Here again, the century-mark emerges as the touchstone—and for kickers, a long run of 100-point seasons is an accurate measure of longevity and accuracy and opportunity. Tennessee's ageless wonder and our former Eagles teammate Gary Anderson, following his 23rd NFL season, was the all-time points leader with 2,434 going into the 2005 season. On a single-season basis you'll see touchdown-scoring machines like Marshall Faulk, Emmitt Smith, or Jerry Rice sometimes leading the way. In the era of the two-way player, which effectively ended in the early 1960s, you'd often see running backs or wide receivers pull double-duty as placekickers, which put those guys in position to really pile on the points. Green Bay's Paul Hornung, one of the all-time greats, still holds the record for most points in a single season—scoring 15 touchdowns and kicking 15 field goals and 41 extra-points for a 1960 season total of 176 points.

KICK RETURN YARDAGE: Another straightforward stat, this one tracks the average distance covered by a kickoff or punt returner, who looks to catch a booming ball in the middle of all kinds of traffic and chaos and somehow advance it into better field position. From where I sit, it looks like one of the scariest assignments on the field, to have to catch the ball and try to run with it in the opposite direction while a thundering herd of coverage defenders bears down for the kill. Typically, a season-long average in the high 20s is considered above par for a kickoff returner, while anything in the double-digits is a strong showing for a punt returner. Football folk still talk about a rookie named Travis Williams who managed to return four kickoffs for touchdowns during his rookie season for Green Bay in 1967, helping him to an incredible 41.06 average for the year, a record that still stands. The top single-season punt returner of all time: Baltimore's Herb Rich, who averaged 23.0 yards per return in 1950, which was also *his* rookie season. The best kick returner in today's game? For my money it's Kansas City's Daunte Hall, who has been known to change a game or two just by positioning himself downfield to receive the kick.

FUMBLE RECOVERIES: This is another right-place-at-the-right-time category, although it can still be a useful indicator of a defensive player's grit and determination. Collect a half-dozen loose balls in a single season, and it generally means you're where the action is, and willing to give up your body and take one for the team. To my mind, though, the better stat would be *fumbles caused,* although the league doesn't track this one on any kind of official basis. Coaches and fans take note, though, and if you can strip your opponents of the ball on anything resembling a regular basis, I want you on my team.

10

ALL-TIME GREAT FOOTBALL BUTTS

Okay, so I have no shame. In my defense, let me just point out that these guys are required to wear second-skin-tight pants, so how can we help but notice? This is one list where 10 just isn't enough! Nice bottoms are an epidemic in the NFL.

In my long and dubious career as a football-fan-turned-NFL-wife, I have seen my share of cute butts. I'd be doing a disservice to my girls if I didn't share my findings, right? So, pay attention and play along as I present my "Golden Cheeks" awards to . . .

RODNEY PEETE: Predictable? Yes. Deserving? Yes, yes, yes! Along with his other terrific attributes, my honey has the best butt in the biz.

TONY GONZALEZ: And not just because he *is* one of the best tight ends in the league . . . he also happens to *have* one.

MARCUS ALLEN: Now that's a Hall of Fame boo-tay!

TERRELL OWENS: In some circles, T.O. stands for "Tush Outrageous!"

EDDIE GEORGE: This former Titan has a bodacious bum.

JOHNNY MORTON: This chief has fabulous cheeks!

DARREN SHARPER: This Green Bay Booty is sharp!

CURTIS MARTIN: What can I say? (I'm running out of one-liners!) This running back got back!

CHARLES WOODSON: Charles is "in charge" with those buns!

TOM BRADY: Super Bowl MVB (most val— well, you get it!)

9

TEAM HISTORIES

A Short Course

The winds of change have blown through the NFL conference and divisional alignments so many times over the past 4 decades that it's almost impossible to recognize the traditional east-west lineups of my growing up. And if a lifelong fanatic like myself has had a hard time tracking those changes, I can just imagine how confusing it must be for the casual fan.

I check out the standings and I sometimes don't recognize what I'm seeing, with familiar names in all kinds of unfamiliar places. The Cardinals used to play in St. Louis against the Eagles, Giants, Redskins, and Cowboys as part of the National Football Conference (NFC) East. But now they're relocated to Arizona and pitted against their new rivals in the NFC West, the Rams and the 49ers, along with the Seahawks, who jumped from the AFC West in 2002. The Colts, who used to play in

Baltimore in the NFL's Eastern Conference, and later in the American Football Conference (AFC) East, now play in Indianapolis, assigned to the AFC South with the expansion Jaguars and Texans—and the Titans, who used to play in the "black-and-blue" AFC Central as the Houston Oilers, before moving to Tennessee in 1997.

It's all a little crazy-making, don't you think? And yet the more things change, the more they remain the same. Storied intra-division rivalries continue to play out each season between Minnesota and Green Bay, Dallas and Washington, Pittsburgh and Cleveland—and on and on across the league. You might need a scorecard (or a chapter in a primer on pro football . . . hint, hint) to keep track of all the teams, but the endgame remains the same—to be the last team standing at the end of the long season. No matter what team you play in any division, you want to hoist the Super Bowl trophy high above your head in one hand and hold up the index finger of your other hand in the universal "We're Number One!" gesture, and to announce joyfully that you're going to Disney World, whether or not you in fact ever make it to the Magic Kingdom.

Until recently, the NFC and AFC conferences were broken into three lopsided divisions—East, West, and Central—featuring four, five, or six teams each. As the NFL gradually expanded to include 31 teams, it all made for an imbalanced, imperfect schedule. Compounding that, tradition holds that each team plays two regular-season games against every other team in its division each season—one at home and one away—which gave the schedule-makers headaches trying to even things out and the odds-makers fits trying to determine which teams had the most favorable matchups going into the start of each new season.

In a league that had come to pride itself on order and stability, the variations in teams' schedules and the inequality in some of its divisions were nagging concerns, until finally, just prior to the 2002 season, some great minds hit on a formula that made the kind of sense even we fans could understand. And so, in its newly found and hardly infinite wisdom, the NFL added an expansion franchise in Houston (the Texans) to replace the Oilers, giving the league 32 teams and the chance to do something about its quirky scheduling and alignment problems. (An expansion franchise is the designation given to any team that joined the league after it was initially formed.) It all came down to simple math. With 32 teams, it was now possible to break down each conference into four divisions of four teams each. There was order and balance and symmetry all around. Teams would continue to play their intra-division rivals twice each season, leaving 10 games of the 16-game schedule unaccounted for, and ensuring that each team meets every other team in the league at least once every 4 years. And, where a natural geographic rivalry exists, such as the one between the NFC East New York Giants and the AFC East New York Jets, it would be possible for those teams to meet, say, every other season.

Under this new format, the four division winners of each conference would advance to the play-offs. Two "wild card" teams from each conference with the best remaining overall records would also advance, giving 12 of the league's 32 teams a shot at the Super Bowl title. In the first round of the play-offs, the two wild card teams from each conference would face the third- and fourth-ranked division winners from the same conference; the top two division winners in each conference would receive a "bye" and move automatically into the second or "divisional" round of the play-offs, awaiting the winners of the first-round games. Winners of the divisional play-offs would meet in a conference championship game, which would in turn produce an AFC Champion and an NFC Champion to face off in the Super Bowl.

On paper at least, it seemed the league had hit on a workable solution to a mess of problems—but seven clubs were required to switch divisions, some long-standing and fan-friendly rivalries were effectively quashed, and the Seattle Seahawks were asked to move from the AFC to the NFC. It was tough for most fans to tell who was coming, who was going, and who was staying put, but when the dust finally settled, the league was left with a clean, logical, balanced format that now looks like this:

AMERICAN FOOTBALL CONFERENCE

AFC EAST

Buffalo Bills
Miami Dolphins
New England Patriots
New York Jets

AFC NORTH

Baltimore Ravens
Cincinnati Bengals
Cleveland Browns
Pittsburgh Steelers

AFC SOUTH

Houston Texans
Indianapolis Colts
Jacksonville Jaguars
Tennessee Titans

AFC WEST

Denver Broncos
Kansas City Chiefs
Oakland Raiders
San Diego Chargers

NATIONAL FOOTBALL CONFERENCE

NFC EAST

Dallas Cowboys
New York Giants
Philadelphia Eagles
Washington Redskins

NFC NORTH

Chicago Bears
Detroit Lions
Green Bay Packers
Minnesota Vikings

NFC SOUTH

Atlanta Falcons
Carolina Panthers
New Orleans Saints
Tampa Bay Buccaneers

NFC WEST

Arizona Cardinals
St. Louis Rams
San Francisco 49ers
Seattle Seahawks

Study the alignments carefully, and you'll still notice some pairings that don't make a whole lot of sense and take some getting used to. Last I checked, St. Louis was located substantially east of such NFC cities as Chicago, Detroit, and Green Bay, but the Rams are nevertheless assigned to the NFC West division—primarily because they used to be known as the Los Angeles Rams and over the years had developed a natural, downstate rivalry with the San Fran-

HISTORY OF THE GAME

THE NFL AS WE KNOW IT

Following Joe Namath's rookie season, and a great deal of speculation in the media and in barrooms across the country, ownership groups from both leagues started meeting secretly to discuss a possible merger between the two leagues. On June 8, 1966, Commissioner Pete Rozelle announced that the AFL and the NFL would combine to form a 24-team league. The merger would take place gradually over the next 3 years, with the two leagues meeting only in a world championship game at the close of each league's season, pitting the AFL champion against the NFL champion in a bowl game to crown a true national champion. There would also be a combined college draft beginning the following year, eliminating the bidding wars for top players. After 3 years, it was decided that the new league would operate as the National Football League, with an American Football Conference comprised primarily of former AFL teams and a National Football Conference comprised of former NFL teams.

Finally, three full seasons after the announced merger and only 9 years after the AFL opened for business, the two leagues joined forces for a combined, integrated schedule. The Browns, Colts, and Steelers switched stripes to join the new AFC alignment. And, to further herald the new age in professional football, the league decided to play one featured game each Monday night of the season, breaking from the traditional game day of Sunday, and selling the broadcast rights to those games to ABC-TV. For the first time, professional football would be played each week on a grand scale, on prime-time television, and ABC's *Monday Night Football* broadcasts became an instant hit.

Not much has changed from that basic blueprint developed for the 1969 season, except in terms of scale. The 14-game season has grown to include 16 games, with "bye" weeks built in to the schedule to allow players to regroup and recover from injuries, and to allow television networks to maximize their regular season exposure. The league has expanded from 24 teams to its current 32. Play-off berths are now awarded to "wild card" teams that don't manage to win their divisions, keeping more teams in the play-off picture deeper into each season. And the Super Bowl has grown each year to where it is now watched by nearly 150 million Americans—and beamed all over the world as one of the premier sporting events of the year.

cisco 49ers. Similarly, you'll note that Miami sits substantially south of such AFC cities as Baltimore, Nashville, and Jacksonville, and yet the Dolphins continue to play in the AFC East with their long-standing northeast rivals, the Buffalo Bills, and New England Patriots, and the New York Jets.

Perhaps the best way to understand these alignments is to look at them in context, and with that in mind I offer up a team-by-team thumbnail of every NFL franchise—on the theory that the more we fans know about each team and its history, the more we can appreciate each game as it unfolds.

Each of these sketch histories—presented in alphabetical order by division—is crammed with what I hope is just the right amount of information to help you pass yourself off as a knowledgeable fan. There's a lot of stuff here, so tread lightly if you're not all that interested in knowing, say, who coached the Tampa Bay Buccaneers to their first NFC title game. But go for it if you've got a head for details, and if you mean to impress the football fan in your life with your (sort of) extensive knowledge of the game. Really, the best way to read this chapter, which was suggested to me by one of my girlfriends, is on a need-to-know basis; if you're about to attend a Super Bowl party featuring a rematch of Super Bowl XXXIX, for example, you might want to check out the entries for the New England Patriots and the Philadelphia Eagles, the same way you used to study for a pop quiz back in school. Truth be told, I wish I had a reference like this when I was first learning the game, because it's all so *right here*. Pick and choose your spots, or grab it all at once—either way, you'll probably know a thing or two more than your guy when you reach the other end.

AFC East

BUFFALO BILLS: One of the American Football League's original eight teams . . . won AFL championships in 1964 and 1965, before losing to Kansas City in the 1966 AFL title game and thereby missing the opportunity to represent the league in the first Super Bowl . . . led in those early years by quarterback Jack Kemp, the future congressman and Democratic Vice Presidential nominee . . . struggled throughout the early 1970s, and hoped to turn things around with star running back O.J. Simpson, who helped to make the team competitive once more, in the process establishing a single-season rushing record of 2,003 yards in 1973 that continues to stand for a 14-game schedule . . . under head coach Chuck Knox, the Bills returned to the play-offs in the early 1980s, but it wasn't until the late 1980s, under head coach Marv Levy, that they were once again considered a top team . . . beginning in 1988, the Bills won five consecutive AFC East titles . . . under Levy, and led by quarterback Jim Kelly, running back Thurman Thomas, and defensive end Bruce Smith, the Bills became the first team to appear in four straight Super Bowls, losing each time but nevertheless setting a standard of overall excellence that will likely remain unmatched in conference play . . . head coach Mike Mularkey joined the Bills in 2004 . . . **TEAM COLORS:** Royal blue, scarlet, white . . . **RETIRED JERSEYS:** None . . .

MIAMI DOLPHINS: The expansion Dolphins joined the AFL in 1967 and became competitive in 1970 under head coach Don Shula, behind a nucleus of players that included quarterback Bob Griese, wide receiver Paul Warfield, running backs Larry Csonka and Jim Kiick, linebacker Nick Buoniconti, and guard Larry Little . . . Shula's Dolphins became the first AFC team to win three straight AFC championships (1971–1973) and back-to-back Super Bowls (VII and VIII) . . . also, the first team in NFL history to record an undefeated championship season, going 14–0 in the 1972 regular season, and running up an incredible 17 consecutive wins, capped by the first of the two successive Super Bowl victories . . . the accomplishment was all the more remarkable considering the relative youth of the franchise, affectionately dubbed "The Fish" by local fans and sportswriters . . . remained competitive for more than 2 decades under coach Shula, who retired in 1995 with more wins than any other coach in NFL history (328, including an earlier stint with the Baltimore Colts) . . . consistently finished at or near the top of their division throughout the '70s, '80s, and early

'90s, with only two losing seasons . . . the Griese-era Dolphins, known for their so-called "No-Name Defense" and systematic ground game, eventually gave way to an aerial assault led by quarterback Dan Marino, who carried the team to AFC Championships in 1982 and 1984, and by the time he retired, he was the only quarterback to amass more than 60,000 total passing yards, and to pass for more than 400 career touchdowns . . . fans are counting on new head coach Nick Saban to bring back some of the glory days . . . **TEAM COLORS:** Aqua, coral, blue, white . . . **RETIRED JERSEYS:** Bob Griese (#12), Dan Marino (#13) . . .

NEW ENGLAND PATRIOTS: Another one of the original AFL teams, the "Pats" bounced from Boston University to Harvard University and eventually to Fenway Park in search of a permanent home stadium . . . enjoyed modest success throughout the 1960s, mostly on the strength of their star wide receiver/placekicker Gino Cappelletti, who would go on to become the AFL's all-time leading scorer . . . running back Jim Nance won back-to-back league rushing titles in 1966 and 1967 . . . upon joining the NFL, the team fared poorly, but in 1971 managed to secure a stadium lease to call its own, 25 miles south of Boston in the working-class suburb of Foxborough . . . to reflect the move, the franchise changed its name to the New England Patriots, a harbinger of things to come in all of professional sports as teams abandoned run-down inner-city stadiums for the wide-open spaces of the suburbs and outlying areas . . . not much changed on the field, however, as the team managed only one AFC Eastern Division title until 1985, when the Patriots parlayed a wild-card play-off berth into an AFC Championship, only to lose out in Super Bowl XX to the Chicago Bears . . . more recently, under coaches Bill Parcells and especially Bill Belichick, the team has enjoyed a competitive run, led initially by quarterback Drew Bledsoe and currently by quarterback Tom Brady . . . its 21 consecutive wins, which included a 2003 post-season run, mark an NFL record . . . some say this team is shaping up to be the next dynasty, winning three out of four recent Super Bowls (XXXVI, XXXVIII, and XXXIX) . . . **TEAM COLORS:** Blue, red, silver, white . . . **RETIRED JERSEYS:** Steve

Grogan (#14), Gino Cappelletti (#20), Mike Haynes (#40), Steve Nelson (#57), John Hannah (#73), Jim Hunt (#79), Bob Dee (#89) . . .

NEW YORK JETS: Originally known as the Titans as an AFL charter franchise, the team moved to the newly opened Shea Stadium in 1963 and changed its name to acknowledge nearby LaGuardia Airport and its Shea Stadium co-tenant, baseball's New York Mets . . . (soon basketball's New York Nets began playing on Long Island, and for a brief time there was a Team Tennis franchise known as the New York Sets, giving the city four professional teams linked in rhyme for no good reason) . . . Hall of Fame coach Weeb Ewbank built his program around high-profile Alabama quarterback Joe Namath, who signed before the 1966 season for a reported $400,000, an astronomical sum at the time . . . football historians regard the Namath signing as a key impetus for the AFL-NFL merger talks that began the following season . . . "Broadway Joe" Namath led the team to its first AFL Championship in 1968, teaming with wide receiver Don Maynard to form one of the most effective passing combinations in the game . . . the brash young quarterback famously predicted that the Jets would prevail in Super Bowl III, over a veteran Baltimore Colts squad representing the NFL, at a time when most people didn't think the AFL could compete . . . the Jets' 16–7 victory shocked pundits and fans alike, and hastened the merger between the two leagues . . . the Jets managed to repeat as division champs the following season, but were eliminated in the first play-off round and began a long stretch of disappointing seasons that lasted through the 1970s . . . the 1980s saw a return to competitiveness, coinciding with the team's move to the Meadowlands Sports Complex in New Jersey, which it began sharing with the NFC East New York Giants in 1984 . . . led by quarterback Ken O'Brien and running back Freeman McNeil, and inspired by a defensive unit known as "Gang Green" and spear-headed by linemen Mark Gastineau and Joe Klecko, the team became a fixture in post-season play . . . current coach Herm Edwards looks to quarterback Chad Pennington and ex-Pat running back Curtis Martin to lead the offense . . . **TEAM COLORS:** Green and white . . . **RETIRED JERSEYS:** Joe Namath (#12), Don Maynard (#13) . . .

AFC North

BALTIMORE RAVENS: Joining the league in 1996 as an offshoot of the storied Cleveland Browns franchise, the team took its name from a famous poem written by Baltimore denizen Edgar Allen Poe, after a phone-in poll conducted by a local newspaper . . . (stay with me on this one because it gets a little complicated) . . . Browns owner Art Modell looked to boost his fortunes by relocating his team to Baltimore . . . the league retained the rights to the Cleveland Browns name and team history, which it revived a couple years later with an expansion franchise (see below) . . . led initially by former Baltimore Colts coach Ted Marchibroda and veteran quarterback Vinny Testaverde, a holdover from the 1995 Browns, the Ravens struggled in their new home . . . the team moved into a new, football-only stadium in 1998, adjacent to Camden Yards, home of baseball's Baltimore Orioles, and turned things around in 2000 under coach Brian Billick, capping its successful season with a resounding 34–7 victory over the New York Giants in Super Bowl XXXV, led by running back Jamal Lewis, linebacker Ray Lewis, and offensive lineman Jonathan Ogden, the team's first-ever draft pick . . . **TEAM COLORS:** Black, purple, gold . . . **RETIRED JERSEYS:** None . . .

CINCINNATI BENGALS: An AFL expansion team dating to 1968, when the AFL-NFL merger was already on the horizon . . . the Bengals were brought to life by Paul Brown, the legendary coach of the cross-state Cleveland Browns, who had retired from football in 1962 . . . Brown led the investor group that purchased the franchise, helped to win approvals for a new stadium, and brought instant credibility to the enterprise . . . he also signed on as head coach, a position he would fill for the next 8 years, and as general manager, a position he filled until his death in 1991 . . . despite Brown's pedigree, the Bengals got off to a slow start, until they selected quarterback Ken Anderson from tiny Augustana College in Rock Island, Illinois, in the third round of the 1971 draft . . . Anderson became one of the top quarterbacks in the league over the next 14 seasons and helped the team to a run of successful campaigns, culminating in

1981 with the AFC Championship . . . the Bengals would go on to lose 26–21 to the San Francisco 49ers in Super Bowl XVI . . . the team also suffered one of the most disappointing losses in Super Bowl history, succumbing again to the 49ers in Super Bowl XXII, this time on a last-minute touchdown pass by Joe Montana . . . that same year the Bengals inspired a national dance craze known as "The Ickey Shuffle," named for running back Ickey Woods in honor of his unusual touchdown celebration—a precursor to the over-the-top scoring salutes of today's players . . . Boomer Esiason succeeded Anderson as quarterback and managed to post several winning seasons for the Bengals throughout the late-1980s, under the tutelage of head coach Sam Wyche . . . running back Corey Dillon established the single-game rushing mark of 278 yards as a member of the 2000 Bengals . . . head coach Marv Lewis brought on in 2003, is one of just a handful of African American head coaches in the NFL (hopefully there will be more to come) . . . QB Carson Palmer and WR Chad Johnson made the 2005 offense one to watch . . . **TEAM COLORS:** Black, orange, white . . . **RETIRED JERSEYS:** Bob Johnson (#54) . . .

CLEVELAND BROWNS: Compiled a 52–4–3 winning record during four seasons atop the All-America Football Conference, a rival league that briefly threatened the pro game in the late 1940s, capturing all four league championships . . . led by quarterback Otto Graham, fullback Marion Motley, and tackle/placekicker Lou Groza, the Browns moved to the NFL after the two leagues agreed to merge prior to the 1950 season . . . coached by the legendary Paul Brown, the team finished atop the NFL's Eastern Conference for six consecutive seasons, from 1950 to 1955 . . . they collected another important trophy in 1957 after adding star Syracuse running back Jim Brown, who would rewrite the record books, setting the standard for career rushing yards (12,312) and retiring at the top of his game after only nine seasons to pursue a film career . . . incredibly, the Browns made the play-offs more often than not, notching 22 post-season appearances in their first 40 years in the league . . . highlights included NFL championships in 1950, 1954, 1955, and 1964, and NFL Eastern Conference championships in 1950–55, 1957, 1964, 1965, 1968, and 1969 . . .

in 1971, the Browns agreed to join the newly formed American Football Conference as part of the merger agreement between the AFL and the NFL . . . finished atop the AFC Central Division in 1971, the first year of combined play . . . the AFC Browns have continued to win, under coaches Sam Rutigliano, Marty Schottenheimer, and Bill Belichick, but they have fallen short of the ultimate prize in the modern era—a trip to the Super Bowl . . . in 1995, Browns owner Art Modell set off a firestorm when he announced plans to move the team to Baltimore, angering hard-core Browns fans, most especially the die-hard and slightly crazy season ticket holders known as "the Dog Pound" because of their rowdy enthusiasm . . . local fans lobbied to keep the team in Cleveland, and ultimately prevailed when the league declared the franchise "suspended," allowing Modell to establish a new franchise in Baltimore with his old personnel, and creating a new franchise that would inherit the Browns' name, colors, and team history . . . these born-again Cleveland Browns resumed play in 1999 . . . TEAM COLORS: Brown (duh!), orange, white . . . look out for new coach Romeo Crennel (2005) who brings his defensive expertise from the Patriots to breathe some life into this team . . . RETIRED JERSEYS: Otto Graham (#14), Jim Brown (#32), Ernie Davis (#45), Don Fleming (#46), Lou Groza (#76) . . .

PITTSBURGH STEELERS: Sixth-oldest franchise in the NFL, originally known as the Pirates until 1940, when its name was changed to reflect the city's reliance on the steel industry . . . under the stewardship of original owner Art Rooney, the Steelers often landed in the bottom half of the league standings . . . among the most prominent Pittsburgh players of the late 1930s was future U.S. Supreme Court Justice Byron "Whizzer" White . . . by the mid-50s, the team boasted a bona fide star in quarterback Bobby Layne, and for several years challenged for the divisional title, but it took nearly 40 years for the team to win its first championship, the 1972 AFC Central Division crown, beginning a run of eight consecutive play-off appearances, including a then unprecedented four Super Bowl victories (IX, X, XIII, XIV) . . . first team to win back-to-back Super Bowls on two separate occasions . . . along with Cincinnati, Cleveland, and Houston in the AFC Central, formed the fabled "black and blue" division, so named because intra-division games were always hard-fought affairs and teams were closely matched . . . "the team of the '70s" was known for its "Steel Curtain" defense, featuring stalwarts like "Mean" Joe Greene, L.C. Greenwood, and Dwight White on the line and Pro Bowlers Jack Ham, Jack Lambert, and Andy Russell in the linebacking corps . . . cornerback Mel Blount shut down opposing receivers . . . the offense was led by quarterback Terry Bradshaw, wide receivers Lynn Swann and John Stallworth, and running back Franco Harris, whose loyal band of Italian-American fans called themselves "Franco's Italian Army" and turned each game into a party . . . coached by Chuck Noll for 23 years, beginning with an awful 1–13 1969 season, the Steelers were the dominant team on the NFL stage for such an impressive span that many experts consider it a true sports dynasty, and one of the best football teams ever assembled . . . Coach Bill Cowher succeeded Noll in 1992, and has managed to lead the team to AFC Central Division Championships in 1992, 1994, 1995, 1996, and 1997, including a then-record fifth Super Bowl appearance, which it lost to the Dallas Cowboys . . . Cowher's teams continue to be marked by a grind-it-out offense and sound defenses . . . in the late 1990s, quarterback Kordell "Slash" Stewart emerged as an unlikely star, and took his nickname from his all-purpose ability to run/pass/receive the ball, while running back Jerome Bettis helped to establish the running game . . . in 2004, the team looked to begin a new chapter in its storied history, with the addition of highly touted quarterback Ben Roethlisberger . . . **TEAM COLORS:** Black and gold . . . **RETIRED JERSEYS:** Ernie Stautner (#70) . . .

AFC South

HOUSTON TEXANS: The expansion Texans joined the NFL in 2002, 5 years after the Oilers quit the city for the greener grass of Tennessee . . . nickname calls to mind the Dallas Texans of the original AFL (now known as the Kansas City Chiefs) . . . the newest Houston franchise is led on the field by David Carr, the young quarterback out of Fresno State, and off the field by coach Dom

Capers, who guided the expansion Carolina Panthers to the NFC Championship game in the team's 2nd year of play . . . the Texans got off to a strong start, besting their cross-state rival Cowboys 19–10 in the first regular-season game in franchise history . . . rookie QB Carr connected on a touchdown pass to Billy Miller on his very first NFL pass . . . the game had been billed as a "Texas Super Bowl," although there had never been much of a rivalry between the Cowboys and the Oilers (the two teams met only eight times in 37 years) . . . inevitably, the young Texans could not sustain the momentum of their opening-day victory, and finished 4–12 . . . one other first-year highlight: the Texans boasted one of the league's top pass defenses, led by defensive lineman Gary Walker, a former Oiler who returned to Houston and earned a spot in the Pro Bowl . . . **TEAM COLORS:** Red, white, steel blue . . . **RETIRED JERSEYS:** None . . .

INDIANAPOLIS COLTS: Originally of Baltimore, this team's got *some history* . . . current franchise dates back to the 1953 NFL season, under original owner Carroll Rosenbloom . . . a new ownership group led by Carroll Rosenbloom was awarded this second-chance franchise . . . by 1957, coach Weeb Ewbank (who later coached the New York Jets) had built a winning team, with a foundation of future Hall of Famers that would not post another losing season for 14 years . . . quarterback Johnny Unitas, a Baltimore icon considered one of the greatest to play the game, steered the Colts to the NFL championship in 1958, 1959, and 1968 . . . the 1958 championship game, a 23–17 overtime victory against the New York Giants, was an all-time classic, played before a record television audience and capped by a dramatic game-tying field goal and touchdown drive that cemented the Unitas legend . . . backup quarterback Earl Morrall filled in for the injured Unitas in 1968 and helped the team to a 13–1 record and an ill-fated Super Bowl appearance against Ewbank's upstart New York Jets of the AFL . . . the Colts were now coached by Don Shula, who would go on to tremendous success with the Miami Dolphins . . . in fact, the Colts followed Shula to the AFC Eastern Division following the AFL-NFL merger, winning the first-ever AFC East championship and representing the AFC for the first time in the Super Bowl, beating the Dallas Cowboys 16–13 in Super Bowl V . . .

the Super Bowl Champion Colts were a defensive-minded bunch, led by Pro Bowlers Mike Curtis at linebacker, Bubba Smith on the line, and Jerry Logan in the secondary . . . in 1972, owner Rosenbloom engineered one of the strangest trades in the history of professional sports, swapping *entire teams* with Robert Irsay, who had just purchased the Los Angeles Rams . . . after his new Colts struggled on the field, Irsay followed this strange deal with another curious transaction, moving the franchise to Indianapolis in 1984 in a middle-of-the-night dodge to avoid the fan protest he knew would follow . . . sure enough, Irsay's name continues to invoke the wrath of Baltimore football fans . . . the current crop of Indianapolis Colts are coached by Tony Dungy, and led by quarterback Peyton Manning (who set a record for touchdown passes in a single season, with 49, in 2004, breaking Dan Marino's long-standing mark of 48), running back Edgerrin James, wide receiver Marvin Harrison (who set a record for pass receptions in a single season, with 143 in 2002), and lineman Dwight Freeney . . . **TEAM COLORS:** Royal blue and white . . . **RETIRED JERSEYS:** Johnny Unitas (#19), Buddy Young (#22), Lenny Moore (#24), Art Donovan (#70), Jim Parker (#77), Raymond Berry (#82), Gino Marchetti (#89) . . .

JACKSONVILLE JAGUARS: The NFL's 30th franchise, awarded to an investment group headed by local businessmen Tom Petway and J. Wayne Weaver, the club's current chairman and CEO . . . joined the league for the 1995 season, along with my current favorite team, the Carolina Panthers . . . fared better than previous expansion teams in its inaugural season, owing to a rich expansion draft and a strong free-agent market . . . led initially by coach Tom Coughlin and quarterback Mark Brunell, the Jaguars posted a winning record in just their second season, capturing a wild card play-off berth and clawing their way past Buffalo and Denver in the first and second round to a showdown with New England for the AFC Championship game . . . the Jaguars wound up losing that game, 20–6, but their incredible second-season run announced their arrival in a big way . . . Brunell emerged as one of the league's top QBs, with wide receiver Jimmy Smith as a top target and perennial Pro Bowler . . . more recently, coach Jack del Rio joined the team in 2003, running back Fred Taylor has stepped in to complement the offense, while young quarterback Byron Leftwich has played like a star-in-the-making . . . **TEAM COLORS:** Teal, black, gold . . . **RETIRED JERSEYS:** None . . .

TENNESSEE TITANS: One of the AFL's original franchises, then known as the Houston Oilers . . . signed reigning Heisman Trophy winner Billy Cannon prior to the team's first season; the Louisiana State running back became one of the league's first marquee attractions . . . ran the table in the league's early years, winning the first two AFL championships, and losing out on a third-straight championship to the Dallas Texans in a historic, double-overtime 1962 title game . . . quarterbacked early on by Hall of Famer George Blanda, with wide receiver Charley Hennigan as a favorite target, the Oilers soon struggled through a string of disappointing seasons . . . defensive back Ken Houston was a fixture in the Houston secondary during this period, and widely regarded as one of the best safeties in the game, despite playing most of his career on mediocre teams . . . finally, under coach "Bum" Phillips, the Oilers returned to the play-offs in the late 1970s, making three-straight wild card appearances beginning in 1978 . . . behind veteran quarterback Dan Pastorini and punishing running back Earl Campbell, they managed to reach the AFC Championship game in 1978 and 1979, only to lose out each year to the rival Steelers . . . quarterback Warren Moon guided the team to consistent success throughout the 1980s and early 1990s, coached by Jerry Glanville and Jack Pardee, but it wasn't until Jeff Fisher signed on as head coach and the emergence of quarterback Steve McNair and running back Eddie George that the team would again contend for a championship . . . relocated in 1997 to Nashville, which had long been a haven for college football but had yet to host a professional football franchise . . . played for two seasons as the Tennessee Oilers before retiring the old nickname . . . in the team's first year as the Titans, McNair & Co. managed to grab the AFC Championship, with a defense stamped by Pro Bowl lineman Jevon Kearse, but lost to the St. Louis Rams in Super Bowl XXXIV, 23–16, despite one of the most thrilling last-second drives in Super Bowl history . . . **TEAM COLORS:** Navy, "Titans" blue, red, silver . . . **RETIRED JERSEYS:**

Earl Campbell (#34), Jim Norton (#43), Mike Munchak (#63), Elvin Bethea (#65) . . .

AFC West

DENVER BRONCOS: Won the first AFL game ever played, with a 13–10 victory over the Boston Patriots on September 9, 1960 . . . also notched the first-ever win for an AFL franchise over an NFL team, with a 13–7 exhibition win over the Detroit Lions on August 5, 1967 . . . still, managed to record the worst record of any of the AFL's original eight teams during the league's 10-year history . . . completed its first winning season in 1973, and proceeded to post winning marks in 17 of the next 20 seasons . . . enjoyed greatest success under coach Dan Reeves following the 1983 arrival of quarterback John Elway, a two-sport star at Stanford who was at one time under contract with the New York Yankees . . . over his Hall of Fame career, Elway became known for his strong passing arm and for his dramatic come-from-behind scoring drives in a game's waning minutes . . . Elway led the Broncos to five Super Bowl appearances, including back-to-back wins in Super Bowls XXXII and XXXIII . . . the Broncos defense became known as "Orange Crush" during this period for the team colors and for its swarming, punishing style of play . . . the team continues to thrive under long-term coach Mike Shanahan, backed by quarterback Jake Plummer and a solid defensive unit that has remained a hallmark of the franchise . . . **TEAM COLORS:** Orange, navy, white . . . **RETIRED JERSEYS:** John Elway (#7), Frank Tripucka (#18), Floyd Little (#44) . . .

KANSAS CITY CHIEFS: Originally known as the Dallas Texans, and owned and operated by Texas businessman Lamar Hunt, the founder of the AFL and its first president . . . the team moved to Kansas City in 1963 to avoid direct competition with the NFL's newest expansion team, the Dallas Cowboys, but it didn't shrink from competition on the field . . . perhaps the most successful of the AFL teams, with league championships in 1962 (a 20–17 double-overtime victory over the Houston Oilers—the longest professional football game ever played to that point), 1966 (leading to an appearance at the first-ever Super Bowl, against the powerful Green Bay Packers), and 1969 (culminating in a Super Bowl IV victory over a heavily favored Minnesota team to cap the AFL's final year of operation) . . . pioneering coach Hank Stram was the only coach to lead the same team throughout the AFL's entire 10-year history, and he continued to coach the Chiefs in the NFL with consistent success . . . Stram's great weapons were quarterback Len Dawson, wide receiver Otis Taylor, defensive end Buck Buchanan, and linebackers Willie Lanier and Bobby Bell . . . placekicker Jan Stenerud became the first kicker elected to the Hall of Fame, and remains the only special teams player to receive the honor . . . perennial play-off contenders throughout the 1990s, under head coach Marty Shottenheimer . . . Hall of Fame quarterback Joe Montana and Hall of Fame running back Marcus Allen completed their careers in Kansas City uniforms . . . the acquisition of running back Priest Holmes prior to the 2001 season gave current coach Dick Vermeil one of the league's most feared all-purpose threats, to round out one of the most potent offenses . . . **TEAM COLORS:** Red, gold, white . . . **RETIRED JERSEYS:** Jan Stenerud (#3), Len Dawson (#16), Abner Haynes (#28), Stone Johnson (#33), Mack Lee Hill (#36), Willie Lanier (#63), Bobby Bell (#78), Buck Buchanan (#86) . . .

OAKLAND RAIDERS: A last-minute replacement to the AFL's original eight-team lineup, after the Minneapolis franchise bolted for an expansion slot in the NFL . . . the Raiders struggled early but enjoyed instant success under new head coach Al Davis in 1963 . . . Davis would go on to become the league's commissioner during the 1966 AFL-NFL merger and return to the Raiders as managing general partner, a position he continues to hold . . . John Madden signed on as coach before the 1969 season, and led the team during an impressive run of winning seasons with help from gun-slinging quarterback Daryl Lamonica and sure-handed wide receiver Fred Biletnikoff . . . defensive backs Willie Brown and Jack Tatum were among the most feared "assassins" in any defensive secondary throughout the Madden years, and offensive linemen Jim Otto, Gene Upshaw, and Art Shell became household names, symbolizing their coach's hard-nosed style of play in the trenches . . . Lamonica's run gave way to left-handed quarterback Ken Stabler, and Madden was eventually succeeded by former Raiders QB Tom Flores, and the team continued to win . . . beginning in 1965, the Raiders posted a winning record for 19 of the next 20 years . . . Super Bowl XI, XV, and XVII Champions (MVP Marcus Allen lit that last game on fire), and the only team to make Super Bowl appearances in the '60s, '70s, and '80s . . . moved from Oakland to Los Angeles in 1982, but returned to Oakland following the 1994 season . . . Peete family trivia: my brother-in-law, Skip Peete, is the current running backs' coach . . . under Davis, the team has developed a "renegade" or "outlaw" personality unmatched in professional sports, as the Raiders have become known for taking on talented players with troubled histories off the field and providing a second chance at glory on the field . . . the talented, yet moody, WR Randy Moss joined the team in 2005 . . . **TEAM COLORS:** Silver and black . . . **RETIRED JERSEYS:** None . . .

SAN DIEGO CHARGERS: Captured the first AFL Western Division championship as the Los Angeles Chargers, but moved to San Diego the following season in search of greater fan support . . . originally owned by hotel tycoon Barron Hilton . . . under coach Sid Gillman, the Chargers demonstrated more personality and flair than any other of the original AFL teams, deploying an exciting passing game behind quarterback John Hadl and his favorite target, wide receiver Lance Alworth, and running up big scores, including a 51–10 rout of Boston in the 1963 AFL Championship game . . . the same free-wheeling style of play continued in the 1970s under coach Don Coryell, who had an uncanny weapon in the arm of future Hall of Famer Dan Fouts . . . the Chargers' relentless passing attack became known as "Air Coryell," and featured an aerial assault that frequently ended up in the sure hands of tight end Kellen Winslow and wide receiver Charlie Joiner, both future Hall of Famers . . . returned to championship level in 1994, with a ground game led by running back Natrone

THE SUPER BOWL

Despite the merger, it was still widely believed that AFL teams were a notch below NFL teams in terms of talent. Much of the reason for the disparity was the all-out dominance of Vince Lombardi's Green Bay Packers dynasty—although for the previous few seasons, even the stronger NFL teams were no match for the Packers. Still, sportswriters and Vegas odds-makers gave the younger, weaker AFL teams no chance against their NFL rivals. That first world championship game, nicknamed "The Super Bowl" by an NFL executive who bent and borrowed the name from a rubberized ball that was a popular children's toy at the time, was played on January 15, 1967, at the Los Angeles Memorial Coliseum, a neutral site chosen before the contestants had been determined. Lombardi's Packers trounced Lamar Hunt's Kansas City Chiefs by a score of 35-10, adding further fuel to the argument that AFL teams didn't belong on the same field with their NFL counterparts.

The following year, in the second world championship game, the Packers again domi-nated the AFL champs, this time by a 33-14 score over the Oakland Raiders. The game, held in Miami, was referred to as Super Bowl II by sportswriters and pundits, but it was still known formally around the league as a world championship. (The Roman numerals came later.) As in the first "Super Bowl," the game was never in doubt, and fans, sportswriters, and league officials alike began to wonder about the logic of combining the two leagues.

By the 3rd year of the gradual merger, AFL fans were primed for an upset. Lombardi had retired as the head coach of the aging Packers, and the NFL sent the Baltimore Colts to the title game. The Colts, led by a legendary quarterback named Johnny Unitas who had also been slowed by age, were to face off against Joe Namath's brash young New York Jets—and Namath himself guaranteed a victory. This time, league organizers realized they had stumbled across a sure-fire handle and formally recognized the game as Super Bowl III. And this time, again in Miami, the AFL champs managed to prevail. The Jets beat the Colts by a score of 16-7, bringing instant credibility to the AFL and justifying the decision to merge the two leagues.

Means and a tenacious defense sparked by linebacker Junior Seau, grinding out a 17–13 victory over the Pittsburgh Steelers in the AFC title game, only to lose to Steve Young and the San Francisco 49ers in Super Bowl XXIX . . . the current crop of Chargers is led by coach Marty Schottenheimer, Pro Bowl running back LaDainian Tomlinson, and 2004 comeback player of the year, QB Drew Brees . . . **TEAM COLORS:** Navy, gold, white . . . **RETIRED JERSEYS:** Dan Fouts (#14) . . .

NFC East

DALLAS COWBOYS: "America's Team" . . . expansion franchise based in Dallas to compete for fans with Lamar Hunt's AFL Dallas Texans . . . posted losing seasons for first 5 years, but began a record run of 20 consecutive winning seasons in 1966 . . . coaching icon Tom Landry, known for his trademark hat and stoic sideline ways, led his team to sustained excellence as football came of age as "America's Game" . . . pioneered use of track athletes in skill positions with the signing of wide receiver "Bullet" Bob Hayes . . . also pioneered use of glamorous cheerleaders in the NFL with the introduction of the Dallas Cowboys Cheerleaders . . . division champions in 1967–70, falling short each year in the title game, with "Dandy" Don Meredith at quarterback, and Cornell Green and Mel Renfro in the secondary . . . a heartbreaking last-minute loss to the Colts in Super Bowl V cemented the team's reputation, but the Cowboys rebounded in 1971 with a 24–3 trouncing of Miami in Super Bowl VI, behind quarterback Roger Staubach . . . running backs Calvin Hill and Duane Thomas helped the Cowboys to a league-best offense, while Chuck Howley and Bob Lilly led the way on defense . . . returned to the Super Bowl three more times in the 1970s, losing to Pittsburgh in Super Bowls X and XIII, but besting the Broncos, 27–10, in Super Bowl XII . . . lineman Randy White became a force, and running back Tony Dorsett developed into one of the game's greats . . . reached the post-season for the next 5 years, adding quarterback Danny White, lineman Ed "Too Tall" Jones, and receivers Drew Pearson, Tony Hill, and Doug

Cosbie to the mix, but the Landry-era was on the wane . . . 1989 was both a low-water mark and a turning point, as the team sank to 1–15 under first-year coach Jimmy Johnson while rookie quarterback Troy Aikman looked like the real deal . . . Aikman teamed with career rushing leader Emmitt Smith and wide receiver Michael Irvin to form one of the league's most explosive offenses, with six division championships in the '90s, and a resounding three Super Bowl victories in 4 years (XXVII, XXVIII, and XXX) . . . coach Bill Parcells reversed three straight 5–11 seasons in 2003 to lead the team to a wild card berth in his first season . . . newly acquired veteran QB, Drew Bledsoe, will try to turn up the volume for the 2005 season . . . **TEAM COLORS:** Royal blue, metallic blue, white . . . **RETIRED JERSEYS:** None . . .

NEW YORK GIANTS: Franchise granted in 1925 to NFL pioneer Tim Mara, whose teams were known for their defense . . . began play in New York City's Polo Grounds, later moved to Yankee Stadium in the Bronx, before crossing the river to New Jersey to take up residence at Giants Stadium in the Meadowlands Sports Complex . . . first NFL championship came in 1927 when a stingy Giants defense led by Steve Owen held opponents to an incredible 20 points *for the entire season* . . . Owen became head coach in 1931, and continued in that role for 23 seasons, delivering division championships in eight of his first 16 seasons, and NFL championships in 1934 and 1938 . . . two-way threat Mel Hein, at center/linebacker, didn't miss a game in 15 standout seasons during this period . . . backed by New York legends Frank Gifford, Roosevelt Brown, Emlen Tunnell, Andy Robustelli, and Y.A. Tittle, the Giants of the '50s again emerged as perennial contenders, coached initially by Jim Lee Howell and later by Allie Sherman . . . sank to the bottom of the standings in mid '60s, despite brief reign of Hall of Fame quarterback Fran Tarkenton . . . signs of a turnaround appeared in 1979 with the promising play of quarterback Phil Simms, and linebackers Harry Carson and Brad Van Pelt, but it wasn't until 1981 and the addition of game-changing linebacker Lawrence Taylor that the Giants posted a winning record and a play-off run . . . despite his troubled personal life off the field, Taylor was generally considered one of the greatest linebackers to ever play the game . . . 2nd-year coach Bill Parcells took the team to the divisional play-offs in 1984, with Pro Bowl defensive back Mark Haynes and linebacker Carl Banks rounding out an already tenacious defense . . . victories in Super Bowls XXI and XXV soon followed, the last in a thrilling 20–19 contest over the Bills . . . coach Jim Fassel returned the team to the Super Bowl in 2000 on the back of strong defensive play from linebacker Jesse Armstead and lineman Michael Strahan, with quarterback Kerry Collins, running back Tiki Barber, and wide receiver Amani Toomer driving the offense . . . in the 2004 college draft, the team traded several future draft picks and other considerations in order to claim the top pick, which they used to draft their quarterback-of-the-future, Eli Manning . . . **TEAM COLORS:** Blue, red, white . . . **RETIRED JERSEYS:** Ray Flaherty (#1), Tuffy Leemans (#4), Mel Hein (#7), Phil Simms (#11), Y.A. Tittle (#14), Al Blozis (#32), Joe Morrison (#40), Charlie Conerly (#42), Ken Strong (#50), Lawrence Taylor (#56) . . .

PHILADELPHIA EAGLES: A losing franchise for much of its early history, the Eagles finally put together an impressive string in the 1940s under coach Greasy Neale, collecting back-to-back championships in 1948 and 1949 . . . those Eagles teams were led by center-linebacker Chuck Bednarik and running back Steve Van Buren . . . age and injuries put a sudden stop to the team's winning run, but coach Lawrence "Buck" Shaw brought the team another championship in 1960, with a boost on the field from linebacker Maxie Baughan . . . played at the University of Pennsylvania's Franklin Field until 1971, when they moved to Veterans Stadium . . . in the late '60s and early '70s, the Eagles were known for disappointing their fans, and for signing past-their-prime veterans for key positions . . . it would be 18 years before the team was in a position to repeat as champions, posting a 9–7 record for 3rd-year coach Dick Vermeil in 1978, good for a wild card play-off berth and the chance for this particular Eagles fan to dream . . . Vermeil's Eagles played in four consecutive post-seasons and were led by quarterback Ron Jaworski, wide receiver Harold Carmichael, and running back Wilbert Montgomery . . . lost out in Super Bowl XV to Oakland, despite a league-best defense led by lineman Charlie Johnson . . . the

Eagles reclaimed the top of the NFL Eastern Division under coach Buddy Ryan, this time on the arm of quarterback Randall Cunningham, who also led the team in rushing for four consecutive seasons . . . acquired Rodney Peete in 1995 and finished 10–6 to earn a wild card spot (go Rodney!) . . . scored an impressive 58–37 first-round play-off victory over Detroit, before losing to the Super Bowl–bound Cowboys . . . returned to NFC Championship game in 2001 under coach Andy Reid, this time led by current quarterback Donovan McNabb and Pro Bowl defensive backs Brian Dawkins and Troy Vincent . . . moved to Lincoln Financial Field before the 2003 season . . . lost three consecutive NFC Championships before making it to Super Bowl XXXIX . . . star wide receiver Terrell Owens played with an injury, only to lose to the Patriots, 24–21 . . . **TEAM COLORS:** "Eagles" green, silver, black, white . . . **RETIRED JERSEYS:** Steve Van Buren (#15), Tom Brookshier (#40), Pete Retzlaff (#44), Chuck Bednarik (#60), Al Wistert (#70), Jerome Brown (#99) . . .

WASHINGTON REDSKINS: One of the most popular teams in the NFL, with a rabid fan base and a record streak of consecutive home sellouts dating to 1966 . . . known for one season as the Boston Braves before adopting the Redskins name in 1933 . . . moved from Boston to Washington, DC, for the 1937 season to play at Griffith Stadium . . . "Slingin'" Sammy Baugh joined the team that same year and quickly transformed the quarterback position . . . with Baugh at the helm, the "Skins" grabbed five Eastern Division titles in the '30s and '40s, including NFL championships in 1937 and 1942 . . . moved to RFK Stadium (then known as DC Stadium) in 1961 . . . football legend Otto Graham tried his hand at coaching in the late '60s, with middling success behind quarterback Sonny Jurgenson and wide receiver Charley Taylor, an eight-time Pro Bowl selection . . . another legendary Packer coach, Vince Lombardi, took the reins in 1969 for a single season, helping the Skins to a winning record for the first time in 14 years . . . returned to post-season play in 1971 under coach George Allen after a 26-year drought, with quarterback Billy Kilmer and running back Larry Brown as key additions . . . lost to Miami Dolphins in Super Bowl VII, 14–7 . . . quarterback Joe Theisman began his long career with the

Redskins in 1974, and played a featured role for three strong coaches—Allen, Jack Pardee, and Joe Gibbs—with a lineup that soon featured running back John Riggins, wide receiver Charlie Brown, linebacker Dexter Manley, and defensive back Darrell Green . . . Gibbs's Redskins won Super Bowls XVII, XXII, and XXVI, and posted winning marks in 10 of his 12 seasons . . . the 1991 Redskins, quarterbacked by Mark Rypien, with an offense built around Earnest Byner and wide receiver Art Monk, and a defense still anchored by Green, tallied a 14–2 regular season on its way to a Super Bowl victory over Buffalo, but the season signaled the end of a winning era . . . moved in 1997 to FedEx Field, initially known as Jack Kent Cooke Stadium, in honor of the team's long-time owner . . . currently owned and operated by Dan Snyder, a brash, outspoken champion of his players and the franchise who has eagerly signed big-name free agents to big-money contracts . . . indeed, in 2004, Snyder was able to persuade Gibbs to come out of a 12-year retirement to coach the Skins to the next level . . . **TEAM COLORS:** Burgundy and gold . . . **RETIRED JERSEYS:** Sammy Baugh (#33) . . .

NFC North

CHICAGO BEARS: Charter NFL franchise, originally known as the Decatur (Illinois) Staleys, named for a local starch company . . . moved to Chicago in 1921 under the direction of player-coach (and, soon, owner) George Halas, who rechristened the team in a nod to Chicago's beloved Cubs baseball team, the Bears' Wrigley Field co-tenants . . . signed All-American Red Grange in 1925 and staged a series of attendance-breaking exhibition games across the country, helping to establish the professional game . . . "Papa Bear" Halas served as head coach until 1967, with only a 2-year hiatus in 1956–57, compiling an astounding 318–148–32 regular season record, and an incredible eight championships . . . Halas's 1934 Bears were the first NFL team to notch a perfect regular season, going 13–0 behind legendary running back Bronko Nagurski . . . appeared in four consecutive NFL Championship games in the 1940s, including the famous 73–0 drubbing of the Washington Redskins in 1940, led by quarterback Sid Luckman . . . went without a championship for 17 years before besting the New York Giants in the 1963 title game, this time sparked by tight end Mike Ditka and quarterback Billy Wade . . . the 1960s saw the emergence of running back Gale Sayers as one of the most graceful and powerful to ever play the game, and middle linebacker Dick Butkus as one of the most tenacious and bruising defenders to ever line up on the other side of the ball . . . the 1970s were mostly disappointing, save for the signing of running back Walter Payton (soon and forever after known as "Sweetness" to adoring Bears fans) . . . moved to Soldier Field in 1971 . . . the 1980s marked the return of Ditka, this time as head coach, and the scrappy play of the new "Monsters of the Midway" led by Payton, quarterback Jim McMahon, and linebacker Mike Singletary . . . Super Bowl XX champions, noted for the folk hero status of defensive lineman William "The Refrigerator" Perry, who barreled in for a touchdown after being called in to run a play from scrimmage . . . the 2001 Bears managed a 13–3 record under coach Dick Jauron, sparked by linebacker Brian Urlacher and a league-best defense . . . currently owned and operated by Halas's grandson, Michael McCaskey . . . **TEAM COLORS:** Navy, orange, white . . . **RETIRED JERSEYS:** Bronko Nagurski (#3), George McAfee (#5), George Halas (#7), Willie Galimore (#28), Walter Payton (#34), Gale Sayers (#40), Brian Piccolo (#41), Sid Luckman (#42), Dick Butkus (#51), Bill Hewitt (#56), Bill George (#61), Bulldog Turner (#66), Red Grange (#77) . . .

DETROIT LIONS: Established in 1930 as the Portsmouth (Ohio) Spartans, the franchise moved to Detroit in 1934 with the sale of the team to local radio executive George A. Richards . . . headlining the new Detroit Lions was the versatile Dutch Clark, a charter member of the Pro Football Hall of Fame . . . began tradition of hosting a regular season game on Thanksgiving Day in its first season in Detroit . . . captured first NFL Championship in 1935 . . . posted forgettable 0–11 season in 1942 . . . enjoyed first real run of success in the 1950s, under coach Raymond Parker, with Bobby Layne at quarterback, racking up league titles in 1952–54 and 1957 . . . the Lions teams of the 1950s also featured running back Doak Walker and safety Jack Christiansen . . . posted second-division finishes throughout most of '60s and '70s, despite standout individual performances from future Hall of Famers Lem Barney and Dick "Night Train" Lane . . . coach Wayne Fontes brought the team to respectability beginning in 1989, coinciding with the arrival of franchise running back Barry Sanders (and, not incidentally, my own personal "franchise" quarterback Rodney Peete) . . . known throughout the Peete household as the team that let Rodney get away . . . (Rodney's best year in a Detroit uniform was 1990, his second year in the league, when he completed 52.4 percent of his passes for 1,974 yards and 13 touchdowns, to go along with 363 yards rushing and six rushing touchdowns) . . . Sanders abruptly retired in 1998 sending the team into a tailspin . . . currently coached by former San Francisco 49ers head coach Steve Mariucci and quarterbacked by young gun Joey Harrington . . . **TEAM COLORS:** Blue and silver . . . **RETIRED JERSEYS:** Dutch Clark (#7), Bobby Layne (#22), Doak Walker (#37), Joe Schmidt (#56), Chuck Hughes (#85), Charlie Sanders (#88) . . .

GREEN BAY PACKERS: "The Pack" . . . third oldest team in pro football, dating to 1919, when a Wisconsin packing company backed a local pro team coached by Earl (Curly) Lambeau . . . widely considered one of the most successful franchises in the game, with a team history stamped by two legendary coaches—Lambeau and Vince Lombardi . . . captured first NFL Championship in 1929, beginning a run of three straight titles for Lambeau's Packers . . . during Lambeau's 30-year tenure, he coached such Hall of Fame players as Cal Hubbard, John "Blood" McNally, Tony Canadeo, and Don Hutson, one of the great wide receivers of his era . . . consistently finished at or near the top of the league throughout the '30s and '40s, including championships in 1936, 1939, and 1944 . . . lost more games than they won in only one season in Lambeau's first 28 years as coach . . . Lombardi era distinguished by Jim Taylor, Paul Hornung, Willie Davis, Jim Ringo, and Forrest Gregg . . . Ray Nitschke redefined the linebacker position during his great career, and long-time quarterback Bart Starr was a gritty team symbol . . . Lombardi's signature play, the "Packer

Sweep," was soon copied on high school football fields and in pickup games across the country . . . home stadium dedicated as Lambeau Field in 1965 . . . Lombardi's Packers matched Lambeau with three straight NFL Championships, in 1965, 1966, and 1967, the last two leading to victories in Super Bowls I and II . . . only community-owned franchise in professional sports . . . fan favorites Starr and Gregg returned as coaches in the '70s and '80s, with only modest success . . . arrival of Mike Holmgren as coach in 1992 signaled a new winning era, which coincided neatly with the arrival of future Hall of Fame quarterback Brett Favre . . . lineman Reggie White anchored one of the league's best defenses during this period . . . reached the play-offs for six consecutive seasons beginning in 1993, including back-to-back Super Bowl appearances and a victory over New England in Super Bowl XXXI, before losing to Denver in Super Bowl XXXII . . . wide receiver Sterling Sharpe was a favorite target during Favre's early career, and in recent years running back Ahman Greene has helped to spread the offense . . . current coach Mike Sherman took the helm in 2000 and recorded 43 regular season victories in his first four seasons . . . **TEAM COLORS:** Dark green, gold, white . . . **RETIRED JERSEYS:** Tony Canadeo (#3), Don Hutson (#14), Bart Starr (#15), Ray Nitschke (#66) . . .

MINNESOTA VIKINGS: Consistent winners since the late 1960s, after joining the league as an expansion franchise in 1961 . . . the Vikings ownership group had been awarded an AFL franchise, but rejected the opportunity in favor of an NFL berth . . . in the team's first regular-season contest, coach Norm Van Brocklin substituted rookie quarterback Fran Tarkenton into the game, and the future Hall of Famer and one-time career passing leader proceeded to throw four touchdown passes and run for a fifth in a 37–13 rout of the powerhouse Bears . . . it was to be one of the few highlights for the next while . . . veteran Canadian Football League coach Bud Grant succeeded Van Brocklin in 1967 and quickly turned the "Vikes" into winners . . . quarterback Joe Kapp was brought in to replace the popular Tarkenton, who was shipped to the New York Giants, and the team set off on a record run that was notable for its bruising front-line defense known as "the Purple People Eaters," led by Carl Eller, Alan

Page, and Jim Marshall . . . Grant took the team to Super Bowl IV in just his third season with them, his first of four appearances in the next 7 years—all losses . . . Tarkenton returned to the fold in 1972 and remained with the Vikings until his retirement in 1978, after amassing 47,003 career passing yards . . . he was joined in the backfield by running back Chuck Foreman, one of the great receiving backs of all time . . . Central Division Championships followed under new head coach Dennis Green in 1992, 1994, and 1998, behind a franchise-best 15–1 record in 1998 . . . the Green era was marked by the arrival of super-star wide receiver Randy Moss and Pro Bowl quarterback Daunte Culpepper, who formed one of the league's most potent passing combinations under current coach Mike Tice . . . the 2001 training camp death of offensive lineman Korey Stringer, coming off a Pro Bowl season, inspired NFL teams to reassess their harsh, relentless practice schedules . . . **TEAM COLORS:** Purple, gold, white . . . **RETIRED JERSEYS:** Fran Tarkenton (#10), Mick Tingelhoff (#53), Jim Marshall (#70), Korey Stringer (#77), Alan Page (#88) . . .

NFC South

ATLANTA FALCONS: The 15th NFL franchise, beginning league play in 1966 . . . first-ever draft pick Tommy Nobis quickly became one of the league's best linebackers, and gave head coach Norb Hecker a strong defensive foundation, but it would be 6 years before the team could put together a winning season, which it finally did under coach Norm Van Brocklin in 1973 . . . set an NFL team mark in 1977 for fewest points allowed in a 14-game season, led by Nobis and six-time Pro Bowler Claude Humphrey . . . it wasn't until new coach Leeman Bennett figured out a way to put points on the board, helped by franchise quarterback Steve Bartkowski and running back William Andrews, that the Falcons managed to reach the post-season . . . flashy wide receiver Billy "White Shoes" Johnson emerged as one of the league's most popular players—and its most explosive punt returner, netting more yards than any other punt returner in NFL history . . . captured the NFC Western Division Championship in 1980, and, under coach Dan Reeves, the NFC Championship in 1998, but lost in Super Bowl XXXIII to the Denver Broncos . . . more recently, under coach Jim Mora Jr. and behind the all-around athleticism of superstar quarterback Michael Vick, the 2004 Falcons reached the NFC Championship game but lost to the Super Bowl bound Eagles . . . **TEAM COLORS:** Black, red, silver, white . . . **RETIRED JERSEYS:** Steve Bartkowski (#10), William Andrews (#31), Jeff Van Note (#57), Tommy Nobis (#60) . . .

CAROLINA PANTHERS: Joined the NFL in 1995 as its 29th franchise, bringing professional football at long last to the Carolinas . . . played first-ever game in Canton, Ohio, besting the expansion Jaguars in the NFL's annual Hall of Fame exhibition game, 20–14 . . . finished inaugural season an impressive 7–9, behind quarterback Kerry Collins, a record showing for an expansion franchise . . . linebacker Lamar Lathon helped to set the tone for the defense under head coach Dom Capers . . . followed with an even stronger 1996 season, posting a 12–4 mark and losing out in the NFC Championship game to the Green Bay Packers—still an unprecedented showing for a 2nd-year team . . . coach John Fox took over from George Seifert in 2002 and installed a menacing defensive system, led by linemen Julius Peppers and Kris Jenkins, that has helped to make the Panthers perennial contenders . . . Fox's offense was initially led by my #1 play caller quarterback Rodney Peete, originally signed as a backup after 12 NFL seasons, who recorded the best season of his career in 2002 at the age of 36 to put the Panthers in position to contend . . . Peete resumed his reserve role the following season, helping establish young quarterback Jake Delhomme as one of the top QBs in the league . . . with Delhomme and running back Stephen Davis leading the way, Fox's Panthers posted an 11–5 mark in 2003, and earned a trip to Super Bowl XXXVIII . . . the Panthers lost a thrilling game to the New England Patriots juggernaut, 32–29, but nevertheless captured the hearts and minds of fans in Charlotte and throughout the region . . . **TEAM COLORS:** Black, blue, silver . . . **RETIRED JERSEYS:** None . . .

NEW ORLEANS SAINTS: The NFL's 16th franchise, beginning play in 1967 . . . New Orleans fans couldn't get enough of their first taste of professional sports, and the team averaged over 75,000 fans per game in their first season . . . selected NFL legend and former Louisiana State star Jim Taylor from the Green Bay Packers in the expansion draft . . . wide receiver John Gilliam recorded an exhilarating 94-yard touchdown return on the opening kickoff in the team's first-ever game . . . victories were few and far between, so team management turned each home game into an event . . . halftime shows were like mini-versions of New Orleans's springtime Mardi Gras ritual, with high school marching bands and special appearances by celebrated trumpet player and Saints part-owner Al Hirt . . . in 1970, placekicker Tom Dempsey, who wore a special orthopedic device in his right cleat to compensate for a deformed kicking foot, established an NFL record with a 63-yard field goal to beat Detroit 19–17 as time ran out in one of the Saints' most memorable games . . . quarterback Archie Manning—the top 1972 draft pick and father of Peyton and Eli—became the team's first homegrown star . . . in 1975 the team began playing in the Louisiana Superdome, a state-of-the-art domed stadium that would be the neutral site of several future Super Bowls . . . posted first winning season in 1987, the Saints' 21st in the NFL, under head coach Jim Mora, going on to reach the play-offs four times in the next six seasons, capped by their first-ever NFC West crown in 1991 . . . under coach Jim Haslett and the stellar play of QB Aaron Brooks, they repeated as NFC West champs in 2000 . . . **TEAM COLORS:** Gold, black, white . . . **RETIRED JERSEYS:** Archie Manning (#8), Rickey Jackson (#57), Doug Atkins (#81) . . .

TAMPA BAY BUCCANEERS: The NFL's 27th franchise, commencing play in 1976, although it took a bit longer for the "Bucs" to get going, losing a league-record 26 consecutive games to start their NFL career . . . despite these early struggles, head coach John McKay, who signed on to helm the team in a public relations coup after notching a record four national championships at USC, laid a strong defensive foundation . . . on the field, the team was led by defensive end Lee Roy Selmon, the number one pick of the 1976 college draft, and a true foundation player . . . just 2 years after recording its first regular-season victory, the franchise shut down opposing offenses and reached the post-season by winning a series of hard-fought, low-scoring battles . . . in the final regular season game, the Bucs clinched the 1979 NFC Central title with a 3–0 victory over Kansas City, but lost in the NFC Championship to the Los Angeles Rams by another low score, 9–0 . . . the offense was led by quarterback Doug Williams and running back Ricky Bell, but the team was known around the league for its defense . . . along with Selmon, the NFL's Defensive Player of the Year in 1979 and a future Hall of Famer, McKay's teams featured Wally Chambers and Dave Pear on the line, and David Lewis on the linebacking corps . . . the team struggled upon the departure of McKay following the 1984 season, but returned to the top of the NFC Central in 1999 under coach Tony Dungy, only to lose out again to the Rams in the NFC Championship game, 11–6 . . . defense remained a hallmark, this time with linemen Warren Sapp and Simeon Rice leading the way . . . under coach Jon Gruden, and behind the league's top-ranked defense, the team defeated the Oakland Raiders, 48–21, in Super Bowl XXXVII . . . **TEAM COLORS:** "Buccaneer" red and pewter . . . **RETIRED JERSEYS:** Lee Roy Selmon (#63) . . .

NFC West

ARIZONA CARDINALS: The oldest continually operating franchise in football, dating from an 1898 Chicago club team known as the Racine Street Cardinals to the American Professional Football Association and on to the NFL, where the team recorded its first NFL Championship in 1925 as the Chicago Cardinals . . . despite its long history, the team has enjoyed only occasional success on the field . . . in 1929, star running back Ernie Nevers turned in one of the greatest single-game performances in NFL history, scoring all 40 points in a 40–6 victory over the cross-town rival Chicago Bears, setting a record that might never be broken . . . purchased by Charles W. Bidwill in 1932 . . . team is now owned and operated by William V. Bidwill, marking one of the longest runs of single-family ownership in professional team sports . . . Hall of Fame quarterback Charlie Trippi led the team to its first NFL Championship in

1947 . . . returned to championship game in 1948, but lost to Philadelphia, beginning a string of losing seasons that reached into the 1960s . . . as the relocated St. Louis Cardinals, the team shared a name, logo, and colors with the St. Louis Cardinals baseball team, and soon began to mirror that team's winning ways as well . . . under head coach Wally Lemm, the "Redbirds" posted several winning seasons in the early 1960s, and with the addition of four-time Pro Bowler Jim Hart at quarterback, the Cardinals were poised to remain competitive for the next decade, winning the NFC Eastern Division Championship in 1974 and 1975 . . . offensive lineman-turned-analyst Dan Dierdorf was a standout player during this period, with defensive back Larry Wilson leading the way in the secondary . . . running back Stump Mitchell was one of the club's most popular players in the 1980s, along with quarterback Neil Lomax . . . relocated to Phoenix's Sun Devil Stadium prior to the 1988 season, and as the Arizona Cardinals, quarterbacked by Jake Plummer, managed to win a 1998 wild card play-off game against Dallas before losing out in the divisional round to Minnesota . . . storied head coach Dennis Green came aboard in 2004 . . . former league and Super Bowl MVP Kurt Warner joined the cards in 2005 . . . **TEAM COLORS:** "Cardinal" red, black, white . . . **RETIRED JERSEYS:** Larry Wilson (#8), Stan Mauldin (#77), J.V. Cain (#88), Marshall Goldberg (#99) . . .

ST. LOUIS RAMS: Replaced the Cardinals in the hearts of St. Louis fans in 1995 after nearly 50 years in Los Angeles . . . launched as the Cleveland Rams in 1937 . . . enjoyed first success on the arm of rookie UCLA quarterback Bobby Waterfield, who took the team to a stunning 15–14 victory over Washington in the 1945 NFL title game . . . moved to Los Angeles for the 1946 season, and played to modest success behind the passing combination of Waterfield and Elroy "Crazy Legs" Hirsch . . . quarterback Norm Van Brocklin continued the Rams' exciting West Coast style of football . . . under coach George Allen, the team became a defensive powerhouse . . . the defensive line became known as the "Fearsome Foursome," as Deacon Jones, Merlin Olsen, Rosey Grier, and Lamar Lundy intimidated opponents around the league . . . quarterback Roman Gabriel led the team to the divisional play-offs in 1967 and 1969 . . . other half of the historic 1972 swap of franchises between owner Robert Irsay and Colts owner Carroll Rosenbloom . . . the team enjoyed its greatest sustained success under coach Chuck Knox in the early 1970s, winning 49 regular season games during his 5-year tenure, but the Rams didn't notch an NFC Championship until 1979, with a lineup that included Pat Haden at quarterback, Fred Dryer, and Jack Youngblood on the defensive line and Jim Youngblood (no relation) at linebacker . . . coach John Robinson shepherded the team through most of the 1980s, with mostly first-division success, in an era marked by the emergence of Eric Dickerson as one of the game's all-time great running backs . . . coach Knox returned to Los Angeles for three sub-.500 seasons, just prior to the team's move to St. Louis in 1995 . . . there, under coach Dick Vermeil, the Rams received dominant Pro Bowl performances from quarterback Kurt Warner and running back Marshall Faulk, culminating in a Super Bowl XXXIV victory over Tennessee . . . in 1999, Warner was both league and Super Bowl MVP . . . posted the league's best offense in terms of total yards and total points for three consecutive seasons, from 1999–2001 . . . Marc Bulger has since replaced Warner at quarterback, with Mike Martz at coach . . . **TEAM COLORS:** Royal blue, gold, white . . . **RETIRED JERSEYS:** Bob Waterfield (#7), Eric Dickerson (#29), Merlin Olsen (#74), Jackie Slater (#78), Jack Youngblood (#85) . . .

SAN FRANCISCO 49ERS: Charter members of the All-America Football Conference . . . joined the NFL in 1950 . . . early NFL days marked by strong individual play from quarterback Y.A. Tittle, running backs Hugh McElhenny, Joe Perry, and John Henry Johnson, and defensive tackle Leo Nomellini . . . team success had to wait until the late 1950s, with a first-ever play-off appearance in a 1957 season marked by the debut of John Brodie, who would remain the team's starting quarterback for the next 15 seasons . . . following an ownership change in 1977, when Edward DeBartolo Jr. took the helm and dedicated himself to winning championships, the 49ers began to enjoy unparalleled success on the field . . . the team's first great run came in the 1980s under coach Bill Walsh and Hall of Fame quarterback Joe Montana, who combined with running back Roger Craig and wide receiver Jerry Rice to form one of the most explosive offenses in league history, and form the template of the West Coast style of offense that would soon be copied around the league . . . defensive back Ronnie Lott set the tone in the secondary . . . Rice would go on to rewrite the record books for receivers . . . these 49ers captured the NFC Western Division Championship a stunning 13 times from 1981–97, recording victories in Super Bowls XVI, XIX, XXIII, XXIV, and XXIX for a perfect 5–0 record in the biggest game of all . . . two of those Super Bowl victories belonged to Walsh's successor, George Seifert, who continued the West Coast style of play pioneered by his predecessor, and later refined his attack to incorporate the running talents of free-wheeling quarterback Steve Young, who replaced Montana at quarterback beginning in 1991 . . . one of the great characteristics of the franchise was its ability to groom its next generation of stars . . . Walsh-Seifert and Montana-Young are just two prime examples; a third, wide receiver Terrell Owens, became the primary deep threat after Jerry Rice . . . indeed, Owens established his own Hall of Fame credentials with the 49ers, before moving on to Philadelphia prior to the 2004 season . . . Steve Mariucci replaced Seifert as head coach in 1997, but after two strong seasons the team began to struggle, as several top players from the team's golden era went into decline . . . quarterback Jeff Garcia managed to help right the ship with three Pro Bowl seasons, and a brief return to postseason play . . . but the 49ers have been on a "rebuilding" path under coach Mike Nolan, son of former 49ers coach Dick Nolan . . . **TEAM COLORS:** Gold and Cardinal red . . . **RETIRED JERSEYS:** John Brodie (#12), Joe Montana (#16), Joe Perry (#34), Jimmy Johnson (#37), Hugh McElhenny (#39), Charlie Krueger (#70), Leo Nomellini (#73), Bob St. Clair (#79), Dwight Clark (#87) . . .

SEATTLE SEAHAWKS: The league's 28th franchise, awarded prior to the 1976 season, the Seahawks have bounced around in their brief NFL career . . . originally assigned to the National Football Conference, the "Hawks" were shuttled to the AFC Western Division for their second season (while Tampa

Bay was reassigned from the AFC to the NFC) ... rookie quarterback Jim Zorn became a fixture for the team's first nine seasons, and one of its most popular players, along with his favorite target, wide receiver Steve Largent, who would go on to become one of the game's all-time greats ... Largent became such a beloved figure that he ran for Congress, serving his home district in Oklahoma from 1994 until 2002, when he left office to pursue an unsuccessful bid for governor ... Hall of Fame defensive lineman Carl Eller, a key to the Vikings of the 1970s, ended his career in a Seahawks uniform ... the team hit its stride under veteran coach Chuck Knox, bolstered by the additions of running back Kurt Warner and quarterback Dave Krieg, reaching the 1983 AFC Championship game in its first run at postseason play, losing out to the Los Angeles Raiders ... returned the following year to avenge that play-off loss, besting the Raiders in the wild card round of the 1984 play-offs, before falling to the Dolphins in the divisional round ... announced itself as a competitive franchise with the hiring of former Packers coach Mike Holmgren, who ushered the team into a new era behind the arm of young quarterback Matt Hasselbeck and the athleticism of running back Shaun Alexander ... earned an NFC wild card spot in 2003, after agreeing to switch conferences in a league-wide realignment ... **TEAM COLORS:** Blue, green, silver ... **RETIRED JERSEYS:** Steve Largent (#80) ...

CHEAT SHEET

10

MORE ALL-TIME ANNOYING THINGS WE SHOULD NEVER SAY TO OUR MEN DURING THE GAME

1. "Why can't you get our lawn to look like that?"

2. "Wow! Forty-eight to nothing. I told you not to bet on the Dolphins."

3. "Those Doritos gave you heartburn so I threw them out. Check out these delicious rice cakes instead."

4. "Can you believe I won your football pool again? I mean, you spend all week reading the sports pages, and I just pick the teams based on which city I like best!"

5. "Honey, meet Carol and Ron. They're Jehovah's Witnesses and they've got some literature they want to share with us."

6. "Okay, I get that a field goal is worth three points, but where's the three-point line?"

7. "You're gonna love the game you asked me to TiVo for you. The Giants won."

8. "Don't tell me 'bout no two-minute warning. That was a half-hour ago!"

9. "Why do they need to keep running out those chains when they've got that yellow line running clear across the field?"

10. "Can we change the channel? NBC has ice-skating."

And (Finally!) the Ultimate Cheat Sheet

A Glossary of Terms

Football has a language all its own. Hang around an NFL locker room long enough and you'll need a phrase book to help you get by—not to mention that yardstick you'll need to help you take the measure of your man. (Sorry, ladies, but I just couldn't resist the easy joke.) Seriously, though: Spend any kind of time on the sidelines, or in a sports bar, or watching the games at home, and you'll still come across words and phrases that make about as much sense as the tax code. Even veteran NFL players and their lovely wives encounter terms that are hard to explain, and just as hard to figure out, and to this lovely wife at least the prospect of subtitles would be one of the game's all-time great innovations.

Throughout this book, I've tried to keep things clear—anyway, to clear things up whenever I've bumped into football terminology that might need some explaining. There are, however, a great many terms and concepts we have yet to cover on this need-to-know basis, so we'll do well to cover a few of them here. Some of them have come up in passing and need a little further clarification, while others have yet to find their way into these pages.

Here goes . . .

ALL-PRO: A term used to describe an all-star at his position . . . the *Associated Press* names its annual "All-Pro" team at the close of each season

" . . . AND LONG": Usually refers to a distance of 6 or more yards that remain to be covered for a first down, as in "third and long," meaning that it is third down and long yardage

AUDIBLE: A play called at the line of scrimmage that changes a play that had been previously called in a huddle or from the sideline

BACKFIELD: The area of the field that begins approximately 2 yards from either side of the line of scrimmage, just beyond the NEUTRAL ZONE (see page 216) . . . can refer to a group of players who line up in the backfield area, or to the area itself . . . certain defensive players such as the safeties and cornerbacks are often referred to as the defensive backfield . . . on offense, running backs and quarterbacks are part of the offensive backfield

BLITZ: An aggressive defensive strategy of rushing six or more players at the quarterback, usually deployed at great risk because if a quarterback manages to complete a pass to one of his downfield receivers, the defense is vulnerable to a long gain

BLOCK: The art and practice of pushing, moving, strong-arming, or otherwise preventing a defender from reaching the quarterback . . . can also refer to the art and practice of pushing, moving, strong-arming, or otherwise repositioning a defender from a predetermined path, through which a ballcarrier might advance up the field . . . the foundation of the game itself, because a team succeeds or fails on the ability of its offensive linemen to execute their blocks and the ability of its defensive linemen and linebackers to crack an opponent's blocking scheme

BLOCKING SLED: A fixture of every football practice field, these platforms of two or more large pads (also known as tackling dummies) are used to practice blocking and tackling techniques . . . usually, these contraptions are set on wheels or runners of some kind, and the whole setup moves backwards with each hit . . . one of my very favorite football things is the sight of big, beefy men barreling into these platforms, over and over and over, while a coach supervises the whole mess from the back of the sled, riding the length of the field like Santa in a warm-up suit

BOOTLEG: A type of deceptive running play designed to momentarily freeze the defense into thinking the quarterback has handed off the ball to a running back, when in fact he has kept the ball and concealed it on his hip and rolled towards the sidelines, after which he will either attempt to run with it or to pass it

BYE: An "off" week in the regular-season schedule, to allow teams a much-needed rest at some early- to mid-point of the season, and to allow the league to extend the season by 1 full week without adding any additional games . . . can also refer to a play-off team being automatically advanced through a preliminary round play-off game . . . for example, the top two division-winning teams in each conference receive a "bye"—or, free pass—in the wildcard round of the play-offs

CLIPPING: An illegal block, when a player blocks an opponent from behind and below the waist, subject to a 15 yard penalty

DEFENSE: In its simplest form, it refers to the act of preventing or attempting to prevent an advance of the ball by your opponents . . . a player who lines up on the defensive side of the ball is said to be "on defense" . . . "man-to-man," "zone," and "double-coverage" are specific types of defenses . . . (see OFFENSE, page 216)

DELAY OF GAME: Another no-no, this one referring to any intentional action by a player or coach on either team to delay the start of the next play, subject to a 5 yard penalty

DIME BACK: The sixth defensive back in a particular alignment . . . understand, most teams feature four defensive backs in the secondary . . . in a nickel defense, with five defensive backs, the fifth back is known as the nickel back . . . in a dime defense, with six defensive backs, the sixth back is known as the dime back, because he is the second nickel back

DOWN: An attempt, or try, to advance the ball over a set distance . . . can also refer to the period of time from when a ball is put into play from scrimmage to when it is ruled dead . . . a play is ruled dead when a runner is "down by contact," which means that any part of a ballcarrier's body other than his feet or hands has touched the ground as a result of contact with a defender . . . a runner is also considered "down" when he runs out of bounds, or when his forward progress is stopped

ENCROACHMENT: Highfalutin term for when a defender enters the NEUTRAL ZONE (see page 216) and makes contact with an opposing player before the start of a play from scrimmage . . . when I learned the game as a kid, they used to just call this an offside penalty against the defense, but times have changed . . . subject to a 5 yard penalty

END-OVER-END: Usually refers to a sloppily, hastily, or wobbly thrown ball that appears to rotate "end-over-end" in a pinwheeling fashion, as in the opposite of a SPIRAL (see page 220) . . . can also refer to a ball that is kicked in this manner, or to the way it is propelled after bouncing on the field

END ZONE: The 10-yard area at either end of a football field, running the full width of the football field, usually marked by different-colored grass or turf or some kind of logo or design representing the home team . . . each team tries to move the ball toward (and, ultimately, into) the other team's end zone, where touchdowns are scored—and, where touchdown dances, shuffles, and other celebrations ensue

FACE MASK: Also known as a face guard, this refers to the hard-plastic (or sometimes metal) bars that crisscross the front of a football helmet in the area that corresponds to the player's mouth or jawline . . . some players wear helmets with a vertical bar extending from the helmet's forehead area to the horizontal bars . . . it's against the rules (and pretty darn dangerous) for a player to grab an opposing player by the face mask, either on purpose or by accident . . . a *face-masking* foul is subject to a 5 yard penalty, or a 15 yard penalty if an official determines that the violation was flagrant

FAIR CATCH: A truce of sorts, allowing a punt returner to signal that he will not attempt to advance the ball after catching it, provided that the punting team agree not to rip his head off or take his legs out from under him immediately after he does so . . . as rules of engagement go, this is probably one of the more civil provisions in the NFL code . . . without such a fair catch signal (usually indicated by one arm pointing skyward), the punting team is able to pummel the punt returner immediately upon touching the ball, putting the returner at particular risk on especially short kicks . . . in a fair catch, once the ball is caught, it is considered downed and the play is dead . . . if the punt is fumbled or mishandled, each team is equally entitled to the loose ball

FALSE START: Illegal motion called against the offense when a player moves off the line before the ball is snapped . . . unlike its defensive counterpart—encroachment—it doesn't matter if the offending player actually crosses the line of scrimmage or makes contact with an opposing player . . . subject to a 5 yard penalty

FIELD GOAL: A scoring try, usually attempted on fourth down after a team's offensive unit has failed to cross the ball over the goal line for a touchdown or fails to make a first down . . . a kicker attempts to send the ball through the uprights extending from the goalpost at the back of the end zone . . . if he succeeds, a field goal is recorded and the offense is awarded three points . . . if he fails, the defensive team takes possession of the ball at the spot of the attempted kick, or at its own 20-yard line, whichever is more favorable

FLAT: Area of the field extending from the hash marks to the sideline (about 20 yards long, 5 to 7 yards wide), within several yards of the line of scrimmage . . . a pass thrown to a receiver in this area is said to be thrown "in the flat"

FLEA FLICKER: A trick play, usually a passing play designed to look initially like a running play . . . frequently involves a running back or a wide receiver, who receives the ball in a handoff before sending it back to the quarterback for a pass downfield

FOUR-POINT STANCE: Refers to a player's crouch position with both hands on the ground at the start of a play from scrimmage . . . the four "points" refer to the two hands and two feet . . . (see also THREE-POINT STANCE and TWO-POINT STANCE, page 221)

FUMBLE: A loose ball that is dropped or knocked from a ballcarrier's hands . . . can also be used as a verb, meaning to drop the ball . . . not a phrase you particularly want to hear when your team has the ball

"GOAL TO GO": Refers to a series of downs that begin inside the opponents' 10-yard line—meaning that there are fewer than 10 yards to go before crossing the goal line . . . in this situation, there is no need to mark the distance to a subsequent first down because the remaining shorter distance will result in a touchdown

GRIDIRON: Old-fashioned term to describe the field itself, for the way the hash marks and yard markers can sometimes look from a distance

HAIL MARY: A desperation play, usually deployed as time is running out, usually involving a long, hope-for-the-best pass to a receiver

HEAD SLAP: You don't see too many of these anymore, since the move was outlawed by the league in 1977, but back in the day, players would slap the helmets of their opponents to rattle their cages and knock them off guard . . . it was an effective move, too . . . from time to time, you'll still catch an overly aggressive defensive lineman head slapping an opposing tackle, but he'll rarely get away with it—and if he does, there'll usually be some bend-the-rules, hope-the-official-is-looking-the-other-way payback

HOLDING: Another major no-no, probably one of the most frequently called penalties in the game . . . refers to the illegal grabbing of an opponent's jersey, or the intentional locking of arms with an opponent, or bear-hugging him in any way that might restrict his movement . . . subject to a 10-yard penalty, and the wrath of your coaches and teammates

"I" FORMATION: One of those too-simple football names that pretty much describes the action or formation to which it refers . . . an offensive formation, wherein the two running backs line up directly behind the quarterback, in a row—hence, the "I"

INCIDENTAL CONTACT: Official-sounding term that essentially means "no harm, no foul" . . . describes contact between a receiver and a defender that falls outside the rules of the game but that nevertheless fails to impact the play or hurt the receiver's chances to make a catch . . . not incidentally, defenders are allowed (and even encouraged) to make contact with opposing receivers within the first 5 yards beyond the line of scrimmage

INTERFERENCE: A good thing or a bad thing, depending on the usage . . . in a case of "pass interference," it refers to a situation where a defensive player hits a receiver while a ball is on its way to him, inhibiting his chances to make a catch . . . such unlawful obstruction is subject to a first down at the point of infraction . . . can also be used to describe a block, or a series of blocks, as in "the offensive line ran interference for the running back"

KICKOFF: The method of starting and restarting the game, at the start of each half and after each score . . .

LATE HIT: Not a good thing, if you're the guy getting hit late, or a teammate of the guy doing the late-hitting . . . occurs when a defensive player makes contact with the ballcarrier after a play has been ruled dead . . . also known as unnecessary roughness, one of the more delightful football terms for the way it suggests that some roughness is indeed necessary . . . a personal foul, subject to a 15 yard penalty

LINE STUNT: Two defensive linemen who switch assignments and attack positions at the snap . . . in success, it can be an effective way to confuse the opposing linemen . . . unfortunately, if not executed properly, it can also confuse the defense

NEUTRAL ZONE: The very small area immediately surrounding the line of scrimmage, extending the width of the field from the back end of the football to the front end of the football . . . a safe harbor, into which no defensive player can enter until the ball is snapped, and upon which no offensive player other than the center can line up

NICKEL BACK: See DIME BACK (page 212)

NO-HUDDLE OFFENSE: A "hurry-up" style of offense where a sequence of plays is called in advance, or plays are signaled from the sidelines by a coaching staff member, or called at the line of scrimmage by the quarterback, instead of in a traditional huddle

OFFENSE: The act of advancing or attempting to advance the ball against your opponents, towards your own goal line . . . a player who lines up on the offensive side of the ball is said to be "on offense" . . . (see DEFENSE, page 211)

OFFSETTING PENALTIES: When penalties are committed on both sides of the ball on the same play . . . typically, the penalties cancel each other out and the play is allowed to stand, unless one of the violations is considered a major penalty and the other a minor penalty, in which case the major penalty is assessed

ONSIDE KICK: A special teams play, deployed by the kicking team on a kickoff and designed to give the kicking team a chance to retain possession of the ball . . . it used to be that the kicking team could recover the ball only once it had traveled 10 yards and been touched by the receiving team, but under current rules the ball is up for grabs once it has traveled the minimum 10-yard distance from the kicking tee . . . in an onside kick, the ball is usually kicked on the ground, or end-over-end, or on a line drive, to give the coverage team an opportunity to retrieve the ball before the receiving team can take possession . . . in some parts of the country, and on some broadcasts, I have heard this referred to as an *onsides* kick, with no explanation given for that extra *s* . . .

PASSING LANE: A direct path between the quarterback and the intended receiver

PASS INTERFERENCE: See INTERFERENCE (page 215)

PERSONAL FOUL: Any of several violations committed by an individual player against an opponent, including piling on, running into the kicker, face-masking, kicking, illegal use of the hands, illegal blocking . . . also, illegal use of the helmet as a weapon, meaning after it has left a player's head and been deployed as a blunt instrument, which I have never seen in all my years watching football . . . subject to a 15 yard penalty and, in certain cases, disqualification

PIGSKIN: Commonly used term to describe the football itself, presumably because at one time or another the balls were made from pigskin leather

POCKET: A ring or semicircle formed by the offensive line to protect the quarterback as he moves back to pass

POINT-AFTER-TOUCHDOWN: Another scoring try, awarded to a team after a touchdown . . . also known by its acronym, PAT . . . as the name implies, it offers an opportunity at a single extra point, to combine with the six points awarded for a touchdown for a seven-point scoring opportunity . . . as in a field goal, a kicker attempts to send the ball through the uprights extending from the goalpost at the back of the end zone . . . if he succeeds, a point after touchdown is recorded and the offense is awarded an additional point . . .

PREVENT DEFENSE: Type of defense that guards against a long-yardage play, usually in the waning minutes of a close game . . . often, this means deploying five or six players in the defensive backfield, conceding a short-yardage gain on the ground while protecting against the threat of a long pass . . . roughly akin to "guarding the line" in baseball, when an infielder positions himself to protect against an extra-base hit while conceding a single . . . what I've always loved about this set is the way it's referred to in a thick southern drawl, no matter what part of the country the person doing the referring is from . . . it's the "pre-vent defense," hard accent on the *pre* . . . it is also acceptable to refer to this defensive strategy in the shorthand, as in, "there was only a minute left on the clock, so we went into the pre-vent"

RED ZONE: Area inside an opponent's 20-yard line . . . significant because offenses are judged by how effective they are at scoring once they close within 20 yards of the goal line, and because defenses are judged by how effective they are at preventing their opponents from doing so

ROUGHING THE KICKER: When a member of the receiving team makes significant contact with the kicker that doesn't also block the kick in the same motion . . . protective rule to keep kickers safe when and where they are most vulnerable, with only one leg on the ground while the other swings forward in the kicking motion . . . subject to a 15-yard penalty, which is often enough to earn the kicking team a first down, allowing them to maintain possession

ROUGHING THE PASSER: When a defender makes contact with the quarterback just after the ball has been thrown . . . as above, this protective rule requires defensive players to pull back at the precise moment when the quarterback is most vulnerable . . . officials will allow a certain amount of incidental contact owing to momentum and such, but if a defender takes a second step and hits a quarterback after a pass has been thrown, he'll most likely get a flag . . . subject to a 15-yard penalty, and an automatic first down

RUN AND SHOOT: A free-wheeling, wide-open style of offense, featuring up to four wide receivers and no tight ends, with a lone running back positioned in the backfield . . . so named for the way it allows a running option in support of a likely pass

SACK: When a quarterback, attempting to pass, is tackled behind the line of scrimmage . . . when a quarterback, attempting to run, is tackled behind the line of scrimmage, it goes down merely as a really, really good play

SAFETY: This is another one of those football terms that can refer to a play or a player, with different meanings and associations for each . . . as a play, it describes the situation where an offensive player is tackled behind his *own* goal line . . . when this happens, a safety is recorded and the defensive team is awarded two points *and possession of the ball* . . . as a player, it describes the defensive player who frequently lines up in the deepest part of the defensive backfield, where he is positioned as a defender of last resort on long pass plays

SCRAMBLE: All-purpose term for when a quarterback is made to run out of the pocket to avoid a sack and to somehow *scramble* to safety . . . keep in mind, coaches never set out to design such a play, but sometimes a quarterback scramble can effectively counter a swarming defensive attack . . . some of the game's most effective quarterbacks have been those with the athletic instinct and ability to move swiftly out of the pocket . . . a quarterback can scramble behind the line of scrimmage to buy sufficient time to find an open receiver down the field, or he can scramble past the line of scrimmage and advance the ball on the ground himself

SCRIMMAGE, LINE OF: A yard line or plane passing through the end of the ball nearest a team's own goal line . . . the line marks the start of each new play

SECONDARY: Another term to describe the defensive backfield

SHOTGUN FORMATION: An offensive alignment wherein the quarterback lines up 3 to 5 yards behind the center to receive the "snap" to start the play . . . not to be confused with position of the groom when the bride is 7 months pregnant on her wedding day

SNAP: The start of a new play from scrimmage . . . can also refer to the act of "hiking" the ball from the center to the quarterback, or to the holder on a field goal or extra-point attempt, or to the punter

SPECIAL TEAMS: Players assigned to the receiving or kicking units on a punt or kickoff, or players assigned to blocking or kicking units on field goal or point-after-touchdown attempts, are said to be on the special teams unit

SPIRAL: A perfectly thrown ball that travels in the shape of the ball itself, usually with the laces rotating like a pig on a spit . . . a thing of beauty to fans, coaches, and receivers, who frankly find it much easier to catch a tight spiral than an ugly end-over-end toss

SPOT: The placement of the ball on the field following each play . . . a spot can be said to favor the defensive team or the offensive team, depending on its position relative to the first-down marker, or to the goal line

TAILGATING: Refers to the pregame and postgame parties in the stadium parking lot that have become standard around the league on game days . . . the term comes from the practice of lifting a hatchback or dropping the tailgate on a station wagon and using the rear of the vehicle as a picnic table/park bench/portable kitchen . . . these days, serious fans dress up the routine with charcoal or mini gas grills and ice chests and beach umbrellas and lawn chairs . . . the only thing missing is the big-screen TV

TERRITORY: Like any good turf war, football is about protecting your own land against intruders, and each team has its own territory to defend . . . technically, a team's territory refers to the 50 yards between the end zone it's attempting to defend and midfield . . . the 40-yard line closest to its own end zone, for example, is considered its own 40-yard line . . . the 40-yard line closest to its opponent's end zone is considered its opponent's 40-yard line

"T" FORMATION (ALSO KNOWN AS PRO SET): Standard offensive formation featuring two running backs positioned several feet apart at approximately the same depth behind the quarterback

THREE-POINT STANCE: refers to a player's crouch position with one hand on the ground at the start of a play from scrimmage . . . (see also FOUR-POINT STANCE, page 214, and TWO-POINT STANCE, below)

TOUCHBACK: Another truce, this time on a kickoff that reaches the opponent's end zone—or, in some cases, sails past the end zone, over the back line, and beyond the field of play . . . following a touchback, the ball is spotted on the receiving team's 20-yard line . . . when a kickoff returner catches the ball in his own end zone, he is entitled to drop to one knee and signal for a touchback . . . this always strikes me as one of the best rolls of the dice in football, when the receiver calculates his chances of returning a kick *beyond* his own 20 against his chances of being stopped *inside* his own 20; if he doesn't like his chances, he can take a knee; if he likes his chances, he can run the ball out of the end zone and take them; and, of course, if he doesn't reach the 20, there is once again the wrath of his coaches and teammates, one of the game's great equalizers

TURNOVER: Make mine apple . . . actually, refers to any situation that results in possession switching to the other team, as in a fumble, interception, or failure to advance the ball the necessary yardage on fourth down

TURNSTILE: Pejorative term used to describe an ineffective offensive lineman, who barely manages to slow an onrushing defender

TWO-MINUTE WARNING: An "official" time-out called by the officials when there are 2 minutes left to play in either half . . . if the 2-minute mark is passed during the unfolding of a play, the play is allowed to continue while the clock continues to run, and the 2-minute warning is sounded once the play has been whistled dead

TWO-POINT STANCE: Refers to a player's upright position at the start of a play from scrimmage, as opposed to the crouch positions described above . . . (see also THREE-POINT STANCE, above, and FOUR-POINT STANCE, page 214)

WEST COAST OFFENSE: Another freewheeling style of offense popularized in the NFL by coach Bill Walsh of the Joe Montana–era San Francisco 49ers, but somewhat less wide open than the run-and-shoot offense . . . characterized by short passes underneath the defense, and featuring a quick-release, high-percentage passing attack on first- and second-down . . . deployed successfully, this type of passing game can have the same effect as a grind-it-out running game, with short-yardage gains to maintain possession and run the clock and push the ball downfield

WISHBONE OFFENSE: Similar to a "T" formation, with a fourth backfield player added to the mix . . . an offensive set that features the quarterback, fullback, and two halfbacks lined up in a formation that loosely resembles a chicken wishbone

ZEBRA: A derisive nickname for an official, a reference to his not-always-flattering black-and-white vertical striped uniform . . . (stripes, as we all know, can be slimming, but the jailbird lines do not always get along with the potbellies and occasional out-of-shapeness we see on some of these guys) . . . usage is akin to calling a businessman a *suit* or a corrections officer *the man*

Index

Boldface page references indicate illustrations.
Underscored references indicate boxed text.